W9-BHE-315

Praise for *Connectable*

A must-read. Tackling loneliness and improving belonging at work should be a priority for every organization and leader. This book is timely, crucial, and practical.

—**Daymond John**, founder of FUBU
and star of ABC's *Shark Tank*

Loneliness is a crisis, and it's past time for teams to address the issue. With its moving stories and wise insights, this book is an important read for workplaces everywhere.

—**Daniel H. Pink**, *New York Times* bestselling author of
When, Drive, and *To Sell Is Human*

Connectable is fascinating, compelling, and extremely readable. But its greatest quality is that it is so darn important. Even though I've spent much of my career working to help people find dignity in their work, after reading the book I found myself with a newfound desire to reach out to the people I work with and have a greater impact on their lives. Every leader and manager needs to read this.

—**Patrick Lencioni**, *New York Times* bestselling author of
The Five Dysfunctions of a Team, The Advantage,
and the assessment, *The 6 Types of Working Genius*

Connectable is an indispensable resource for every team member, manager, and leader. A connected team is an inclusive, thriving team. Ryan Jenkins and Steve Van Cohen give us the much-needed road map to a healthier and united workforce whether the team is in-person, fully remote, or hybrid.

—**Marissa Andrada**, Chief Diversity,
Inclusion and People Officer
at Chipotle Mexican Grill

Connectable is utterly groundbreaking. It opened my eyes in ways I wouldn't have imagined. I am now equipped to intervene and turn the tide on loneliness and focus on building a more connected organization with improved engagement. I was moved to proactively make meaningful changes to enable employees to feel valued and a deeper sense of belonging!

—**Melissa Bernstein**, Cofounder of
Melissa & Doug and author of *LifeLines*

This book brims with inspiring stories, eye-opening statistics, and practical steps to move teams from disconnected to connected. Human connection is more critical than ever before, and *Connectable* delivers the answer for today's teams.

—**Keith Ferrazzi**, #1 *New York Times* bestselling author
of *Never Eat Alone* and *Who's Got Your Back*
and Founder/Chairman of Ferrazzi Greenlight

Connectable provides leaders with the tools they need to drive today's global workforce success by helping lessen employees' loneliness and improving their sense of belonging. It helps leaders create connected, driven, and high-performing teams.

—**Mariana Fagnilli**, Vice President, Global Office of Diversity,
Equity & Inclusion at Liberty Mutual Insurance

Loneliness is an epidemic, and it's one of those things that tends to build on itself. When you find yourself feeling lonely, you think, "I should spend some time alone trying to figure out this loneliness" instead of reaching out to community. I'm so glad that Ryan and Steven have provided a fresh approach to address an issue every business leader needs to be ready to solve.

—**Jon Acuff**, *New York Times* bestselling author of
Soundtracks: The Surprising Solution to Overthinking

We are in the midst of a seismic shift toward hybrid work, creating the propensity of an even more socially detached workforce. As a result, the topic of belonging has never been more essential. In this book, Ryan Jenkins and Steven Van Cohen provide us with an engaging, yet practical perspective on how to nurture these social connections. It is a must-read for any leader.

—**Michael Arena**, author of *Adaptive Space* and
former Chief Talent Officer for General Motors

A fascinating, accessible, and hopeful approach to addressing loneliness at work. Since loneliness lives at the cross-section of inclusion and wellness, *Connectable* couldn't be more relevant and essential. Required reading for any people-focused organization.

—**Claude Silver**, Chief Heart Officer at VaynerMedia

With workplace loneliness on the rise, *Connectable* is a timely, valuable book. It does a great job of normalizing a difficult, undiscussed topic and has practical tools that will help leaders reconnect with a disconnected workforce.

—**Carter Cast**, Clinical Professor at
Kellogg School of Management and author
of *The Right—and Wrong—Stuff*

This book not only describes the loneliness trend in our organizations, it calls on leaders to do something about it—to create connectedness. With powerful stories and practical approaches for the workplace, the authors sparked insights and ideas that I can apply in my team and across our company.

—**Donna Kimmel**, Executive Vice President
and Chief People Officer at Citrix

Connectable is an essential book for our modern world. A breakthrough guide to combating loneliness and fostering belonging, it's a must-read for leaders of startups to Fortune 500 companies.

—**Erica Dhawan**, *Wall Street Journal* bestselling
author of *Digital Body Language*

Loneliness is an epidemic with real consequences to our physical, mental, and emotional health. Considering that most of us spend significant time at work, the workplace is key to tackling the isolation that many are experiencing. *Connectable* provides the strategies that managers need to create strong team cultures that encourage connection and belonging. The result is happier, healthier, and more engaged teams!

—**Jen Fisher**, Chief Well-Being Officer at Deloitte
and author of *Work Better Together*

CONNECTABLE

CONNECTABLE

HOW LEADERS CAN MOVE TEAMS FROM ISOLATED TO ALL IN

RYAN JENKINS + STEVEN VAN COHEN

Mc
Graw
Hill

NEW YORK   CHICAGO   SAN FRANCISCO   ATHENS   LONDON
MADRID   MEXICO CITY   MILAN   NEW DELHI
SINGAPORE   SYDNEY   TORONTO

1 2 3 4 5 6 7 8 9   LCR   27 26 25 24 23 22

ISBN   978-1-264-27750-6
MHID   1-264-27750-4

e-ISBN   978-1-264-27751-3
e-MHID   1-264-27751-2

This publication is designed to provide accurate and authoritative information in regard to the subject matter covered. It is sold with the understanding that neither the author nor the publisher is engaged in rendering legal, accounting, securities trading, or other professional services. If legal advice or other expert assistance is required, the services of a competent professional person should be sought.

—*From a Declaration of Principles Jointly Adopted*
by a Committee of theAmerican Bar Association
and a Committee of Publishers and Associations

Library of Congress Cataloging-in-Publication Data

Names: Jenkins, Ryan (Millennial keynote speaker), author. | Van Cohen, Steven, author.
Title: Connectable : how leaders can move teams from isolated to all in / Ryan Jenkins, Steven Van Cohen.
Description: New York : McGraw-Hill Education, [2022] | Includes bibliographical references and index.
Identifiers: LCCN 2021049964 (print) | LCCN 2021049965 (ebook) | ISBN 9781264277506 (hardback) | ISBN 9781264277513 (ebook)
Subjects: LCSH: Loneliness in the workplace. | Social isolation. | Employees—Psychology. | Teams in the workplace. | Telecommuting.
Classification: LCC HF5549.5.L65 J46 2022 (print) | LCC HF5549.5.L65 (ebook) | DDC 658.3/14—dc23/eng/20211013
LC record available at https://lccn.loc.gov/2021049964
LC ebook record available at https://lccn.loc.gov/2021049965

McGraw Hill books are available at special quantity discounts to use as premiums and sales promotions or for use in corporate training programs. To contact a representative, please visit the Contact Us pages at www.mhprofessional.com.

McGraw Hill is committed to making our products accessible to all learners. To learn more about the available support and accommodations we offer, please contact us at accessibility@mheducation.com. We also participate in the Access Text Network (www.accesstext.org), and ATN members may submit requests through ATN.

To Ashley and Jennifer,
our most cherished connections.

CONTENTS

PART TWO
BELONGING, THE ANTIDOTE TO LONELINESS

PART THREE
HOW TO LESSEN LONELINESS
AND BOOST BELONGING AT WORK

INTRODUCTION

Alone we can do so little;
together we can do so much.
HELEN KELLER

On the brink of ruin, the people of a remote Arctic town in Canada recently banded together to save their community. It wasn't education, public policy, or economics that saved them, but rather a sport.

Near the edge of the world, inside the frigid Arctic Circle, exists a small human settlement called Kugluktuk (pronounced kug-luck-tuck). Bordering the Arctic Ocean, it's part of Canada's largest and most northerly territory, Nunavut. Kugluktuk can be an unforgiving place with temperatures reaching 50 degrees below zero, darkness lingering for more than 20 hours a day in the winter, and meal delivery via a fishing line and a hole in the ice. It's a setting that lends itself to extreme isolation and loneliness.

This tiny community of indigenous people of northern Canada had one of the highest teen suicide rates in the world for many years—that is, until Canada's national sport took root.

Ice hockey? No. Canada's other national sport—lacrosse.

In the early 2000s, Russ Sheppard, a teacher at Kugluktuk High School, established the Kugluktuk Grizzlies, the school's first-ever lacrosse team. Sheppard hoped to provide the students with a spark—an ignition that would light the flame of teamwork, commitment, and dedication. He wanted to create a feeling of togetherness, a bond shared through sport, that would give the students a desperately needed sense of belonging and purpose.

"I was probably about 15 or 16 when I first heard about [the team]," says Adam Kikpak,[1] who was one of the original players and now a coach of the Grizzlies. "Before that I was heavily into drugs and alcohol, missing so much school."

Because Kugluktuk is so remote, it proved very difficult to acquire lacrosse gear. Coaches and members of the community went to great lengths to ensure the team had what they needed. A group of chief mates who were part of the Arctic sealift, a resupply system involving a fleet of ships, loaded large barges with lacrosse gear and pushed them with tugboats through ice-ridden waters, braving the treacherous conditions. All in the name of greater belonging. Due to the commitment of many, it didn't take long before the Grizzlies were fully equipped and practicing on their icy Arctic playing fields.

The lesson for us all: cultivating a culture of belonging takes intentional (and sometimes extreme) effort. But the effort pays off.

Not only did the Grizzlies find their way to the National Lacrosse Championship, but Kugluktuk's teen suicide rate, once one of the world's highest, *fell to zero.*[2]

For the people of Kugluktuk, lacrosse wasn't a game, it was survival. Belonging and purpose turned a lonely town plagued by mental illness into a unified town filled with hope.

Isolation battered.

Loneliness ravaged.

Purpose lifted.

Belonging healed.

Similar to the students at Kugluktuk High School, the global workforce is lonelier than ever before, resulting in disengaged, dissatisfied, and disloyal employees. The increase in remote work, the growing importance of inclusion, and the need for better well-being make addressing loneliness paramount. This book uncovers the modern causes of loneliness at work, the crucial role inclusion plays in solving it, and the strategies leaders can use to reduce loneliness among their teams. By following these strategies, we believe leaders can build more connected organizations with improved engagement, health, and performance at work.

Much like Kugluktuk, today's workspaces are cold and barren, in need of leaders to provide belonging. Your team might not be as remote as the Arctic Circle or facing such dire survival circumstances as the people of Kugluktuk, but rest assured, loneliness is battering your team. It plagues us all. Loneliness is a universal human condition—a condition that is silently seeping into the workplace like never before, causing immense and invisible damage to workers' well-being and performance.

If you or your team is experiencing loneliness, you are not alone. A colossal 72 percent of global workers feel lonely at least monthly, with 55 percent saying they feel lonely weekly. The impact of loneliness is stark. Loneliness *shaves 15 years off of a person's life*[3]—an eye-opening statistic that should motivate all of us, from individuals to business leaders to policy makers, to address the issue.

In the workplace, employee productivity, loyalty, collaboration, and engagement all decrease when employees are lonely. Reducing isolation is good business. Ninety-four percent of leaders say that their teams are growing lonelier while working remotely. Leaders can sense the escalating loneliness among their teams, but they haven't had a resource for how to handle it. Until now.

Psychologists have studied the negative impacts of loneliness for years, but very little has been written about how loneliness shows up at work—even though most people spend a bulk of their waking hours working. This is the first book to tackle loneliness in the workplace. As a business leader, you can become a pioneer in addressing the unaddressed loneliness problem. Way to go!

Without concerted action, loneliness is likely to get worse in the years ahead. With work cycles spinning faster, remote work becoming more prevalent, technology advancing, and a digital native generation flooding the workforce, workplace loneliness will turn from a simmer to a boil. Fast.

Workplace loneliness is defined by the distress caused by the perceived inadequacy of a quality connection to teammates, leaders, the organization, and work itself. Remote workers who feel connected to their work and team will experience less loneliness than someone who works in an office surrounded by people but lacks quality connections.

Loneliness should be as important to managers, directors, and CEOs as it is to therapists. Loneliness isn't shameful. It's a signal. A signal that we need each other. Humanity's strength has always been in our ability to work together. Collaboration is what makes humanity the dominate species.

Communication and collaboration are humanity's greatest asset.

If we were successful in seeking isolation, nothing would exist. The book you read, the phone you check, the building you sit in, and the car you drive all came into existence because a group of people came together to build it. Nothing of significance is ever created alone. Together we dream, build, and prosper.

We seek each other. We help each other. We heal each other.

We build together. We grow together. We thrive together.

While this book will help you build a stronger team, it's more than that. It's about why we must work as a team. And how a team on a mission is the most powerful force on the planet. Creating environments where people are seen, heard, and valued so they can perform at their best and as their whole selves is the foundation for building an exciting and fulfilling future. Connecting people to a team, their work, and a purpose is a worthy mission.

Too much hangs in the balance if we don't act now. We'll splinter apart and drift further into isolation if we don't build strong and authentic social connections at work. Instead of uniting and creating an exceptional future together, we'll retreat away from each other and become frustrated, sick, and lonesome. We must put in the effort now to create the connections that lead to better teams, better companies, better communities, and a healthier us. Humanity and your team are only as unified as its loneliest member.

As the Kugluktuk Grizzlies can attest, no matter how remote or disconnected people are, it only takes one leader with a vision to rescue a team from loneliness.

In the Kugluktuk story, the coach represents you, a capable leader who is committed to helping your team. The Grizzlies represent your team who are in need of more belonging. The town of Kugluktuk represents your organization, which gets better by improving the well-being of your people. Lastly, the Arctic sealift that provided the necessary gear to the coach and team represents this book.

This book is your sealift. It's the supply ship that will deliver the critical cargo to the shores of your organization. We've traversed the ice-ridden waters of worker isolation to deliver it just for you.

For over a decade as global leadership speakers and consultants, we've* helped companies prepare for the future of work by humanizing their business so they can better leverage their greatest asset— their people. Over the last two years, we've surveyed more than 2,000 employees and leaders around the world about their experience with loneliness at work. We've interviewed more than 50 global leaders about how they lessen loneliness and boost belonging inside their organizations. And we've worked alongside many of the world's leading organizations like The Home Depot, Liberty Mutual Insurance, Catalent Pharma Solutions, Kaiser Permanente, Bruster's Ice Cream, Blackstone, and Texas A&M University to strengthen belonging across their workforces whether they are in-person, remote, or hybrid.

We've distilled everything we've learned into this book to equip you with strategies, assessments, and our proprietary framework to lessen loneliness and boost belonging. You'll find the right balance of science, statistics, stories, and strategies to effectively move your team from isolated to all in.

The title of this book, *Connectable*, means to link together. Our aim in this book is to create stronger links between workers and their team, the work, and their leaders. When people are teachable, they are ready and willing to be taught. Similarly, when people are connectable, they are ready and willing to be connected. A connectable leader is ready and willing to establish and facilitate team connections. A connectable team member is ready and willing to connect with teammates. A connectable culture is ready and willing to foster deeper human connection across the team or organization.

Today's smart devices are connectable. Users can connect their smartphone, for example, to a smart TV, Wi-Fi network, or charging station. When a device is connected it becomes more powerful, intelligent, and useful. A connectable team experiences similar benefits. When workers are connected to their team, the work, and their

---

* **The use of "we" in this book:** *Connectable* is written by two authors, Ryan (the introvert) and Steven (the extrovert). You will see first-person plural throughout the book, except when we're telling personal stories.

leader, they are stronger, healthier, and more useful. Just like a smartphone was built to connect with other technology, humans are built to connect with other humans. We are all connectable.

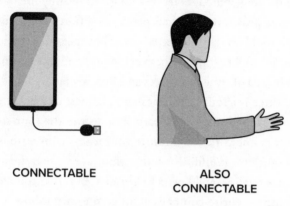

CONNECTABLE   **ALSO CONNECTABLE**

Social connections charge humanity.

However, without the appropriate action, our collective connectability will become dormant, stripping humanity of its very essence. Leaders like you can awaken the renewed sense of connection that humanity is silently screaming for. Work is the most fertile ground where more connection can spring forth.

Here's an overview of the upcoming journey toward making teams and the workplace more connectable than ever before.

Part One of the book focuses on understanding loneliness and its impact on work and well-being. You'll find out how the "father of 24-hour banking" unknowingly reformed the social norms of connecting, why research shows that more people today ignore their doorbell, what pervasive condition caused 9 out of 10 people to ignore a person in need, the peculiar way a solitary Gen Zer learned to use a manual can opener, how an extroverted consultant unexpectedly slipped into loneliness while visiting Elko, Nevada, and how email caused a Millennial to experience deep differential loneliness.

Part Two examines how belonging is the antidote to loneliness. You'll gain an understanding of belonging, why it's needed at work, and how to identify workers who are in need of more connection.

You'll also find out what woolly mammoths teach us about the power of belonging, how two neuroscientists used cocaine to understand the origin of loneliness, how your future self can be certain that relationships are the undisputed secret to a long and healthy life, how neural seesawing proves your brain is playing favorites toward humanity, why Maslow's Hierarchy of Needs should be replaced in order to save our collective well-being, and how belonging can occur even among the most heated of rivals—Yankees and Red Sox fans.

Part Three is about how to lessen loneliness and boost belonging among your team. You'll learn how to use the four-step Less Loneliness Framework™ to improve your team's connections. You'll also find out how an unlikely connection saved a man from a near 100 percent fatality rate, how a first-time CEO used connection to turn around an entire company (and community), how a record-breaking astronaut wards off isolation and loneliness while 254 miles from civilization, how "social snacking" is tricking the masses with the illusion of social sustenance, and how a young Native American warrior sparked the first social network. We close by reflecting on how humans can harness their greatest resource to reduce loneliness and an invaluable lesson about togetherness discovered in the middle of the Alaskan wilderness.

Loneliness is increasing. But that means it's malleable. What increases can also decrease. And it takes much less effort than you might expect to lessen loneliness and boost belonging at work. In fact, it only takes 0.6, 1, and 5.

You'll discover what these numbers mean in the coming chapters. Let's dive in.

PART ONE

LONELINESS,
A SILENT SWEEPING
EPIDEMIC

1

THE LONELINESS LOWDOWN

Loneliness adds beauty to life.
It puts a special burn on sunsets
and makes night air smell better.

HENRY ROLLINS

In New York in 1969, an invention was unveiled that sparked a revolution of convenience. What was once a process requiring face-to-face interaction was now a completely autonomous experience thanks to the sophistication of this invention. Today there are over 3 million of these inventions worldwide, including one at a height of 15,397 feet at the Khunjerab Pass in Pakistan, where the invention can work in temperatures as low as −40° Celsius.

What was this groundbreaking invention?

It was the automated teller machine, or ATM. The American businessman Donald Wetzel holds the US patent for the ATM. In 1968 the 40-year-old Wetzel had the idea for the ATM while standing in a long line at a bank in Dallas, Texas. He grew agitated by the long wait since he only needed to make a simple withdrawal for an upcoming weekend trip.

Wetzel pondered how he could make this process more convenient. With his background in the banking industry and experience with engineering, he figured he could build a machine that would perform at least 90 percent of all the transactions processed by a bank teller. He brought his idea back to his employer, assembled a small team of mechanical and electrical engineers, and began working on the project.

Wetzel's ATM was unveiled 11 months later at a Chemical Bank branch in Rockville Centre, Long Island, New York, on September 2, 1969. Advertisements for the first "cash box" read: "On Sept. 2 our bank will open at 9:00 and never close again." Wetzel became known as the "father of 24-hour banking."[1]

Convenience, efficiency, and time saving were attractive traits of the ATM, making it easy for people to adopt the new technology. ATMs soon became one of the first computers that were widely used by people. ATMs eventually became available in shopping malls, gas stations, airports, cruise ships, restaurants, military ships, and even in rural areas of Africa operating via solar power.

So, what does the invention and proliferation of the ATM teach us about loneliness?

It's estimated that the ATM has collectively saved people around the world billions of hours by eliminating waiting in long lines and speeding up the transaction process. However, there's an opportunity cost associated with avoiding lines, and that cost is social connection. If you choose to use the ATM instead of entering the bank, you miss the opportunity to speak with fellow customers, tellers, or other bank employees. Ultimately, you trade connection for convenience. In fact, this is a primary reason why Wetzel's wife, Eleanor, took a very shocking stance on ATMs—a stance that is a masterclass in how to lessen loneliness. More on Eleanor's stance later in the book.

The Catch of Convenience

If you were presented with the peculiar opportunity to press a big red button that reads "Delete the internet," would you push that button and erase the internet from the face of the planet?

While tempting for some people, most people we've polled have said they would not push the button. Why? Because the benefits of the internet outweigh the risks. As long as the benefits of an invention or technology outweigh the risks (even if just slightly), then people will continue to adopt and integrate it into their lives.

A few decades ago, listening to a new music album took determination, human connection, and one-too-many steps for today's "why is Netflix taking a minute to load" society. You started your new music quest by requesting an album recommendation from a friend (connection #1), finding a record store near you, asking the store employee (connection #2) if they had the album, winding your way through a labyrinth of genre rows, grabbing the album, standing in the checkout line complimenting the music taste of fellow customers (connection #3), purchasing the album from the store clerk (connection #4), then heading to a friend's house to enjoy the album together (connection #5).

This process required connection.

Listening to an album today takes two words, "Alexa play . . ." This process is convenient. But while we're marveling at the ease and novelty of today's innovations, the fabric of our social connections is fraying.

We are subtly turning our backs on humanity every day. We do this when we choose automation like mobile banking, Siri, on-demand food delivery, or self-checkout kiosks. Just a generation ago, we could never have imagined just how convenient it would be to avoid connecting with people. And while many are embracing this ubiquitous world, others, like David Byrne, the front man of the band Talking Heads, are deeply nervous for what it will do to humanity. In an article titled "Eliminating the Human" Byrne wrote, "We are an animal that flourishes because we are social, and you wonder what will happen when that aspect of our deep makeup starts to be taken away from us."[2]

Automation and technology aren't bad. They're incredibly useful and at times are better suited to carry out a task than humans are. However, if we are automating out humans, we'd better start automating in more connectable habits, such as calling a friend or having lunch with a new hire. After all, isn't the purpose of automation to regain time? But instead of using that time to connect more deeply with others, too many of us spend it on solitary pursuits.

Regressing to pre-internet times to regain more social connection isn't realistic, viable, or even desirable for most. What sane person would intentionally choose to refold those tricky road maps instead of relying on the real-time traffic updates of Google Maps?

However, now more than ever, we need to be more vigilant about fighting for less loneliness and more belonging in a world full of convenience and tempting distractions. Today's ATMs come in many forms. Smartphones, email, remote working, social media, one-click ordering, binge-watching, and texting present us with subtle daily choices to trade connection for convenience. Left unaware and unchecked, these modern tools can unknowingly march humanity into the deep dark sea of loneliness.

Loneliness isn't a problem to solve, however, but rather a tension to manage. It will be a tension to be managed as long as humans are fully human. Then again, if humans eventually merge with machines, perhaps we'll still experience loneliness like the solitary robot in Walt Disney Pictures' film *WALL-E*.

Loneliness isn't easily solved. Belonging must be fought for. In this book, we'll arm you with the knowledge, perspective, and tools to mount a winning fight against loneliness at work.

The Definition and Distressing Dimensions of Loneliness

Loneliness is the absence of connection.

Loneliness is a subjective feeling of the lack of trust, closeness, and affection of loved ones, close friends, and community. Loneliness is not defined by the lack of people, because someone can be lonely even while surrounded by others. As a social species, humans require more than the mere presence of others. We require the presence of others to dream, strategize, and work toward common goals with. We need to be in the presence of others who value, appreciate, and "see" us for everything we are. Loneliness is being seen through; connection is being seen as.

Unfortunately, being seen through is all too common in the workplace. Connection is traded for the convenience of moving fast. While seeing through someone greases the wheels of productivity, it leaves an organization feeling hollow, ultimately making employee disengagement and burnout a high probability.

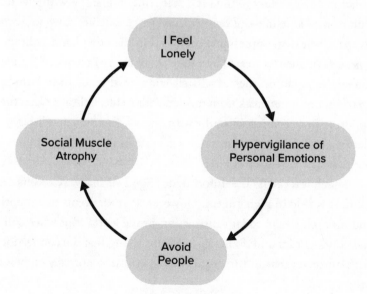

The cycle of loneliness.

Researchers Peplau and Perlman state, "Loneliness corresponds to a discrepancy between an individual's preferred and actual social relations."[3] Everyone craves and needs connection, but the size of discrepancy varies for each individual. The discrepancy for extroverts might be much larger than introverts. The discrepancy also varies across stages of life (single, married with kids, empty nesters, etc.). No matter the person or situation, humans seek belonging by securing strong relationships. The frequency of social contact or the number of relationships doesn't matter as much as the quality of connection.

Loneliness is also measured by one's personal comfort level of being isolated. Isolation is the physical state of being separated or apart from other people. Isolation decreases the opportunities to interact with other people, thus increasing the risk of loneliness. However, people can be isolated without experiencing loneliness. For example, remote workers who are isolated from other team members can experience little to no loneliness while involved in a project that interests them.

The negative state of isolation is loneliness. The positive state of isolation is solitude. Solitude is a state of being alone without the emotions of loneliness. When we experience loneliness, we want to escape it as it is an unpleasant emotion. On the other hand, solitude is peaceful aloneness created by a state of voluntary isolation. Solitude can take many forms such as self-reflection, meditation, mindfulness exercises, or a quiet break from the demands of life. Solitude offers the opportunity to connect inwardly with oneself. Emotional well-being, clarity, creativity, and perspective are some of the benefits of intentional and healthy solitude.

Loneliness carries the unfortunate stigma of shame. Conversely, solitude is held in high esteem. However, solitude seems to be more and more elusive in today's distraction-prone world. But when solitude is fought for and done right, it helps strengthen the connection with ourselves that in turn equips us to connect more deeply with others.

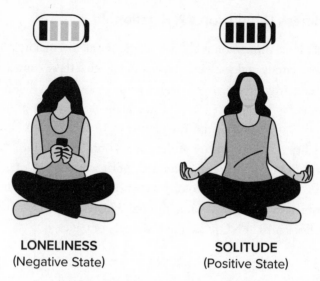

LONELINESS
(Negative State)

SOLITUDE
(Positive State)

Loneliness is depleting. Solitude is restoring.

Ironically, solitude is insurance against loneliness. And as we'll explore in this book, solitude is leaders' first line of defense in protecting against loneliness in themselves and ultimately their team.

Loneliness is a complex condition. Researchers have categorized loneliness into three dimensions that are defined by the type of relationship that is missing.[4] These three dimensions have been identified in people young and old across the globe.

Loneliness Dimension #1: Intimate

The intimate dimension is defined by the absence of a significant someone (e.g., parent, spouse, mentor, best friend). A significant someone is a person who affirms an individual's value, provides emotional support, reciprocates a mutual bond, and extends assistance during a crisis. A person's significant others can include up to five people, according to Robin Ian MacDonald Dunbar, the head of the Social and Evolutionary Neuroscience Research Group at the University of Oxford.[5]

Loneliness Dimension #2: Relational

The relational dimension is defined by the absence of quality friend-ships and family connections. Dunbar has labeled these connections as a "sympathy group" from whom people can obtain "high-cost instrumental support" (e.g., childcare, loans, help with a project).[6] A person's "sympathy group" can consist of 15 to 20 people, but it's the quality not the quantity of the connections that counts. While all three dimensions are important to both women and men, the relational dimension tends to play a slightly greater role in influenc-ing women than men according to Louise Hawkley, PhD, principal research scientist at NORC at the University of Chicago.[7]

Loneliness Dimension #3: Collective

The collective dimension is defined by the absence of community, social identities, or active networks (e.g., school, team, national iden-tity). Such networks allow individuals to connect with others with similarities, shared purpose, and common interests. Loneliness is lower the more voluntary the association. A person's active network can include 150 to 1,500 people according to Dunbar.[8] This dimen-sion tends to play a slightly greater role in influencing men than women according to Hawkley.[9]

Having healthy social connections in each of these dimensions is ideal and leads to the highest quality of life. However, many peo-ple find they are deficient in one or more of the dimensions. This explains why someone can have a supportive family at home but still feel lonely with friends or at work.

Organizational leaders play a critical role in lessening loneliness because they carry the position and influence to fulfill each loneliness dimension for the individuals on their team. The collective dimen-sion is the most likely dimension to be fulfilled by workplace teams. However, team members can still experience collective loneliness if they don't know much about their teammates, haven't identified common interests, or are unaware of the purpose of the team or organization.

While leaders themselves can fulfill the relational dimension for a team member, it may be more comfortable or appropriate for leaders to help their team members establish high-quality friendships among the team or throughout the wider organization. Establishing employee resource groups or encouraging meetups around common team interests are examples of how leaders can facilitate greater connection in the relational dimension.

The intimate dimension can be satisfied by leaders becoming a mentor for a team member. Establishing a "significant someone" status among a team is the pinnacle of leadership. When an individual is fully seen, heard, and valued by a leader, the leader's influence can extend well beyond the walls of work, providing the individual with a secure sense of belonging.

Leaders have the unique opportunity to ease one of the most distressing human conditions and help workers bring a new sense of vigor, focus, and hope to work and life. Throughout this book, we provide strategies that will enable you to satisfy each loneliness dimension of your workforce. Specifically, in Chapter 3, we'll discuss how loneliness is impacting work and the important role that work and leaders play in lessening loneliness among a team.

A Physical and Mental Health Bully

As the research on loneliness mounts, it's clear the issue goes well beyond just social issues; the physical impacts of loneliness are some of the most profound in modern medicine. As alluded to in the Introduction, 15 years is how much loneliness can shorten a person's life, equivalent to smoking 15 cigarettes a day according to a study in *Perspectives of Psychological Science*.[10]

Loneliness hinders health. According to University of Chicago psychology professor John T. Cacioppo, coauthor of *Loneliness: Human Nature and the Need for Social Connection*, loneliness may actually alter genetic activity in the human body.[11] Cacioppo discovered that inflammation and suppressed antiviral responses occur when people experience loneliness. Loneliness also hinders mental health. Older people who are lonely are 64 percent more likely to develop dementia than people of similar age who are more connected.[12] Simply put, social connections improve health.

Loneliness also decreases longevity. Feelings of loneliness can increase the risk of death by a shocking 45 percent.[13] That's greater than air pollution (6 percent), obesity (23 percent), and excessive alcohol use (37 percent). People with strong connections to family, friends, and coworkers have a 50 percent greater chance of outliving people who have fewer social connections.[14] Social connections increase longevity.

If loneliness had a side effect label, it would read like the following figure.

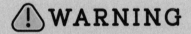

⚠ WARNING

LONELINESS MAY CAUSE:
Increase of inflammation, disrupted sleep, abnormal immune response, depression, anxiety, higher stress levels, early cognitive decline, alcoholism, cardiovascular disease, stroke, Alzheimer's disease, diabetes, and even early death or suicide.

The warning label of loneliness.

How could anyone expect a workforce to show up fully to work when these ailments are occurring? Considering loneliness is a universal human condition, it's very likely that people on your team are experiencing loneliness and struggling to bring their full and capable selves to work to deliver for their teammates, customers, and clients. It's as if we are asking workers to fully focus on the task at hand or deliver delightful customer experiences while they are being physically and mentally assaulted by an invisible bully.

It's not an exaggeration to say that loneliness is devastating workers and their organizations, silently incapacitating many and wreaking havoc on engagement, retention, and overall performance.

Who Is Lonely? (Hint: Almost Everyone)

If you're ever lonely, you're not alone. In fact, 61 percent of American adults report they are lonely, a 7 percent increase since 2018.[15] In 2020, during the Covid-19 global pandemic, 47 percent of Americans reported having lost touch with at least a few friends.[16]

Here's a flow chart to help you determine if loneliness is normal.

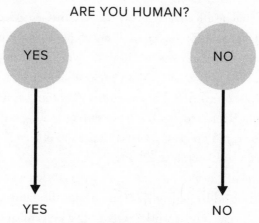

ARE YOU HUMAN?

Only the inhuman are immune.

Anyone, anywhere, anytime can feel lonely. Loneliness is not a respecter of persons, and its impact is felt worldwide. In Canada, 54 percent of adults report being lonely or isolated.[17] In Australia, one in four people report feeling lonely at least one day a week.[18]

In England, 45 percent of adults feel occasionally, sometimes, or often lonely.[19] In Hungary and Greece, over 40 percent socialize with friends and family only once a month or less.[20] In Lithuania, Estonia, and Poland, 35 percent socialize with friends and family once a month or less. In Italy, 13 percent of adults report having no one to ask for help.[21] In Latin America and the Caribbean, about one in six students reported being lonely most or all of the time and/or having no close friends.[22] In Japan, half a million people live as "modern-day hermits" or recluses who withdraw from all social contact and often don't leave their houses for years at a time.[23]

Who's lonely? Everyone. Who's loneliest? Generation Z.

The Next Generation of Loneliness

A connected world that's leaving so many feeling disconnected is counterintuitive and troublesome, yet it's humanity's new reality. And this new reality is impacting the next-generation workforce at an alarming rate. Seventy-three percent of Gen Z report sometimes or always feeling alone,[24] a 4 percent increase since 2019—the highest level of any generation.

The mental health challenges experienced by Gen Z are like nothing any other generation has faced. Only 45 percent of Gen Z report "excellent" or "very good" mental health,[25] which is the lowest of any generation. Ninety-one percent of Gen Z adults say they have experienced at least one physical or emotional symptom because of stress such as feeling depressed or sad (58 percent) or lacking interest, motivation, or energy (55 percent).[26] And 68 percent of Gen Z report feeling significant stress about the future.[27]

While mental health has previously been labeled a personal issue that should be addressed on personal time, the ramifications are showing up negatively at work. Seventy-five percent of Gen Z and half of Millennials left a job because of mental health reasons,[28] compared with 34 percent of other generations. For employers, the implications are clear: employee engagement and retention issues will loom large if loneliness isn't addressed.

These numbers become increasingly concerning when you consider that 75 percent of the global workforce will be Millennials and Gen Z by 2030.[29] Even if mental health and loneliness aren't concerns that are vocalized by your current team. . . . It. Is. Coming.

Gen Z will be the first generation in the workplace that has never been offline. The entire generation is younger than Google. That makes our Millennial hips hurt just writing that. Despite Gen Z's digital upbringing and the inevitable advances of virtual reality, artificial intelligence, and blockchain inside the workplace, Gen Z wants human elements at work.

The human elements of "supportive leadership" and "positive relationships at work" were Gen Z's top two most important factors to consider in a job.[30] And when it comes to workplace communication, our research discovered that 72 percent of Gen Z want to communicate via face-to-face at work. In addition, 83 percent of Gen Z workers prefer to engage with managers in person, yet 82 percent of managers believe their Gen Z employees prefer to communicate via instant message.[31] Further, 57 percent of Gen Z want to receive feedback several times a week, but only 50 percent of their managers provide feedback to them that frequently.[32]

Most leaders seem to be deaf to Gen Z's cries for more human connection. Effective leaders of the future will need to couple high-tech and high-touch among their teams. They will need to serve up the technology that the next generation has come to expect while delivering the human elements they crave and need.

While loneliness impacts all generations, it is intensified among the emerging generations. Although the insights and tools discussed in this book are generationally agnostic, all of us need to keep a close eye on the next generation because we don't know what hangs in the balance if we fail to address the human connection needs of the most technologically advanced generation in human history.

Our Brains Are Fueling the Raging Fire of Loneliness

On any given Friday evening in the 1990s, most families who were fully immersed in watching TGIF, the hilarious two-hour television sitcom programming block that stood for Thank God It's Friday, would gladly answer an unexpected ring of the doorbell. Urkel, Topanga, and Uncle Jesse were set aside as the whole family ran to the door to see what delightful surprise awaited on the other side. It wasn't their latest Amazon Prime package, but something even more delightful—a guest. Someone who was "just in the neighborhood" and wanted to stop by. The family gladly ignored phone calls on the landline, brought out the guest-only glassware, and gave the guest their undivided attention.

How people answer an unexpected ring of the doorbell today is completely different. Many become suspicious and hope the quasi-intruder doesn't get a glimpse of any movement inside the house. Residents discreetly peek through window blinds in the hope they'll see an Amazon driver heading back into their van.

Today people have the power to pause any program they are watching to direct their attention toward the person on the other side of the door, and yet they react to the doorbell ringing as a bigger inconvenience than the pre-TiVo TGIF-watching family did. Similarly at work, phone calls or office visitors are met with the same acts of avoidance.

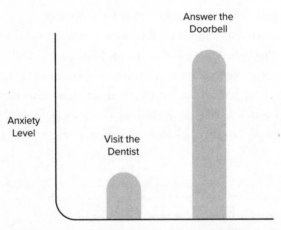

These days few things in life strike as much dread as the doorbell ring.

What's happened to our openness to connect with unexpected visitors? The research of Nick Epley, a University of Chicago Booth School of Business professor and behavioral scientist, provides a possible explanation.

When Epley rode the train into Chicago, he was fascinated by why people ignored each other every day on the 45-minute commute. He wondered why it was so deathly quiet on a train full of people who carried so much knowledge, stories, and jokes. His curiosity led him to partner with Juliana Schroeder, an assistant professor at the University of California, Berkeley, Haas School of Business, in 2014 to conduct research aimed at discovering how people benefit from spontaneous social interaction.[33]

Epley and Schroeder recruited random passengers and divided them into three groups each with a specific condition. The first group was the "solitude condition" where passengers were instructed to keep to themselves, not engage with anyone, and focus on the day ahead. The second group was the "control condition" where passengers were instructed to do whatever they normally did, which was typically not speaking to others. The third group was the "connection condition" where passengers were instructed to make a connection with someone else on the train and get to know something about a stranger.

Epley and Schroeder discovered that people reported the most positive experience in the connection condition and the least positive experience in the solitude condition. Epley and Schroeder thought that maybe the people who were spoken to would report having a negative experience because they were being interrupted—but that was not the case. Even the people who were spoken to reported a more positive experience. Connecting with someone is pleasant whether you're initiating it or receiving it.

Epley and Schroeder repeated this study in other contexts such as city buses, cabs, airports, and waiting rooms. Every environment they tested had the same results: people were happier when they were connecting with others. They also discovered that there was no difference between introverts and extroverts. Introverts enjoyed connecting with others as much as extroverts did. What tends to vary is their expectations. Introverts who expect not to enjoy a conversation will choose not to engage. However, on average, both felt happier when connecting with others.

Epley reported these findings to the head of marketing at the train company thinking marketers might act on his research to create better well-being for Chicago train commuters. Epley learned that they had done their own research and the people surveyed had said they wanted a "quiet [train] car," not one in which they could converse with each other. Epley's surveyed passengers also thought they would be happier not talking to people, but the results proved otherwise.

Epley asked the train company employees if they ever considered creating a "chatty car." They said no, but in the past, they had bar cars where alcohol was served, but they got rid of them because they were "too busy." Meaning they were too popular. For decades, commuters chose newspapers, magazines, books, and music instead of connecting with others. Now they choose YouTube, Spotify, and Netflix.

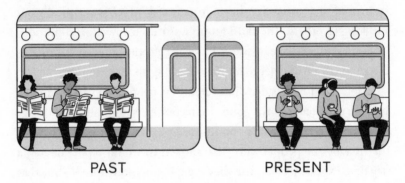

PAST   PRESENT

Evolution of ignoring others on public transit.

Why are people so resistant to social interactions whether it's answering the doorbell or small talk on a train? Because most people wrongly predict that engaging with others won't be pleasant. We think a quick conversation will be awkward, too time consuming, or not worth the effort, but those intuitions are wrong, even for shy people. Our brains mislead us, but the research is clear, that connecting with others, no matter our personality type, makes us feel happier and less lonely.

Where is one of the best places for people to connect with each other? At work—yet there too loneliness is growing. In 1985, 50 percent of people said they had a close friend at work.[34] By 2004, less than a third did. Organizations and leaders will need to divorce the outdated idea that personal well-being is reserved for personal time and instead strive to develop solutions to the loneliness epidemic. In doing so, they will build more connected organizations, with improved employee engagement, well-being, and performance.

The Power Source of Well-Being

You don't necessarily need research to tell you that connecting with others is a well-being booster, because you've likely experienced a lifted spirit after conversing with someone, perhaps even today. Healthy people take time for social connection. Mature leaders take time for team connection.

Think of your team's and your own well-being like the depleting battery of your phone. You don't have a pleasant conversation with someone once and then feel recharged forever. Our well-being batteries are always depleting, and it takes seeking and establishing meaningful connections to replenish the battery. Much like connecting your phone charger to a power source to increase the battery life, you must connect with others to increase your well-being and protect against the empty battery that is loneliness.

We too readily assume that convenience, efficiency, and instant gratification are the roots to happiness. Rather, strong social connections are the power source for our well-being.

Your team's batteries are depleting faster and faster, but before we equip you with the equipment to get your team recharged and reengaged, let's first understand what's draining our batteries and leaving us so lonely.

2

THE MODERN CAUSES OF LONELINESS

Even the technology that promises to unite us,
divides us. Each of us is now electronically connected
to the globe, and yet we feel utterly alone.

DAN BROWN

It's 7:38 a.m., and in a whirlwind you snatch your work bag and head out the door. You're on your way to an important meeting across town that you are in jeopardy of being late to. You'll be playing a critical role in the meeting as the sole presenter of the market analysis for your largest client. On your way to the meeting, you encounter a person injured on the side of the road.

Would you stop and help the injured person and run the risk of being late to your meeting? Or would you assume the person is OK and stay on course to ensure you show up on time?

Considering you have an interest in improving humanity, you would probably say you'd stop to help. However, studies show that most people actually would not stop . . . even under the most ironic of circumstances.

Two behavioral scientists, John Darley and Daniel Batson, conducted an experiment to study what people do in a similar scenario.[1] They tasked a group of students with delivering a public speech on an important topic. It was a topic the students were very familiar with, so it was a fairly straightforward and only mildly stressful request.

The researchers segmented the students into three groups and informed each that the speech was to be delivered across campus at another building. The first group was told that their speech would happen later that day, so they had plenty of time to get there. The second group was told they would have to leave immediately if they wanted to make it on time. The third group was told they were already late for the speech and would need to hurry on over to the other building.

While the students were on their way to deliver their speech, the researchers staged a scenario where an actor lay on the ground pretending to be injured. The actor was strategically placed to block an alleyway on the students' route. The alleyway was only four feet across, so the students could not miss seeing the person in need.

Of the students who had "plenty of time," 63 percent stopped to help the stranger. Of the students who were "on time," 45 percent stopped to help the stranger. And of the students who were "late," only 10 percent stopped to help the stranger.

Astonishingly, 90 percent of the students in a hurry stepped right over the person in need!

Now, there are a few details we left out that make these findings even more astounding. The speech was actually a sermon. The students were priests in training at the Princeton Theological Seminary.

And here's the kicker: the sermon topic they were planning to deliver was about the story of the Good Samaritan from the Bible.

The Good Samaritan story was a parable told by Jesus specifically about a person who was robbed, beaten, and left half dead alongside the road where people (including a priest) passed by without stopping to help. In the parable, it was a Samaritan who finally stopped and was moved with compassion to help the injured person. The Samaritan helped the man up, bound his wounds, took him to an inn to rest, and covered all the costs. In the parable, the Good Samaritan is the person we are all supposed to emulate.

Even when soon-to-be priests were primed to be thinking about the Good Samaritan story, many failed to demonstrate compassion, even when an opportunity presented itself just minutes later. Oh, the irony!

Prior to the students encountering the injured person, they were asked if they were religious primarily for intrinsic reasons ("I am motivated to do good in the world") or extrinsic reasons ("I really want to get into heaven"). These dispositional factors had no bearing on whether the individual helped the injured person or not. The time constraints, on the other hand, had the most impact on the behaviors to help or not,

What makes Darley and Batson's research even more surprising is that the experiment was conducted in the 1970s when the attention of the students stepping over the injured person wasn't divided among work emails, instant messages, or 24-7 news feeds.

Being a good person with good intentions to help others isn't enough to ward off the behaviors that cause us to avoid connecting with others. Situational factors determine our levels of engagement with others. Today's never-ending flow of information has transformed our situational factors in ways that cause us to blindly step over people right in front of us. These new facets are subtly pulling us apart. We have to be vigilant about guarding against these new situations, in life and at work, that steal our attention from those who need it most.

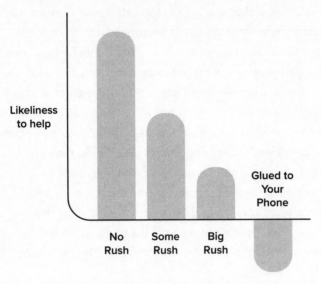

Likeliness to help

Glued to Your Phone

No Rush   Some Rush   Big Rush

Time constraints hinder our willingness to engage with others.

The Rapid Spread of Loneliness

Priests in training stepping over a person in need on their way to tell others how to treat their neighbor is not a good look for humanity. And yet, when tragedy strikes in the form of a hurricane or flood, we show up for our neighbors. Depending on our situational factors, we decide to donate blood, time, money, or sweat to rebuild and serve those in need.

This is what made the Covid-19 pandemic such a paradox for humans. When the disaster struck, a few people fought their neighbors over the last roll of toilet paper at the grocery store. On the other hand, the initial reaction of a larger number of people was to help their neighbors. However, even though we had more in common with our global neighbors than ever before, many of us went in the opposite direction of our instincts—away from others. Loneliness ensued.

By April 2020, according to a global study of more than 2,700 employees across more than 10 industries undertaken by Qualtrics and SAP, 75 percent of people said they felt more socially isolated since the outbreak of the pandemic.[2] Only 6.9 percent of workers said their levels of loneliness decreased since the start of the pandemic according to our research.

Before the pandemic, loneliness was already growing at an alarming pace with rates of loneliness doubling since the 1980s.[3] Additionally, the number of Americans who say they have no close friends has roughly tripled since 1985.[4] When asked in the survey, "How many confidants do you currently have?" the most common response was "zero."[5] And 22 percent of Millennials report having "no friends."[6]

What's causing loneliness to accelerate? Virality. Loneliness has been proven to spread through social networks (not social media but literal social networks). According to professor John T. Cacioppo, "[There's] an extraordinary pattern at the edge of the social network. On the periphery, people have fewer friends, which makes them lonely, but it also drives them to cut the few ties that they have left. But before they do, they tend to transmit the same feeling of loneliness to their remaining friends, starting the cycle anew. These reinforcing effects mean that our social fabric can fray at the edges, like a thread that comes loose at the end of a crocheted sweater."[7] Too many sweaters have begun unraveling, due to how contagious loneliness is. A loose thread at the end of a sweater, if not mended immediately, unravels until the sweater is no longer recognizable and useful.

You've probably seen the virality of loneliness play out in real life. For example, if a team member at work is lonely, he becomes less committed and less approachable, thus making it less likely that others will reach out to help. Ultimately, this compounds the problem making the individual more lonesome and the team more susceptible to loneliness. This is bad news for an already lonely workforce, as loneliness begets loneliness, creating a downward spiral that becomes difficult to surmount.

While loneliness abounds, there is good news. In the same way that loneliness is contagious, so is kindness, which is an antidote for loneliness.

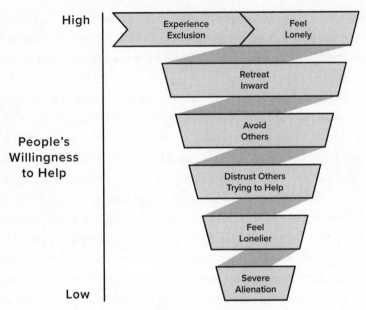

The severe spiral of loneliness.
The unhealthy transition from exclusion to alienation.

According to Jamil Zaki, director of the Stanford Social Neuroscience Laboratory and the author of *The War for Kindness: Building Empathy in a Fractured World*, "People imitate not only the particulars of positive actions, but also the spirit underlying them. This implies that kindness itself is contagious, and that it can cascade across people, taking on new forms along the way. To be a potent social force, positive conformity requires such flexibility. Not everyone can afford to donate to charity or spend weeks on a service trip to Haiti. Witnessing largesse in others, then, could inhibit would-be do-gooders who feel that they can't measure up. Our work suggests that an individual's kindness can nonetheless trigger people to spread positivity in other ways."[8]

Being other focused thwarts the feelings of loneliness. When we decide to step toward and not over others, we take a massive leap toward belonging.

Imagine you are strolling around one of the busiest plazas in London and you see a man on a sidewalk with a sign offering free hugs. His arms are open wide, he's smiling from cheek to cheek, he looks friendly (and just as important is well-groomed!). He has a warm spirit and pure intentions. Do you feel the need to go in for a hug, or do you avoid making eye contact hoping not to be seen?

While not the first person to attempt the social experiment, Aaron Le Conte, the man with the "free hugs" sign, is keen on spreading kindness to strangers. It does not take long before his first "customer" walks up, thinks for a second, and then goes in for the embrace. What might seem awkward is met with utter joy. Both Aaron and the stranger unlock from their embrace beaming, giving off the impression they were friends reunited.

Aaron posted the video of his social experiment on YouTube.[9] In the 14-minute video, you see people of all ages, genders, and races go in for a hug. Each person leaves the exchange with a smile you can see from outer space. An older woman even leaves the exchange with tears strolling down her face.

While we are not always in a position to give a hug, Aaron's experiment is a helpful reminder of how powerful connection is. The warm embrace a team can extend to a new hire through their presence or a leader can extend to a team member through her full attention can provide the same loneliness-lifting feelings of a physical hug. It's up to leaders to set the example by letting kindness and belonging become a contagion that overtakes the psychological poison that is loneliness.

Loneliness is spreading. But before we give you the practical and easy-to-implement tools to stop the spread, let's first understand the primary modern-day causes. If we understand the cause of an ailment, we can begin to be proactive about rooting out the behaviors to prevent loneliness from occurring. Awareness is curative. Becoming aware of an issue is often enough to help improve it.

The Big Eight Contributors to Modern-Day Loneliness

Some causes of loneliness are unfortunate like growing apart from a close friend or family member. Some causes of loneliness are unavoidable like a health condition that isolates someone in a hospital. Some causes are due to personality disorders that hinders one's capacity to communicate and connect. And some causes of loneliness are self-inflicted and preventable like choosing the convenience of an ATM over connecting with a bank teller.

There are many contributors to loneliness. The following "Big Eight" are the modern-day contributors that you as a leader have direct control over. Controlling those contributors allows you to lessen loneliness among your team and yourself.

Humans have experienced loneliness for centuries. (We'll explore this further in Chapter 4, so for now just take our word for it.) But the following eight causes of loneliness are brand spanking new in the grand scheme of humanity. This is why we have to be more alert than ever before, because there is a growing regime equipped with the latest technology to tactfully and stealthily put our social connections into a sleeper hold.

1. Busyness: Society's New Status Quo

Look no further than the study of the priests at Princeton Theological Seminary to understand how time constraints can severely limit our willingness to engage with others. The students were so preoccupied with being on time to deliver their sermon, they neglected the needs of someone who was right in front of them.

Our preoccupation has skyrocketed in recent years. We are all distracted. We are distracted by work, house chores, progress, social media, the activities of today, the commitments of tomorrow, and then relieving the stress from it all. Our distractions are eating up most of our cognitive resources, leaving little to nothing for focusing on others. We'd all like to think we would never step over a person in need, yet that is what we do every day when we choose an impersonal email over empathy, a text over touch, or Facebook over face-to-face.

Ryan falls victim to neglecting the needs of those around him every time he rushes through an airport to catch his connecting flight. It wasn't until recently that he had enough margin between flights that he was able to spring into action when a woman unknowingly dropped her scarf on the ground. He was able to traverse the terminal to retrieve her scarf and catch up with her before she boarded her flight. If he had been rushing to catch his flight that day, he would have stepped over her scarf, missing the opportunity to experience how relieved and grateful she was.

Are we able to stop for everyone, every time? No, sometimes we need to catch that flight. But at times we need to build in more margin so we can show up for those around us. More margin means more opportunity for meaningful connections.

A top response these days when you ask someone, "How are you?" is "Busy."

Busyness has become a badge of honor, a pseudo status symbol. We falsely assume that having spare time gives the impression of laziness or misguidedness. Spending time in solitude to reflect, think, and journal is an afterthought or pipe dream to most. If we aren't scheduled to the brim, we don't know what to do with ourselves. Somewhere along the way the value of leisure has decreased and the value of busy increased.

We live in a world today where it takes little effort to fill your time. An endless amount of content in the palm of our hands has allowed us to consume news and entertainment whenever and wherever we are. We've become a culture more focused on strengthening our Wi-Fi connections than strengthening our personal connections. How often have you ignored a colleague's invitation to momentarily and serendipitously connect in order to send off an email that in all likelihood could have waited until the next day? We need to trade our connectable technology for a more connectable team.

Culture demands that we do more. Working through lunch, not using all of our allocated vacation days, and consuming countless cups of afternoon coffee point to our propensity for busyness. Not to mention the pull we feel outside of work to "keep up with the Joneses." Our fear of missing out (FOMO) causes us to stockpile new products in our garages and fit new activities and experiences into every open space on our calendars. The ways to spend our precious free time are now endless. And if we're not careful, we'll spend our free time on the immediate instead on the important.

Steve Cole, a genomics researcher at the University of California who studies the effects of loneliness at the molecular level, says "We have created a culture of living which is different from our historical default state. We are relaxed and at ease by default and are bonding oriented in our resting state. But few of us feel this way. It's less common for us to be sitting around a fire talking with neighbors. Instead, we are racing around trying to get work done all the time. Our current state is different from what our physiology is engineered to support."

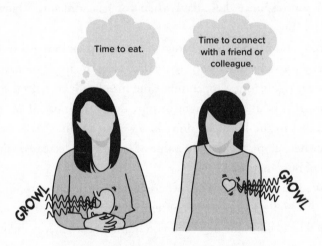

Two different yet critical appetites.
"Is that your 'need for belonging' growling?"

Progress is good. Humans are driven by it. Where we get into trouble is that it's hard to see progress in relationships, which makes it easier at times to turn to our to-do list, respond to a few emails, or level-up in a video game than to lean into a relationship. Thus, today's workers have a tendency to deprioritize relationships at work and instead focus on the busyness of getting it all done or appearing to have it all together.

Is it busyness that causes loneliness, or are we busy to distract from the pain of our loneliness? Either way, busyness is leaving us with less time to connect, making us feel lonelier.

2. Technology: A Social Dilemma

"Maybe I should go to the store like a 'normal person' but I choose delivery for my kumquats. And I choose to have a robot vacuum my floor. I choose to ride the escalator going down. And stream movies I own on DVD. And to let social media remember birthdays for me. I choose to unlock my front door via my smartwatch. I choose to date people by computational algorithms and will never ask for a date in-person like some sort of animal. I choose to buy a car from my couch and have it delivered to my front door because what you call lazy, I call brilliant."[10]

This was a popular US commercial by Carvana, an online car retailer, that aired during Super Bowl XLIX in 2014. It hilariously exemplified how technology has impacted every aspect of our lives, from meal delivery, to dating, to house security, to car buying. It's hard to imagine settings that don't include technology. Even when hiking in the middle of Yosemite National Park in California, far removed from the technological pulse of our day to day, streaming Spotify through a Bluetooth speaker is commonplace. And that's both wonderful and worrisome. It's amazing at what tech can do, but alarming how dependent (and consumed) we've become with it.

Of course, inherently technology and social media aren't bad. They're tools. But just like any tool, such as a hammer, they can be helpful or harmful depending on how you use them. And unfortunately, most of us aren't utilizing technology well. Instead of managing technology, the technology is often managing us. The ping, ding, and ring of our devices causes us to act, versus the other way around.

But in our defense, technology and social media are really new to humanity. In the scheme of humankind, technology and social media is still a blastocyst (a very early stage of a growing embryo). Many of the technological advancements are so new that we're still learning how they're impacting our behaviors—positively and negatively.

While technology and social media can be instrumental in sparking new connections and helping people find communities of like-minded people, they aren't very useful for deepening those connections. It's the old fashioned, time-tested "oldie but goodie" actions like eye contact, empathy, smiling, physical touch, and other emotionally intelligent behaviors that move relationships in the direction we all ultimately crave and need.

According to Erica Keswin, author of *Bring Your Human to Work: 10 Surefire Ways to Design a Workplace That Is Good for People, Great for Business, and Just Might Change the World*, the depth of our conversations is impacted by the simple presence of our smartphones. When a smartphone is in sight, the conversation instantly becomes more trivial and transactional. She calls this the "iPhone Effect." Technology can reduce quality human interactions through distractions and/or by substituting lower quality online connections. This is one of many reasons why most of today's workers believe "technology and social media" contributes most to loneliness (37 percent) according to our research.

All of this begs the question: Why do people continue to adopt new technology if it causes so many barriers between themselves and others? For most of us, the benefits outweigh the risks. And as Carvana illustrated, technology has the power to turn friction-filled daily activities to frictionless. As we continue to integrate more technology into our lives, we must do so through a lens of well-being, because as emerging technologies like virtual reality, blockchain, and artificial intelligence accelerate, our vulnerability to further isolation and loneliness will increase.

When it comes to social media, studies show that very heavy social media users are significantly more likely to feel alone, isolated, left out, and without companionship.[11] Social media has caused a comparison trap. Comparing our life to someone else's highlight reel leads to questions like: am I good enough, smart enough, wealthy enough, etc.? You fill in the blank.

According to Roger Patulny, associate professor of sociology at the University of Wollongong in Australia, while heavy social media users do experience more loneliness, there is also evidence to suggest social media use decreases loneliness among highly social people. Why the contradiction? "Social media is most effective in tackling loneliness when it is used to enhance existing relationships, or forge new meaningful connections. On the other hand, it is counterproductive if used as a substitute for real-life social interaction. Thus, it is not social media itself, but the way we integrate it into our existing lives which impacts loneliness," says Patulny.[12]

The connections available to us are astounding, promising, and for some a great start to boost belonging. But the quantity of connections doesn't make up for the quality of connections needed to lessen loneliness. High-quality connections online are rare because of how status-driven and polished the environments tend to be. However, anonymity can provide a safe haven for some people who need specific help or support.

While technology and social media are clear contributors to loneliness, there are many other cultural shifts afoot that are contributing to our growing sense of isolation.

3. Dependency Shift: The Google Effect

Ryan and his wife recently threw a first birthday party for their youngest son. To help them prepare the food, they enlisted the help of their college-aged family friend, Cassidy (not her real name). Cassidy is a smart, supportive, and self-reliant Gen Zer who has been a helpful part of their family for years.

They asked Cassidy to prepare a portion of a dish that required capers. They handed her a can of capers along with a manual can opener. A few minutes passed, and they noticed there was no progress on Cassidy's dish. When Ryan went to check on her, he noticed she was watching a video on her phone. She wasn't procrastinating—quite the opposite, she was learning. She was watching a YouTube tutorial on how to use a manual can opener. After watching and rewatching the video a few times, she put her phone down and operated the can opener like a pro. Either out of mild shame or being sensitive to not disrupt the tasks of everyone else in the kitchen, she had silently and independently learned how to use the can opener using her device. No human required.

Information is no longer centralized in a family member, neighbor, coworker, or leader. Information is decentralized, empowering humanity to seek knowledge (or help) individually.

Humans are naturally dependent on each other. However, we aren't as dependent as we once were. In the past, if your faucet was leaking in your home, you may have knocked on your neighbor's door to ask for a plumber recommendation. Or you may have called a family member or friend to have them guide you through the process to fix it. Today, your first step would likely be to open YouTube and search for "how to fix a leaky faucet."

The same is true at work. In the past, if you didn't know how to create a pivot table in Excel, you would walk around to the desks of your coworkers to ask who knew how to do such Excel wizardry. Today a simple YouTube search yields a 2:14 minute video that clearly outlines what to do.

Gen Z isn't the only guilty party in leveraging Google or YouTube to gain knowledge. Many of us are now quick to turn to the super-computers in our pockets before we "inconvenience" someone else. This isn't necessarily bad; this is useful and expeditious. But if these subtle non-human-reliant actions are becoming more commonplace, we need to build in more time for connection elsewhere in our lives.

As our dependency shifts more and more to technology, automation, and artificial intelligence—without a counterbalance—our loneliness will grow.

4. Immediacy: Instant Isn't Fast Enough

In December 2020, Mountain Dew and Papa John's announced they were teaming up to create a game controller with a button that allows gamers to instantly order their favorite pizza without disengaging from their gaming session.[13]

If you weren't a weary-eyed and hungry gamer, then you might think this was a bit excessive. Yet, this novelty device isn't the first to feed the immediacy monster that lurks in humans. In 2019 the snack brand Pringles introduced a specialized gaming headset that included a swivel arm that automatically fed the brand's stackable potato chips directly into a wearer's mouth.[14] Bud Light recently created the BL6, a gaming console shaped like a six-pack of brews with built in koozies to fulfill gamers' immediate need for a refreshing drink.[15]

While these inventions are a novelty, cheeky, and a nice branding play, they also provide a glimpse into how infatuated we've become with immediacy. Each kooky invention is a subtle nod to humanity's growing appetite for immediacy, an escalating priority that was seeded by our first use of the microwave oven.

Gamers aren't alone in their insatiable need for immediacy. Most of us are more enraptured with right now than we'd care to admit. Just measure how fast you can go from content to irritated by having to wait a few short minutes in line at the self-checkout kiosk at the grocery store or waiting an extra few seconds for Netflix to load.

In the car, when Steven's three-year-old asks to play her favorite song, Taylor Swift's "Shake It Off," she routinely asks, "Dad what's taking so long!" The few seconds it takes to play the song feels like an eternity for her. Steven has noticed that any request from his daughter that takes longer than six seconds to process creates immediate frustration.

The emerging generations can't remember a world that hasn't been fully on-demand. Millennials have had access to the world's information curated into a search box in the palm of their hand for the majority (if not the entirety) of their life. Gen Z has access to information (thank you, Alexa) at the tip of their tongue. The generation after Gen Z will, in all seriousness, be able to access information at the tip of their brain. (Just imagine ordering your favorite pizza with a double wink of your right eye.)

This immediacy leads to loneliness. According to the 2016 VICELAND UK Census, loneliness was the number one fear of young people—ranking ahead of losing a home or a job.[16] In addition, 42 percent of Millennial women in 2017 said they were more afraid of loneliness than a cancer diagnosis, by far the highest share of any generation.[17]

Millennials were the first generation to feel the impact of an on-demand culture. This caused Millennials to have different perspectives, expectations, and behaviors. On-demand access changed how Millennials searched for jobs, learned, socialized, traveled, communicated, built businesses, networked, entertained themselves, bought and sold goods, and worked. This on-demand, hyperconnected, and fully accessible environment is now every generation's reality.

We now have on-demand access to:

- ▶ Movies
- ▶ Food
- ▶ Transportation
- ▶ New or used cars
- ▶ Jobs
- ▶ Romantic dates
- ▶ Education
- ▶ Event tickets
- ▶ Hotel rooms
- ▶ And anything else from A to Z via Amazon

None of the previous was on-demand just 20 years ago. While today's on-demand capabilities empower us as individual consumers, they make us increasingly susceptible to weaker social ties. "On-demand" by definition is at the convenience of the requester. No coordination or consideration is given (or needed) for anyone else.

Additionally, the immediacy of having all of our contacts in our pocket just a few swipes away can give us a false sense of connection.

Today's on-demand culture has left many people opting for swift transactional digital relationships over the delayed gratification of investing in long-term relationships. A lack of relational investments leaves one prone to loneliness.

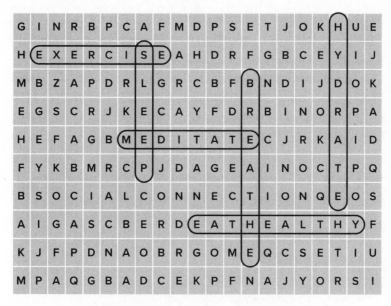

Can you find the self-care activity many people overlook?

5. Remote Work: The Mobilization of a Nation

No longer do people need to be in the same location as their ideal employer, family, or friends. Mobile technology, ubiquitous connectivity, telecommuting, and the rising "gig economy" have created a perfect storm for individuals to be less dependent on their communities and more independent in deciding when and where they live and work. This mobility and independence provides less risk of losing a job if someone chooses to move and seemingly less risk of severing relationships.

Remote work is expected to grow. Eighty-three percent of office workers want to work from home at least one day a week,[18] and 55 percent of employers anticipate that most of their workers will do so. Global Workplace Analytics predicts that 30 million US employees will regularly work from home within the next two years,[19] which is six times as many as did before. Additionally, 81 percent of workers say they would be more loyal to their employer if they had flexible work options.[20] An April 2021 McKinsey & Company remote work survey found that 25 percent of employees said they would consider switching employers if their organization returns to fully on-site work.[21] And one in four workers say the ability to work from home is so important that they are willing to take a 10 to 20 percent pay cut to do so.[22]

Remote work works. Halo Top, the reduced-calorie ice cream brand, grew from $230,000 in revenue in 2013 to more than $100 million in 2018, and it achieved that growth with all 75 employees working remotely.[23] According to FlexJobs' 2020 survey, 95 percent of respondents said that their productivity was higher or the same working from home, and 51 percent report being more productive when working remotely.[24] Their top reasons for increased productivity include:

- ► Fewer interruptions
- ► More focused time
- ► Quieter work environment
- ► More comfortable workspace
- ► Not being involved in office politics

Notice a theme within this list? The reasons why productivity goes up while working at home all stem from spending less time with people. While increased productivity is great for business, it can have a toll on our well-being. Left unchecked, the intoxicating benefits of remote work can leave workers blind to the harmful side effects.

Remote work invites isolation and disconnection. If the 2020 worldwide Covid-19 lockdown taught us anything, it's how soul crushing it can be to work without being able to connect in-person with our teammates and customers. Even if you're someone who typically thrives in a remote work setting, zero human connection can leave you drained and discouraged. Many of us will never again underestimate the restoring value of sharing a meal with a colleague, the playful banter after a successful team presentation, or the comforting pat on the back after experiencing another customer rejection.

People not only have newfound mobility in the way they work but also in the way they live.

Transitoriness is a relationship killer. Just ask any Hallmark movie character. When the busy business executive finds herself back in her small town for just a few weeks to transition her family business, but then falls in love with the longtime local resident, their relationship remains surface level for a time. The temporal only becomes more lasting after she decides to be with her newfound love by moving back home to run her family business.

How can we expect ourselves or those around us to invest fully in a relationship knowing it's fleeting? It's just like when an overeager networker is done with the current conversation and starts looking over your shoulder at the next person he is going to talk to. Mobility can turn our eyes toward the next opportunity or location and leave us with superficial relationships in the meantime.

Stated differently, substitute teachers are far less likely to get to know their students than the full-time teacher is. Not because they don't care, but they simply lack the time.

It's never been easier (and more acceptable) to adopt a transient lifestyle without the risk of losing a job or communal relationships. Less time in a location to invest in communal relationships or the opportunity of leaving at a moment's notice can hinder anyone's ability to invest fully in relationships. Today's high-tech, hyperconnected, and on-demand world makes being transient easy and being susceptible to loneliness even easier.

This loneliness contributor is one that leaders must be aware of as they make decisions on promoting, relocating, and onboarding new employees.

6. Always-on Work: A Never-Ending Routine

The year is 1991. A bowl of Kix, with 2 percent milk, is consumed quickly in the morning. Judi Sheppard's Jazzercise VHS workout tape is playing in the background. Jeff, a middle-aged accountant, puts on his nicest turtleneck and heads to work. Jeff gets to work at 9:00 a.m., works until 5:00 p.m., and heads home. Once home, Jeff isn't tempted to work anymore because he doesn't have the capacity to do so. His work telephone, desk, word processor, manila folders, and filing cabinet are located inside the office building. Jeff can share an uninterrupted meal with his family, toss a football with his kids, and watch an episode of *Seinfeld* and not feel obligated to do anything work related until tomorrow. Must have been nice.

For many back then, work was a single location. Today, work has shifted from a place to a space. The technology shift from fixed communications to mobile communications has redefined how and where we work.

The never-offline and always-available work culture is today's norm. For many people, turning off work at 5:00 p.m. is an anti-quated practice. What's typical for most is checking email prior to getting out of bed in the morning, shopping online while at work, exchanging texts with their managers after 8:00 p.m., and then start-ing the week's projects on Sunday afternoon.

Today's most beloved employers encourage always-on work by including meditation spaces, nap rooms, foosball tables, and fully stocked kitchens inside the workplace to ensure employees never have to leave work. Most of these employers likely have good inten-tions to reduce loneliness by using these perks, but by keeping employees away from their communal relationships and not help-ing protect their personal time, these employers inadvertently have increased worker isolation.

Insert a global pandemic in 2020, and the lines between work and life vanish. Job board searches including the keyword "remote" climbed to all-time highs.[25] Notable companies like Siemens, Twitter, Nielsen, Square, Nationwide Insurance, and Zillow all granted their employees the option to work from home permanently.

According to 2020 data, 61 percent of employers said that they expect their staff to be available outside of regular hours.[26] More employees are working through lunch and logging on to tackle work tasks late into the night than ever before.[27] In addition, 51 percent of employees reported symptoms of burnout in May 2020 (when many were forced to work from home), and by the end of June 2020, the figure had jumped to 69 percent.[28] Even before the arrival of the novel coronavirus our work-life balance was out of control as 42 percent of employees said they feel obligated to check in with work while they're vacationing, and more than one-fourth feel guilty for using all their vacation time.[29] We attempted to capture the new workplace environment in the next illustration.

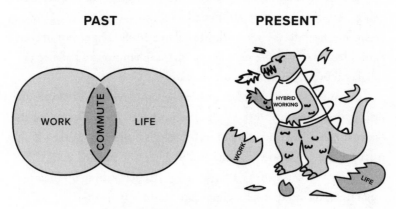

The work-life havoc of hybrid working.

All of this explains why our current relationship between work and life is so tumultuous and why we are having such a hard time establishing the necessary guardrails to protect our personal time and social connections outside of work. We are in a constant and ever-evolving battle to keep work at bay just long enough to maintain our crucial personal relationships while still qualifying for the next promotion.

Of course, working hard and long hours isn't bad—until it leads to burnout. Reaching burnout status is different for everyone and depends on your age, stage of life, personality, role and responsibilities, industry, and so on. What doesn't differ is how quickly burnout can turn an always-on productive employee into an always-off lonely employee.

A recent Gallup study of nearly 7,500 full-time employees found that 76 percent of employees experience burnout on the job at least sometimes, and 28 percent say they are burned out "very often" or "always" at work.[30] According to the 2016 LinkedIn Censuswide Study, nearly half of American workers would forgo the corner-office job and a high salary to gain more flexibility in their schedules.[31] And according to the Center of Generational Kinetics State of Gen Z® 2020 study, after salary, working-age

(16–24) Gen Z individuals are most attracted to jobs that offer flexible scheduling (29 percent) and they place flexible hours at the top of their desired workplace benefits.[32]

Clearly "sometimes on" work is advantageous for worker well-being, as well as talent attraction and retention. Yet, despite a growing desire and need for better work-life balance, only 23 percent of companies feel that they are excellent in helping employees balance personal and professional life/work demands.[33]

Organizations and leaders that expect employees to be always-on, prioritizing work over other important aspects of life, including the establishment and nurturing of relationships outside of work, run the risk of hindering worker health, productivity, and loyalty.

When workers can't guard against work encroaching on their personal time, burnout and loneliness are around the corner.

7. Overly Professional: Leaving Humanity at the Door

Recently Steven was at the airport sitting next to a seemingly rude gentleman who was watching YouTube videos on his phone with the volume turned up loud. It was loud enough to where people around him were rolling their eyes in discontent. All of the other people sitting around him (including Steven) had headphones on so as to not disturb their neighbors. After a few minutes of stewing in his seat, Steven heard an ESPN video on the gentleman's phone that was discussing Steven's favorite team. Steven took off his headphones and asked if he was a fan too. They then spent 20 minutes engaged in a really wonderful conversation. The man shared that he had grown up in Chicago like Steven, was now living in California like Steven, and was getting ready to have his second child, also just like Steven. They established an instant connection, and it felt restorative.

After they said their goodbyes and parted ways, Steven realized how quickly he often seeks solitude behind his headphones. Even though not by intent, when his headphones are in, he is telling the world to leave him alone. This can cause him to misinterpret the inviting actions of others. Perhaps his new friend wasn't wearing his headphones as a way to subtly invite those around him into a conversation or inform them that he was open to connecting.

This is often how the office can look and feel. Everyone is focused on their projects and tasks, and they only pick their heads up to connect with a colleague if they need something. Work environments can feel cold, stoic, and uninviting to those interested in establishing authentic connections.

What professional tasks and duties might you be hiding behind to avoid getting personal with a colleague? Today we seem to prioritize professionalism over connection. Prioritizing professionalism restrains relationships. Of course, there is always the chance to overshare or get too personal, but always choosing professional over personal is too risky amid a workforce that is growing more and more lonely.

Deciding to always close your office door, wearing noise-canceling headphones, or breezing over personal anecdotes during a meeting communicate that you prioritize the profession over the person.

While being professional is important and has its place in communicating confidence to clients and customers as well as setting necessary team boundaries, being professional can also be used as our scapegoat to gloss over the personal and emotional aspects of our teammates' lives that make the work and the organization human. To not have close relationships inside the environment where we spend most of our waking time accentuates our loneliness.

As work and life continue to blur, leaders need to be prepared to address more of their teammates' nonwork "life" at work. We need to lead the whole human, not just the work human. When we're overly professional, we run the risk of sacrificing our humanity at the altar of reputation and success.

Unfortunately, the pervasive myth that emotions don't belong at work and workers should flip a switch and shed all of their fear, joy, sorrow, and hope at the door of work abounds too widely. This myth is stifling to the well-being and performance of work teams. And it leads many to believe that behaving professionally means being cold and stoic.

Not only are feelings part of being human, but research shows that when coworkers drop their polished professional presence, those

How emotions are treated at work. Check your life at the door of work.

around them experience a boost in trust, kindness, performance, and connection.[34] Divorcing ourselves from our personal lives is not only unfortunate, but it's also bad business.

The ability to identify and manage one's personal emotions and the emotions of others is an advantageous skill for leaders to develop as loneliness, depression, and other mental health concerns rise in the modern workforce.

If leaders can't get comfortable shedding some professionalism, showing empathy, and wading into emotional waters, they run the risk of never fully solving the problems of their team or customers.

People have a deep felt need to be valued by other people at work. Yet the cultural norm and default is to keep work relationships at a surface level. Unless leaders model moving beyond professional to more personal connections, work relationships will remain shallow and brittle.

Having leadership authority undermined by driving more depth into work relationships pales in comparison with having a team that feels isolated and detached from each other and their mission.

The cultural norm of being overly professional and having two separate selves—a work self and a nonwork self—discourages genuine relationships and leads to loneliness. If teammates only see a carefully crafted, professionally masked, work-safe version of yourself, then you and your team are likely suffering from loneliness.

8. Lack of Purpose: A Nonexistent North Star

During the global Covid-19 pandemic, few companies were hit as hard as Delta Air Lines. Delta reported $12.4 billion in losses for all of 2020.[35]

How was Delta able to weather such dire conditions? Purpose.

In a recent interview with Deloitte's 2021 Global Human Capital Trends report, Delta's CEO, Ed Bastain, said the following, "We spent a lot of time studying what our mission was and purpose was, which has helped us now post-pandemic. Our mission is to connect people, and we like to say at Delta, no one better connects the world. That's our anthem that we rally to. What we told our team is our purpose has never been more important to bring the world together, and the role we play in bringing the world together, and while it's not safe necessarily to bring the world together the way we would like it [during the pandemic], the world is yearning to be together and that dissonance that we all feel, that lack of clarity, lack of connectivity is going to not only affirm our business purpose even more strongly than ever when we get through this. It's going to make our people feel more empowered by their mission, the role they could play in making that happen. We impact lives and bring people together. Our people really connect with that purpose."[36]

Purpose provided the clarity and motivation Delta needed to weather one of the toughest challenges any company has ever faced. If Bastain neglected to cast vision and point his people toward the preferred future, they'd be left wondering and wandering in the dark. When you're in the dark and can't see the destination or your fellow travelers and you have no map, it's terrifyingly lonely.

Purpose helps us strive for something bigger than ourselves, and when we are focused beyond ourselves, loneliness lessens. Purpose creates a vision that people can unite behind, thus providing a sense of belonging. Purpose is like the North Star during disrupted times, providing people with stability. It enables organizations and leaders to sift through competing priorities in order to provide a clear vision and direction for teams.

Right, wrong, or indifferent—people today are looking to their employers to provide meaningful work and for their leaders to help them individually discover the purpose in their work. Lacking an understanding of how an individual's work impacts the greater community is demoralizing. Teams that lack a clear purpose are at risk of burnout and loneliness. But striving toward a common purpose among a unified team suffocates loneliness.

Stop, Don't Step

Hopefully now you have a better understanding of the causes behind our behaviors that are leaving so many of us feeling lonely. Leverage this new perspective to help yourself and others to circumvent these causes so that we can create a community of people who have the time and wherewithal to not step over people like the busy Princeton priests but to stop and connect.

Three of the modern-day loneliness contributors are directly related to work (always-on work, overly professional, and lack of purpose); and the other contributors indirectly impact work. Needless to say, workplace leaders are in a prime position to address loneliness.

Now that you have a better understanding of loneliness and its causes, let's turn our attention to how loneliness is showing up at work and impacting business results.

CHAPTER

3

LONELINESS
AT WORK

A single leaf working alone provides no shade.

CHUCK PAGE

Open. Click. Tap. Tweet. Compose. Ping. Scan. Post. Send. Import. Sync. Upload. Save. Attach. Cut. Copy. Paste. Like. Open. Close. Subscribe. Search. Snooze. Swipe. Accept. Drag. Drop. Embed. Code. Record. Watch. Write. Decline. Reconnect. Pinch. Trash. Tag. Mention. Filter. Share. Charge. Order. Join. Checkout. Toggle. Screenshot. Mute. Print. Highlight. Hyperlink. Follow. Unfollow. Message. Invite. Poll. Reload. Refresh. Update. Upgrade. Buy. Tether. Forward. Autocorrect. Unsubscribe. Schedule. Scroll. Download. Text. Share. Edit. Play. Pause. Export. Favorite. Read. Delete. Comment. Reply all. Undo! Exhale. Reply. Close.

Our workdays are full of these activities. We can get in touch with dozens of people, all before lunch. These activities require no conversing, in-person communication, or direct collaboration with other humans. The physical workplace is quieter than ever before, yet our virtual workspace has never been noisier. It leaves one wondering, how connected to our coworkers are we?

Should we get rid of these technologies? No. They're useful. Should we rethink our balance or relationships with these technologies? Yes. They're infringing.

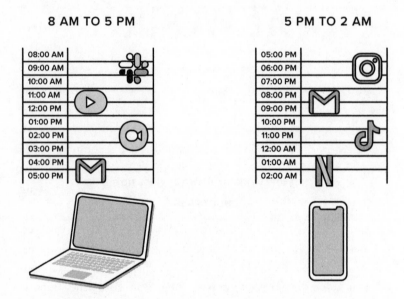

A typical week of work. The endless cycle of technology immersion.

Several decades ago began the rise of the knowledge worker—a person whose main capital is knowledge and who uses convergent and divergent thinking to solve problems. Soon knowledge workers outnumbered workers engaged in manual jobs. Amid this new information age, technology has empowered workers to get much more done without dependence on or interaction with others. It's enabled workers to turn their ergonomic office chairs away from their colleagues and slip into the matrix of spreadsheets, databases, CRMs, email, and messaging platforms.

Researchers, accountants, physicians, engineers, lawyers, programmers, marketers, financial advisors, architects, pharmacists, and sales representatives alike are guilty of choosing convenience over connection, efficiency over empathy, automation over association, and faster over friendly.

Work is social. You'd be very hard-pressed to find a job that is fully independent of other people. Whether remote or not, coworkers, customers, clients, chief leaders, and contractors create a social environment that encircles us at work. This social embeddedness of work often provides a false sense of connectedness. We fall prey to thinking that access to a team and the social context of an organization is enough to ward off loneliness. It is not. In fact, work can be a place where loneliness is felt more extremely—especially if someone feels marginalized.

Even among the perpetual company of others within a company, people are lonely. It's ironic that people aren't finding company inside their company. But loneliness doesn't discriminate. Loneliness doesn't know if you are at work or home, introverted or extroverted, young or old.

Loneliness at work is old. Thousands of years old. However, remote and hybrid work, technology, an emerging generation, and a recent global pandemic have magnified loneliness, dragging it into the spotlight.

Loneliness has long been labeled as shameful, and loneliness at work has been overlooked, stigmatized, and trivialized. Research from the last decade demonstrates how harmful loneliness is to not only our physical well-being but also our work well-being. Addressing loneliness should be as important to leaders as it is to physicians and therapists.

As we've conducted keynote presentations and daylong workshops on the topic of lessening workplace loneliness with thousands of employees across the globe, we've experienced just how ready the workforce is to finally address loneliness. And it's a good thing—because loneliness is bad for business. One-third of all sick days result from mental health issues, such as loneliness.[1] And as you'll discover later in this chapter, loneliness contributes to the decline of employee engagement, loyalty, productivity, and more.

Lonely workers can find a safe haven amid an unsympathetic work environment with just one nurturing coworker. For many, though, finding that one coworker can be challenging, especially considering the relational boundaries that persist inside today's organizations. If overcoming workplace loneliness was as easy as "sucking it up," "getting a pet," "going to a happy hour," or "joining the company softball team," loneliness would not be as prevalent as it is today. It takes much more intentional effort, and that effort starts with an awareness of what loneliness at work looks like and how it surfaces.

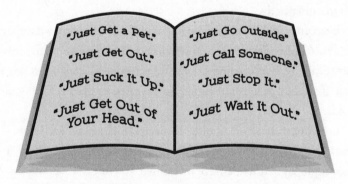

A non-helpful guide to helping a lonely person.

In Part Three, we'll discuss how to identify lonely workers and provide additional tools to assess loneliness levels across teams.

The Universality of Loneliness

No one is immune to feeling lonely at work. Not even your outgoing top sales associate, the customer success representative that brings her dog into the office, or your charming vice president who always declines every happy hour invitation due to "overcommitments." Entry-level employees and managers share the same levels of average loneliness.[2]

Before defining workplace loneliness, here's a snapshot of just how prevalent loneliness is at work according to our research of various global companies.

- ► Seventy-seven percent of leaders believe their teams experience loneliness at least monthly.
- ► Only 4 percent of leaders say that their teams are not growing lonelier while working remotely.
- ► Seventy-two percent of workers feel lonely at least monthly (55 percent saying at least weekly).
- ► Ninety-three percent of workers believe their coworkers are lonely at least monthly (79 percent saying at least weekly).

Workplace loneliness is defined by the distress caused by the perceived inadequacy of a quality connection to teammates, leaders, and the organization itself. Remember, loneliness is the absence of connection. Team members who work remotely but feel connected to the work and their team might experience less loneliness than a team member who works alongside colleagues in an office but lacks a strong connection.

No matter how introverted the person or independent the job function, all people desire social connection at work. The desire to connect and belong is innate in all people. However, loneliness is subjective, and the desire for the quantity of connections at work can vary depending on a person's extroversion or introversion tendencies.

"Personality traits such as extroversion and agreeableness involve the degree to which people orient their interaction with other people and are not characterized by the desire to be valued, included, or accepted by others. As such, these personality characteristics, while related behaviorally, are conceptually independent of the belonging motive and are not the core influence of one's desire for relationships at work. Introversion is not a direct cause of workplace loneliness, but rather sets up behavioural conditions whereby generating actual relationships is more taxing for the individual," writes Sarah Wright, Associate Professor at the University of Canterbury, and Anthony Silard, Associate Professor and Director of the Center for Leadership and Sustainability at Luiss Business School.[3]

Whether introverted or extroverted, young or old, an executive or employee, everyone experiences loneliness and has a desire for belonging.

Loneliness Is a Tenured Team Member

Work is a major source of loneliness. Remote working, switching to a new team, eating lunch while answering emails, or having no one to talk to on an "off" day can all contribute to people feeling lonely. According to our research, the second environment where people experience the most loneliness is at work (25 percent), and 39 percent say they experience the most loneliness at home (where many currently work). However, loneliness and its productivity-sinking ramifications bleed into all aspects of our lives. For example, if we feel alienated in our social lives, we'll carry those feelings into work and vice versa.

Loneliness can be experienced situationally, differentially, or intentionally. Let's explore each and how it's experienced at work.

Situational Loneliness

Situational loneliness occurs as a result of a specific change in circumstances. Examples include switching to a new department, losing a close teammate to a position transfer, or moving to a new location.

In January 2009, Steven (a self-proclaimed extrovert) realized he was no longer the happy, outgoing, enthusiastic, confident, gregarious guy he used to be. He realized he had morphed into someone he did not recognize. He had become reserved, disconnected, and unjoyful. Someone he was uncomfortable being. Someone he didn't like.

The cause of his unraveling and feeling like a stranger inside his own body? Loneliness.

Steven had recently taken a new job working as an internal consultant for the largest gold mining company in the world. He had to move from Chicago, Illinois (population 2.7 million), to Elko, Nevada (population 30,000). Born and raised as a city guy, he entered a world of hunting, fishing, dirt bike racing, and ranching. He was out of his element.

Steven did not have any connections in Elko, but he was confident his strong interpersonal skills would bridge the gap. Six months later he found it hard to get off the couch on the weekends. He had not been successful in establishing connections with his teammates nor anyone in the small mining town. He felt like an outsider in Elko and on his team. He became isolated, irritated, and reclusive much quicker than he could ever have imagined. While his family and friends outside of Elko provided helpful support, the lack of daily connection was devastating. That devastation transferred into unmotivated work where he gave only what was required of him, nothing more.

Loneliness is invisible. Steven's loneliness was hidden from view. But anyone aware of his situation could have connected the dots of his loneliness.

Was it his leaders' responsibility to make sure he made friends? No. Could they have facilitated a couple of introductions with folks on the team or in the community? Yes. Could they have checked in with Steven from time to time to see how he was adjusting? Yes. Could they have helped remind him of the important work he was doing to reinvigorate his drive? Yes. Could they have helped him see beyond his situation to the potential opportunities that lay ahead? Yes.

In her book *Radical Candor*, author Kim Scott explains how her then manager Sheryl Sandberg helped her feel included. Kim said, "Sheryl cared directly for every person that worked for her at a very personal level. She cared about us as human beings, not just employees. When I moved from New York to California to take the job at Google, I did not know anyone or have any friends. Sheryl, knowing that I love to read, asked me to join her book club."

In some situations, loneliness is unavoidable. But with a little bit of forethought, planning, and intentional effort, we can ease situational loneliness among our teams.

Differential Loneliness

Differential loneliness occurs inadvertently when a discrepancy exists between a person or persons and a larger group. The differential is typically unintended and not malicious. Examples include not having a similar amount of time to speak in a meeting as the rest of the team, traveling more and farther than others in a similar role, or not being as proficient with a new technology compared to peers.

Ryan, an older Millennial who had a smartphone-free upbringing, has a very vivid memory of experiencing differential loneliness. It was during his freshman orientation at Miami University in Oxford, Ohio. He and many other wide-eyed, eager freshmen from across the country were gathered in one of the computer labs where they were to sign up for their classes for the semester. They were to check their university email and follow the instructions to select their classes. Ryan had no idea what to do. It was 2003 and he had never used email. He was likely too busy playing ice hockey and Super Mario Kart in high school to prepare for the future. Every classmate around him that day was whizzing around their virtual desktop with ease, bouncing effortlessly back and forth between email, Ask Jeeves, solitaire, and Yahoo News. Not Ryan. He felt stuck. Behind. Embarrassed. Fearful. Alone.

There was a distinct discrepancy between Ryan's knowledge and his skill level compared to those he would be spending the next four years alongside and eventually competing with for job opportunities.

This type of differential loneliness is more and more common today. As technology quickly accelerates, entire generations are feeling like Ryan did—stuck and unsure how to catch up. It's lonesome when everyone else seems to get it but you.

Here are some other modern-day work examples of differential loneliness:

- Someone who is the only parent of young children on the team and has to juggle her children's schedule with her work schedule.
- Someone who does not have the knack for working remotely or lacks a functional work-from-home environment.
- Someone who has to rebuild his business after his biggest client left.
- Someone who knows she doesn't share the same political view as the rest of their team.
- Someone who wants to share more of his personal life but most of the team remains reserved and private.
- Someone who transitioned into a leadership position sooner than her peers.

When there is a difference of knowledge, skill, capacity, or opportunity, it can cause loneliness. While differential loneliness isn't necessarily a problem for leaders to solve, it is a growing tension that leaders must be aware of and manage accordingly.

Intentional Loneliness

Intentional loneliness occurs as a result of a deliberate and malicious act. Examples include blatantly disregarding someone's feedback or suggestion, purposefully excluding someone from a team event, and deliberately overlooking someone for a promotion. Intentional loneliness can be the most hurtful.

Discrimination, bullying, ostracism, or harassment can cause a teammate to feel isolated and alienated especially if the actions are unseen by others. Feeling misunderstood or unable to communicate these hurtful experiences to anyone else leads to individual loneliness and can permeate throughout the entire team.

The negative impact of these types of actions can be even more detrimental when they come from a leader. The broken trust and power inequity can deepen the sense of isolation.

Ethnic minority status, physical disabilities, nonvisible disabilities such as hearing impairment, class differences, or a female in a male-dominated organization are all areas where people can feel marginalized at work. Even realizing your teammates left you off an email thread or group chat can generate the subtle sting of feeling isolated.

Marginalized team members feel excluded, alienated, and disconnected from the collective culture of the team or organization. People's social position within a group not only impacts their ability and desire to interact and contribute inside the group, but also how they relate with others outside the group such as family, friends, and community members. Vice versa is true as well. People who experience exclusion in their community are likely to struggle connecting with their work team. The real or perceived feeling of being excluded from the social network of the organization or being different from the dominant workplace culture causes stress in the body, and this stress leads to a whole host of negative impacts at work.

The Big Dent Loneliness Puts in Business

Loneliness not only negatively impacts people's health, but it slyly wreaks havoc on business. Employee engagement, performance, and loyalty are just a few of its victims.

"The trends shaping how we work—increasing use of technology, more telecommuting and the always-on work culture—are leaving Americans more stressed, less rested, spending more time on social media, and less time with friends and family. For the business community, it is resulting in less engagement, less productivity, and lower retention levels," says David M. Cordani, president and chief executive officer, Cigna.[4]

Here is how loneliness is specifically impacting business.

Employee Engagement Plummets

It would stand to reason that if loneliness impacts human health, then lonely workers would be less motivated to engage. Loneliness is also a major contributor to employee burnout. According to a Cigna study, lonely workers are:

- ▶ Twice as likely to miss a day of work due to illness
- ▶ Five times as likely to miss work due to stress
- ▶ More inclined to believe their work is lower quality (12 percent)[5]

Additionally, Gallup surveyed over 15 million employees around the globe and found employees who have a best friend at work are seven times as likely to be engaged in their jobs, are better at engaging customers, produce higher quality work, have higher well-being, and are less likely to get injured on the job.[6] And those without a workplace best friend have only a one in 12 chance of being engaged at work.

Employee Retention Declines

The lonelier employees feel, the less loyal they are. Lonely workers:

- ▶ Are less committed to their organization[7]
- ▶ Think twice as often about quitting their job[8]
- ▶ Are more likely to leave a job because of mental health reasons, with half of Millennials doing so and 75 percent of Gen Z[9]

Employee Performance Suffers

Without interpersonal networks and a relational support system at work, employee job performance dips. Lonely workers are:

- ▶ Poorer performers, due in part to their low commitment to the organization and low approachability[10]

▶ Limited in their executive mental function (decision making, planning, emotional regulation, analysis, and abstract thinking) because loneliness puts the body in a stress state affecting the prefrontal cortex of the brain where these functions are controlled[11]

▶ Twenty-four percent more likely to have poorer health than workers with positive relationships[12]

▶ Fatigued and irritable because loneliness causes humans to sleep lightly and rouse often, just as our ancestors did to prevent being overtaken by wolves or enemies if they were separated from their tribe[13]

Researchers recently studied loneliness among schoolteachers and found that lonely teachers experienced lower quality "leader-member and organization-member exchanges at work" and in turn were rated as poorer performers than their nonlonely coworkers.[14] The researchers also deduced that loneliness is a significant predictor of educator burnout.

It's not what people do at work as much as who they work with. The momentary experiences throughout the workday that lead to improved well-being and engagement are based on the people you work with. Researchers at MIT monitored the movements and conversations of a group of workers and found that small increases in social cohesiveness, such as idle chitchat, lead to large gains in production.[15]

Employee Collaboration Diminishes

A willingness to collaborate and communicate evaporates when social ties begin to fray among team members. Lonely workers are:

▶ Likely to struggle with introducing themselves, being friendly, making friends, and taking part in groups[16]

▶ Slower to respond during conversation, ask fewer questions, and focus more on themselves[17]

▶ Less creative according to a study conducted at five companies in China[18]

A disengaged, disloyal, underperforming, and uncooperative team member is the last type of person you want on your team. And unfortunately, no individual or industry is immune to the destructive effects of loneliness at work. Workers across a variety of different positions, such as clerks, project managers, truck drivers, accounting specialists, engineers, administrative assistants, police officers, and material handlers were surveyed, and the results were the same: employees who were lonely were less committed to their organization, had lower job performance, and were perceived by their coworkers to be less approachable.[19]

Loneliness is bad for business. The consequences covered in this section make it clear that organizations need to make fostering social connections a strategic priority. Less lonely workers equate to a more engaged, loyal, productive, and collaborative workforce. Here's a flow chart that answers the question, "Should I prioritize social connections?"

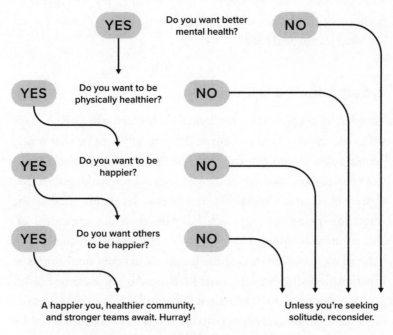

Prioritizing social connections is a no-brainer.

The Workplace Holds the Key

"Yes, loneliness is a growing concern. Yes, loneliness occurs at work. And yes, it hinders the performance of my team. But it's a personal problem, not a problem to be addressed at work or by me, a time-crunched leader."

This is a common response we hear when talking to leaders about addressing loneliness at work. We understand the resistance. However, work is perhaps the best chance humanity has for lessening loneliness at scale.

Here are several specific reasons leaders should not delay in lessening loneliness among their team.

1. Enhanced Team Capability

Look no further than the benefits highlighted earlier in this chapter. Loneliness is a heavy anchor holding so many teams back. Cut loose the anchor so your team can perform like they are capable of. Seeing the performance needle spring forward will be all the convincing some leaders will need.

2. Stop Loneliness Creep

How lonely people respond to loneliness is counterintuitive to how we would expect them to behave. We wrongly assume that lonely people will seek out connections, but the opposite is true. Lonely workers are more likely to pull away from others, making them less approachable and viewed by teammates as less committed to the team. Lower employee approachability leaves an entire team vulnerable to the contagion of loneliness. Loneliness spreads like a virus because most workplaces require interpersonal communications to function. Leaders shouldn't treat loneliness as a private or one-off problem that needs to be addressed individually, but rather as a major organizational threat that potentially can infect an entire team. By

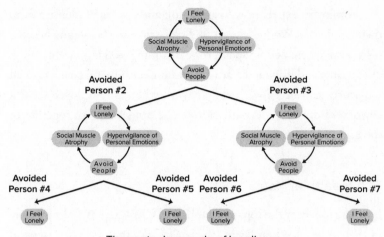

The contagious cycle of loneliness.

providing effective and timely support for lonely workers, leaders can stop a negative loneliness spiral from spreading from one employee to the whole organization.

3. Plentiful Time and Proximity

After sleep, work is the activity humans spend the most time engaged with.[20] On average, people spend more waking hours with their coworkers than with their families. If we are going to create a sense of belonging, it makes sense to build it with people you spend the most time with. In addition, the proximity of our social connections matters to our well-being.[21] People closest to us and whom we see most frequently have more influence on our well-being. We all have stock in each other's well-being, which is why it's critical to strengthen the connections of the entire team.

4. Bolster More Meaning and Worth

Perhaps the two things people want most in life are meaningful relationships and meaningful work. Organizational leaders play a unique role in that they can deliver on both of these items.

Employees expect to gain affiliation and a sense of identity from their employers. Work is a profound place to create belonging because it's a place where people spend time dreaming, solving, overcoming, celebrating, and driving toward a common, meaningful goal. Personal self-worth can be experienced at work when an employee seeks a coworker's opinion on a situation or if employees work together to solve a complex problem.

5. A Healthier You

It can be lonely at the top. In fact, half of CEOs report feeling lonely in their roles.[22] When leaders began to take the necessary steps to lessen loneliness among their team, they'll indirectly be taking steps to address any feelings of isolation that linger in their own work lives. Lessening loneliness is good for the team member, the team as a whole, and the leader.

As discussed in Chapter 1, there are three dimensions to loneliness (intimate, relational, and collective). At a minimum, work teams should fulfill the collective loneliness dimension where everyone feels a secure sense of belonging. Better teams will fulfill the collective and relational dimensions where everyone feels a secure sense of belonging and many individuals have high-quality friendships on the team. The best teams with the most influential leaders create work environments where people can fulfill all three dimensions, including the intimate dimension where leaders become a close confidant and mentor to a few coworkers.

If Not You, Who?

"Lessen loneliness" is likely not written in your job description. But if it's not your responsibility as the leader, who will help the individuals on your team? As the health and economic costs of loneliness become more discussed and visible, the government and healthcare system will play an important role in treating or alleviating the problem. But those resources pale in comparison to the opportunity you have as a leader. Someone who is in close, consistent contact with workers and casting a vision, speaking into their lives, and providing an environment where they can be the best version of themselves is in a position to change lives for the better. Your actions have the power to drive positive societal change, impact families, and set the example of the important role organizations play in lessening loneliness.

Fostering healthy social connections is important if organizations are going to function effectively. And the same is true for societies and families. As social connections grow more and more unhealthy, leaders have an opportunity to turn the tide and provide workers with the example and tools to make an impact at work, in their families, and throughout society. For our health, our work, and our future, it's critical that you address loneliness at work.

PART TWO

BELONGING,
THE ANTIDOTE
TO LONELINESS

4

THE SCIENCE
OF BELONGING

Being engaged in some way for the good
of the community, whatever that community,
is a factor in a meaningful life. We long to belong,
and belonging and caring anchors
our sense of place in the universe.

PATRICIA CHURCHLAND

You step out into the middle of the Ultimate Fighting Championship (UFC) Octagon as 2,600 fans at the Etihad Arena in Abu Dhabi scream your name. You open your arms like the wings of a bird, ushering in all the cheers from the crowd. You're trying to absorb any final energy and confidence you can from the noisy crowd before you clash with your menacing opponent.

The referee motions for both of you to approach the center of the ring. The referee tells you to make it a "clean fight," you touch gloves with your opponent, and you slowly backpedal to your corner—methodically taking in every crude gesture and insulting taunt from your opponent to be used as fuel over the next three 5-minute rounds.

The referee then drops his hand and the fight begins. Throwing technique to the wind and wasting no time, your opponent sprints and lunges toward you, and he lands a crushing kick to your abdomen. You're stunned but bounce back because after all you're a professional fighter and you're at work.

Have you ever been kicked in the gut and then been expected to actively participate in a team meeting? Of course not—that kind of multitasking to be able to take a blow, fight through the pain, and keep enough wits about you is reserved for UFC fighters like Ronda Rousey, not the professionals on your team. However, this participating through physical pain is much more familiar to lonely workers than you may think.

Naomi Eisenberger, associate professor of social psychology at UCLA and director of the Social and Affective Neuroscience Laboratory, conducted an experiment where participants were put through an experience where they were excluded from a group.[1] Being excluded pushes people to the social perimeter, thus decreasing their sense of belonging and increasing feelings of loneliness. Researchers used an fMRI (functional magnetic resonance imaging) scanner to look at the participants' brain activity upon experiencing the exclusion. They discovered that the part of the brain that was activated when being excluded was the same part of the brain that responds to physical pain.

"The brain processes emotional and physical pain in similar ways," Eisenberger says.[2] "Because being connected is so important to us as a species, researchers think the attachment system may have piggybacked onto the physical pain system over the course of our evolutionary history, borrowing the pain signal to highlight when we are socially disconnected." This biological wiring motivates humans to avoid social disconnection in order to maintain close relationships.

In our brains, the sensory fibers that register physical and emotional pain overlap. That means exclusion, disappointment, or loneliness are felt biologically the same as being physically hit. Exclusion, bereavement, or relationship troubles can be just as disruptive or distressing as physical ailments.

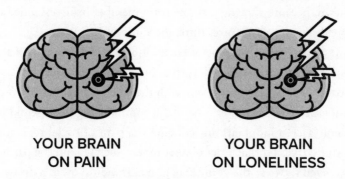

YOUR BRAIN ON PAIN **YOUR BRAIN ON LONELINESS**

Physical pain and loneliness register in the same area of the brain.

Maybe the reason we've ignored addressing emotional needs at work for so long is because they've been hidden from view. If an employee arrived at work with a bleeding appendage, you wouldn't ignore the appendage and ask her to get to work. You'd address the injury and assess if she were fit for duty. The same level of concern and care should be applied to the social and emotional needs of the team.

Humans weave tangled social lives, making addressing emotional needs like loneliness and belonging complex and unfamiliar. But the research makes clear that we have to address these needs if we are going to create a focused, dedicated, and high-performing team.

This research sheds some light on why people typically describe social rejection using words that represent physical pain such as "hurt feelings" or "broken heart." This is not unique to the English language but is common in many different cultures. Outside of words typically reserved to describe physical pain, humanity has very few means to describe and express psychologically distressing events. Perhaps this is another indication of just how inept we can be when it comes to managing our emotions and the emotions of others.

Eisenberger also discovered that simply viewing an image or scene that signals social rejection lights up the pain-related region of the brain.[3] This explains why it's so cringe-worthy to watch sales professionals get hung up on or get a door slammed in their face. The defeating feeling of not being included is painful. At work it's becoming increasingly important that everyone sees and experiences the unity of the team, because viewing just one team member being excluded or ignored can send shockwaves throughout the entire system.

The close relationship between emotional and physical pain also explains why some people will turn to unhealthy substances like opioid painkillers or alcohol to cope with the pain of loneliness. In fact, Eisenberger studied the effects of the common physical painkiller Tylenol (acetaminophen) on reducing the pain of social rejection. The study revealed that Tylenol does reduce social pain. The participants given the over-the-counter pain medication showed a decrease in pain-related brain activity when experiencing exclusion. In addition, over the course of three weeks, the same participants reported fewer hurt feelings in the course of each day. The same dose of painkiller that eases physical aches also eases emotional ones.

In response to her findings, Eisenberger said, "Although certainly painful in the short term, the misery and heartache following broken social relationships serve a valuable function—namely, to ensure the maintenance of close social ties. Over the course of evolutionary history, avoiding social rejection and remaining connected to others likely increased one's chances of staying alive and reproducing. The experience of social pain, while temporarily distressing and hurtful, is an evolutionary adaptation that promotes social bonding and, ultimately, survival."[4]

Loneliness is lethal, connection is vital. Social connection is paramount in the recovery and healing process of addiction as well as the effectiveness and performance of a team. Eisenberger's research makes clear that our urge to connect is one of our most critical survival instincts. Much like our fight-or-flight instinct, we can't turn our social instincts off at work or conveniently compartmentalize them in the "outside of work" bucket.

Belonging is such a strong survival instinct that it's important to address it at work, because left unaddressed, our bodies will react (as if we were alone and lost in the wilderness surrounded by wolves). The hypervigilance that was embedded in our nervous system centuries ago to help us survive isolation will come roaring back, wreaking havoc on our ability to collaborate, innovate, and communicate among a team.

For example, while repeatedly experiencing isolation at work, one real-life worker quit his job to keep his mental health intact and to find a new team with a stronger sense of belonging:

> I worked in a retail store that was farming-based, but had the political atmosphere of *Game of Thrones*. Everyone hated each other and constantly tried to undermine one another. If you were talking to someone that someone else didn't like, it was known across the store, and suddenly, people would stop talking to you. As in, you would stand there and ask a question, and they would literally turn their back on you.
>
> I received zero training, got promoted to "zone manager" (more work with no extra pay), and then injured my foot falling off one of their rickety wooden ladders. This caused everyone to turn on me because the store had to file a workman's comp claim, so they missed out on the annual reward: a visit to the Golden Corral buffet.
>
> After about two weeks of everyone staring daggers at me, while I tried to figure out what I was supposed to be doing, I just quit. I left and never came back. It took me a few months to find another job, but at least I was no longer alternating between openly weeping and feeling physically nauseous.[5]

When a need goes unfulfilled, it's very difficult for humans to avoid stewing about that unfulfilled need. Sort of like when you need to use the restroom during a long road trip. The zeal and zest you had singing along to your favorite road trip playlist rapidly changes to focusing solely on finding the next exit with a public restroom. If individuals on your team are longing for more belonging, they are not able to show up wholly and perform fully. They are distracted at best and debilitated at worst.

This isn't so much of a conversation about making everyone feel good, included, and happy as it is about delivering on a critical human need in order to improve the health and well-being of your neighbor. This isn't a "soft" topic—it's a dire one.

In the same way organizations promote physical fitness to help workers improve their well-being so they can perform at their best, social fitness must also be promoted and practiced. As we learn more and more about the human brain and why humans behave the way they do, be prepared as a leader to navigate and address the social and emotional needs of your team.

So, the next time you conclude a one-on-one or team meeting and get the sense that the person or persons were not fully present, seem distracted, and unmotivated . . . they might be wrestling with loneliness.

In the next chapter, we'll explore how belonging should look at work, but first let's understand the fascinating science behind belonging and loneliness. The following insights will help you better assess the degrees of loneliness that exist on your team and even in yourself.

Surviving Woolly Mammoths

Imagine coming face-to-face with a woolly mammoth. These walking mountains were 13 feet tall, weighed around six tons, and were equipped with massive curved tusks designed to move boulders. Your chances of taking down a woolly mammoth by yourself were practically zero. But with a tribe of humans, equipped with weapons and a plan, your odds would increase exponentially. To survive, eat, and forge a new pair of warm fuzzy slippers, you had to stick with the tribe.

When our ancestors, the early humans who roamed the plains, were separated from their tribe, their chance of survival plummeted.

There was literal safety in numbers. A hunting party could watch each other's back as they traversed new terrain. A tribe could take turns watching for predators at night. While some people hunted and gathered food, others created tools, prepared shelter, or protected the stockpile of food. "We have survived as a species not because we're fast or strong or have natural weapons in our fingertips, but because of social protection," said John Cacioppo, former director of the Center for Cognitive and Social Neuroscience at the University of Chicago. "Our strength is our ability to communicate and work together."[6]

This explains why loneliness is a negative emotion. In the past, when we experienced loneliness, it was a high-threat situation. After all these years, our brain still reacts in the same way when we feel alone—even amid today's modern world. It's our brain's way of protecting ourselves from danger.

Were humans first drawn to the pleasure of being with one another, or were we first repelled by the discomfort of being alone? In other words, what came first, social affinity or loneliness? According to Cacioppo's theory, "The pain of being alone motivates humans to seek the safety of companionship, which in turn benefits the species by encouraging group cooperation and protection."[7] Loneliness is useful for long-term survival; thus, it remains embedded in us.

Loneliness isn't shameful, it's a signal, much like the pain in your stomach is a signal to find a source of food. Loneliness is a signal to find your tribe. Unfortunately, satisfying loneliness isn't as easy as reaching for an apple.

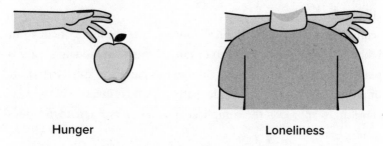

Hunger   **Loneliness**

Social connection is a fundamental human motivation akin to hunger.

When we experience loneliness, our brains detect social threats twice as fast as nonlonely brains.[8] In other words, a lonely brain is more sensitive to potential threats whether real or perceived. While this was helpful for our ancestors to provide an acute attention to the potential predator in the rustling bush while wandering the wilderness alone, this biological trigger can hinder us in today's world. It can cause us to read too much into harmless social situations and ultimately push away helpful people. This self-preservation can cause people to retreat inward at the expense of avoiding social environments and distrusting people with the best of intentions to help. Chronic loneliness will eventually cause people to stop answering texts, phone calls, or social invitations.

Humans may be more susceptible to racial stereotyping, discriminatory practices, or cultural bias when among strangers. Why? Because our stress hormones spike due to loneliness; we don't feel connected to strangers. This can cause us to perceive nonexistent social threats and misinterpret social cues entirely. Loneliness dulls our emotional intelligence.

Dr. Vivek H. Murthy, author of *Together: The Healing Power of Human Connection in a Sometimes Lonely World*, writes, "Hypervigilance also creates an intense preoccupation with our own needs and security, which can appear to others as self-involvement. These two elements—the threat perception shift and the increased focus on self—are key parts of the hypervigilance story that make it difficult to engage with others when we're lonely. . . . Loneliness thus fuels more loneliness until the fracture leads to severe alienation."

When we become chronically lonely, most of us are inclined to withdraw, whether we mean to or not. This is why a lonely person is likely to reject the simple advice of "go to a party" or "call a friend." It often takes someone else, a leader perhaps, who is invested in the relationship to approach the complicated situation and rescue the lonesome person.

We aren't much different from our early ancestors. We still need and seek social connections. We may not be hunting wild game for dinner, but teams likely hunt for its next opportunity. We may not have to keep watch at night for predators, but we do keep watch over our team-mates' health. Loneliness is nature's hint that we belong together.

Loneliness as a signal isn't useful for just survival but for significance. If we were successful in seeking isolation, nothing would exist. Nothing of significance, anyways. The book you read, the phone you check, the building you sit in, the car you drive, the product or service you deliver to customers all came into existence because of a group of people coming together to build it. Nothing of significance is ever created alone. Together we dream, build, and grow.

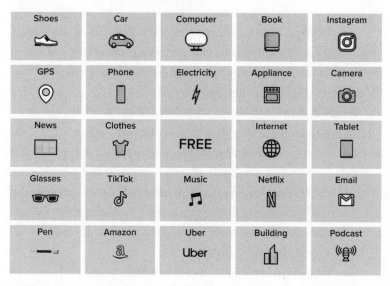

Bingo for things you use today that took a team of people to create.

Mother Teresa offers this beautiful reminder about our interdependence on each other, "If we have no peace, it is because we have forgotten that we belong to each other."

Cocaine, Mice, and the Origin of Loneliness

"I administered cocaine and ended up discovering the source of loneliness."

Said no one ever . . . except two MIT neuroscientists, Kay Tye and Gillian Matthews. By accident in 2012, Matthews and Tye stumbled across the loneliness neurons in the brain while they were studying how cocaine changes the brain in mice.[9]

Before the test, the mice were put through 24 hours of isolation where the researchers focused on the dopamine neurons in the brain region called the dorsal raphe nucleus, best known for its link to depression. The researchers discovered that the neurons were not responding to the cocaine, as they had originally hypothesized, but actually to isolation. This is likely not a coincidence as loneliness is a strong risk factor for depression.

"Maybe these neurons are relaying the experience of loneliness," Matthews said. "I think this reveals something about how our brains may be wired to make us innately social creatures and protect us from the detrimental effects of loneliness."[10]

When Tye and Matthews stimulated these neurons, the mice were more likely to seek social interaction with other mice. And when the neurons were silenced using a process called optogenetics (a method of controlling a neuron's activity using light and genetic engineering), the animals lost the desire to be social. The researchers also found through other tests that the mice were more driven by a desire to avoid pain (loneliness) than to generate pleasure (belonging) in their quest for social interaction.[11]

Like humans, mice are social creatures that have a preference to live in groups.[12] In fact, a mouse will spend more time interacting with other mice after spending time isolated from other mice.[13] This research gives a whole new meaning to the popular children's book, *If You Give a Mouse a Cookie* by Laura Numeroff, because it seems that a mouse really would like to move in with you and be more social given the opportunity. Give cookies cautiously.

Human's basic biological needs like water, food, and sleep are tracked in the background of our brains by a complex homeostatic system seeking a natural balance. Tye and Matthews seemed to have proven a similar system exists for our social connections. The same thing that drives us to eat and drink is similar to what drives us to connect and converse.

In fact, in 2020, researchers proved just that. After 10 hours of social isolation, human participants reported substantially increased social craving, loneliness, discomfort, and dislike of isolation.[14] They also demonstrated decreased happiness compared with when they started isolation. Acute isolation causes social craving, similar to the way fasting causes hunger.

The researchers proved our brains have a biological makeup that drives our desire to be one with the pack. Loneliness isn't just a social phenomenon, but a biological requirement.

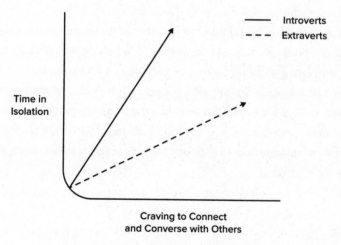

Isolation causes us all to crave connection.

While loneliness is a universal and common condition, the science of loneliness is very new. Due to the subjective nature of loneliness and difficulty in quantifying it, neuroscientists have long avoided studying it. This makes these recent findings truly groundbreaking.

"It's just so exciting to me, because these are all concepts that we've heard about a million times in psychology, and for the very first time, we actually have cells in the brain that we can link to the system," Tye says. "And once you have one cell, you can trace backwards, you can trace forwards; you can figure out what's upstream; you can figure out what all the neurons that are upstream are doing, and what messengers are being sent."[15]

Measuring loneliness in the brain objectively could be the start to better understanding the role loneliness plays in other illnesses such as depression, mental health, addiction, and social anxiety.

Humans' Default State

When you're not casting vision to your team, presenting a solution to a client, or coaching a new hire, but rather find a rare window to relax and do nothing—what state is your brain in?

Research has found that humans rely on two separate networks to process social and nonsocial thinking.[16] When doing activities such as completing expense reports or preparing a PowerPoint presentation, our nonsocial brain pathways are active. When we are having a happy hour with coworkers or helping a teammate with a proposal, our social network within our brain activates. Our brain engages in a form of neural seesawing as we move back and forth between various social settings.

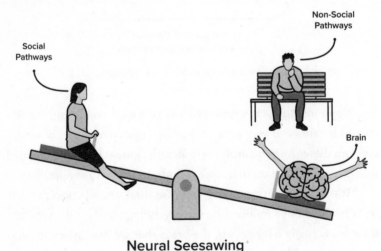

Neural Seesawing

Your brain favors playing with its social pathways.

This isn't that hard to believe or even that fascinating until we realize that our brain plays favorites. Would you believe that your brain has a definitive network preference, no matter if you're introverted or extroverted?

The human brain defaults to the network of social thinking.

When you complete a nonsocial task, such as submitting an expense report, your brain network for social thinking automatically turns on. It's a reflex. "In other words, evolution has placed a bet that the best thing for our brain to do in any spare moment is to get ready to see the world socially. We are built to be social creatures," says Dr. Matthew Lieberman, a UCLA social psychology professor and the bestselling author of *Social: Why Our Brains Are Wired to Connect.*[17]

Connection is the default state of humans. We not only feel good together, but we feel normal. It's home.

Because humans are hardwired this way, we are constantly preparing for our next social encounter whether that is a tough discussion with an upset customer, a team meeting, or exciting news to share with a loved one. We spend a lot of time thinking about other people. Our brains are wired for connection because belonging matters to our well-being.

Humans are tremendous assets to other humans, but they can also be threats. Humans aren't uniformly positive toward each other. We have a very long history of threatening, hurting, and exploiting each other. We need connection, but our capacity for it has limitations.

While our brain nudges us toward connection, there are some natural mechanisms that help us decipher between friend and foe. These mechanisms were established to protect us from befriending an enemy who might kill us.

In the world of organizations, it's important that leaders take the helm in building belonging because when it doesn't exist, people find it elsewhere. And that elsewhere just might be joining a competitor or becoming part of a countercultural group in the company. Creating a culture of belonging is an effective way to create employee engagement and loyalty.

In the same way Tom Hanks in the movie *Cast Away* created Wilson from a volleyball in order to satisfy his need for connection, your team members will use whatever means possible to create connection when it's nonexistent. They'll likely take the path of least resistance to find connections turning to social media or collaboration tools like Slack or Teams that aren't effective for building the necessary human connections that drive the best teams.

In the absence of human connection, people cannot help but create a reproduction with whatever is available to create connection. According to research, people will humanize gadgets (like Wilson or smartphones), gods (socially disconnected people tend to have more faith in deities and are more prone to believe in ghosts), and greyhounds (lonely people attach human behaviors to their pets).[18]

If you don't want your team turning to volleyballs, ghosts, and parrots to superficially satisfy their need for belonging, then be proactive about making them feel connected and valuable to their team. The rest of this book will focus on how to do just that.

Belonging can be perceived as a "soft" topic, conjuring thoughts of being picked last for the kickball team during recess. It can feel childish in a way and something that we should have already gotten over or just need to push through. But hopefully this deeper dive into the science of belonging gives you an appreciative understanding of our profound need for belonging and how delivering it can produce tremendous results.

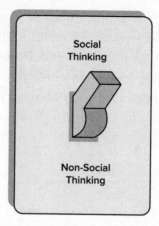

Social
Thinking

Non-Social
Thinking

Connection is the default state of humans.

A Transformational Force

Humans are social creatures. We have a deep desire to be accepted, cared for, and involved in meaningful communities. These desires were (and continue to be) essential for our survival. Our ancestors roamed the plains and lived in tribes. Becoming separated or banished from the tribe made survival unlikely.

This explains why loneliness creates a psychological stress state in humans that leads to higher levels of inflammation in the body, which damages blood vessels and tissues and causes other health problems. Thus, our need and desire for belonging.

Loneliness is unfortunate, especially when it follows a traumatic event such as the death of a loved one, the final child custody ruling, an unexpected diagnosis from a doctor, or a hate-filled statement delivered by a supposed friend. At times loneliness is out of our control and an inevitable part of life.

Loneliness is also healthy. Akin to hunger, loneliness is our biological signal to seek connection. Hunger motivates us to eat. Loneliness motivates us to connect. It's a motivational force to forge strong relationships. It's our innate reminder that our presence matters to others. It's proof we need each other.

Loneliness isn't shameful, it's a signal. It's universal, yet unique. It's not just despairing, it's a motivational force—a force that can transform organizations for the better when belonging is present.

5

BELONGING
AT WORK

Connection is the energy that exists
between people when they feel seen,
heard, and valued; when they can give
and receive without judgment;
and when they derive sustenance
and strength from the relationship.

BRENÉ BROWN

Bang! Screeeeeeech. That's the sound of your future self time-traveling back to the present day to give you the secret to living a long and healthy life. Once your extreme shock and the smoke from the DeLorean DMC-12 dissipates, you lean in close while the future you whispers the answer in your ear.

What answer did you hear?

Make sure to get enough sleep? Focus on the next promotion? Limit unhealthy habits like drinking or smoking? Recognize others for the important work they do? Save as much money as possible? Adopt a mindset of continuous learning? Train the team in the next TikTok dance challenge to ensure it goes viral and everyone achieves fame and fortune?

The answer is none of the above.

The Undisputed Secret for a Long and Healthy Life

The proven answer can actually be found in the Harvard Study of Adult Development, the longest study of adult life that's ever been conducted.[1] The study started in 1938 with 724 men from two different groups. Group one was sophomores at Harvard University. Group two was a group of boys from Boston's poorest neighborhoods. The study is still active today with about 60 participants still alive, most of whom are in their nineties.

Here's how the study works. Every two years, researchers send the participants questionnaires, collect medical records, draw their blood, scan their brains, and in the living rooms of their home, interview the subjects, their spouses, and the now more than 2,000 children of the participants. The researchers ask the participants about their careers, home life, health, and more. The researchers have watched and documented the lives of these former teenagers unfolding over a time span of more than 80 years.

Since 1938, many participants have climbed the socioeconomic ladder, and others backslid down the other way. Some became doctors, bricklayers, lawyers, factory workers, and one became president of the United States (John F. Kennedy). In a recent TEDx talk, psychiatrist Robert Waldinger, the study's fourth director, broke down three specific lessons learned from this incredible study.[2]

Lesson #1: Loneliness Kills, Social Connections Heal

People who are more socially connected to family, friends, and community live happier, healthier, and longer lives than those who aren't as well connected. Additionally, loneliness is extremely toxic. People who are more isolated from others than they'd like to be are less happy, their health declines sooner in midlife, their brain function deteriorates sooner, and they ultimately live shorter lives than those who are not lonely.

Lesson #2: Close and High-Quality Relationships Really Matter

Living amid high-conflict relationships is very detrimental to human health. Conversely, living amid good, warm relationships is protective. The most happily partnered men and women reported that in their eighties, on the days they had more physical pain, their mood stayed just as happy. In contrast, unhappily partnered men and women reported that in their eighties, on the days they had more physical pain, it was magnified by more emotional pain. Healthy relationships buffer us from the trials and tribulations of aging.

Lesson #3: Healthy Relationships Protect Our Brains (Not Just Our Bodies)

When people feel they have someone in their life they can really count on, their memory stays sharper longer. Waldinger said, "The people who were the happiest with their relationships at age 50, were the healthiest at age 80."

So . . . back to your time-traveling future self who is eager to give you the undisputed secret to live a long and healthy life.

The secret is . . . invest in relationships.

Remodeling Maslow's Hierarchy

In 1943, American psychologist Abraham Maslow introduced his now-famous hierarchy of human needs. Maslow's model presented the intrinsic needs of humans and how we prioritize satisfying those needs. The order of needs are as follows.

Maslow's Hierarchy of Needs.

Our physiological needs of food, water, and shelter are critical to our survival. These needs get our immediate attention because they are daily requirements. And fulfilling these needs is obvious, with the payoff being tangible. Feel hungry, eat food. Feel parched, drink water. Feel tired, get sleep.

Fulfilling our needs for belonging and love is much more complex. It takes longer to build trust between two people than to quench your thirst. It's easier to seek food than to seek a friend. This may explain why we don't often discuss our intangible needs like belonging, because they are invisible.

Maslow made physiological needs foundational in his model. While those needs are urgently important, however, the Harvard Study of Adult Development confirms that our need for belonging and love is most dire.

Have you ever heard of someone committing suicide because they were hungry? We haven't. However, many people commit suicide because they are lonely.

Separation is suffering.

Belonging should be a primary priority for humans, not at a stage three priority as indicated in Maslow's hierarchy of needs model. That's why we'd like to introduce a new model that emphasizes the foundational role that belonging plays in our personal and professional lives.

The next figure shows the three core needs of humans and the primary question we ask of ourselves in each phase. We call these the 3 Ls of Life™.

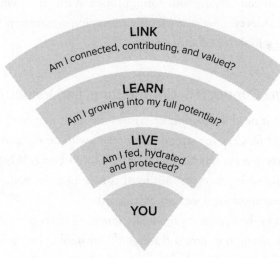

The core needs of humans, the 3 Ls of Life™.

Live: Am I Fed, Hydrated, and Protected?

Meeting our physiological needs of food, water, rest, and shelter is our most urgent need. Humans can live longer without a friend than without food. These needs are personal to you. You can't feed someone else to satisfy your own hunger. While these needs must be met for sustenance, they do not lead to a full and healthy life. They do not satisfy our deeper emotional needs. Without moving to the Learn stage, we don't grow. We remain takers, not able to give or contribute.

Learn: Am I Growing into My Full Potential?

When our Live needs are met, we can then cultivate curiosity, we can advance ourselves. In order to grow, we learn from our surroundings. Learning is continuous, as we never arrive at our full potential or self-actualization. There is always room for more.

Learning gives us hope. It allows for optimism, a brighter future to prevail. Learning allows us to gain knowledge, skill, and perspective that can help advance our communities. Without moving to the Link stage, however, we're stuck only advancing ourselves, ultimately remaining self-absorbed and lonely.

Link: Am I Connected, Contributing, and Valued?

Meeting our need for belonging creates the most longevity and fulfillment in life. Creating strong connections with others provides the most protection for our health and mental well-being. While establishing links with others isn't our most conscious or immediate need, it is the weightiest need we have as humans.

Think of the bars in the model representing layers of a shield. For maximum strength to power through the turmoil of life, we need all three bars. And the Link bar provides the broadest protection. The wider and deeper one's social network, the more dispersed the blows of life become, making one more resilient.

It's not a coincidence that the model mirrors the world's most recognizable sign for connection, the Wi-Fi icon. We hope that the next time you see a Wi-Fi icon, you will be reminded of how vitally important it is to connect with others, not just devices.

If you don't fulfill all three bars, Live/Learn/Link (much like when trying to secure a stronger, more stable Wi-Fi connection), you will be left aimlessly wandering, disappointed, disconnected . . . knowing life has more to offer.

The three things all humans are wired to do are live, learn, and link. These items are the hidden operating system running everyone's work and personal lives.

The Mortar of Strong Teams

"I want people to be afraid of how much they love me."

This was Michael Scott's response when asked, "Would you rather be feared or loved?" Steve Carell played Michael Scott, an odd yet likeable manager at Dunder Mifflin, in the hit TV show *The Office*. Throughout seven seasons, Michael was on a constant quest to gain the trust, respect, and admiration from his team.

Whether Michael was changing the way he wore his tie and did his hair so he looked more like Jim (*The Office*'s "cool guy"), practicing parkour with teammates throughout the entire office, or creating a 5K run called "Michael Scott's Dunder Mifflin Scranton Meredith Palmer Memorial Celebrity Rabies Awareness Pro-Am Fun Run Race for the Cure" to help his team forget about how he hit one of the employees with his car, Michael was always vying for the acceptance of the people he worked with. His physiological desire to belong showed up in both heartwarming and desperate ways.

Michael is not the only worker desperate for more connection. A majority of the modern workforce is longing for more belonging.

Belongingness is defined as the human emotional need to be an accepted member of a group. Belonging varies from diversity, equity, and inclusion. Diversity is having everyone invited to the meeting. Equity is having everyone contribute to the meeting agenda. Inclusion is having everyone have a voice at the meeting. Belonging is having everyone's voice heard.

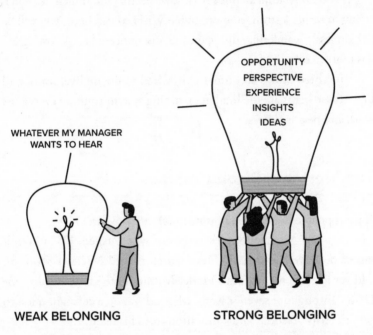

WHATEVER MY MANAGER WANTS TO HEAR

OPPORTUNITY
PERSPECTIVE
EXPERIENCE
INSIGHTS
IDEAS

WEAK BELONGING   **STRONG BELONGING**

What people share when they feel a sense of belonging.

Belonging is also separate from teamwork. Teamwork requires collective effort toward a common goal. Belonging requires collective respect, security, support, and acceptance. Teamwork exists when a teammate helps you at work. Belonging exists when you know the teammate is willing to help you in life. Teams can work together without feeling a sense of belonging. But teams can't reach their highest potential without belonging.

One of the most standout findings from the Harvard Study of Adult Development is that the happiest retirees in the study were those who actively worked to replace workmates with new playmates. The participants in the 80-plus-year study had to make an intentional effort to find new friends after their work life ended. That proposes a unique scenario that for the bulk of our lives, work is the place where we make and maintain friendships—that is, if we're lucky enough to be part of an organization with a strong culture of belonging.

It can be difficult to cultivate and maintain adult friendships as life stages and priorities shift. We move houses, kids join new sports teams, friends transfer to new cities, and so on. However, work is often more stable, remaining constant and providing a common thread as other aspects of life seem to change seasonally. Therefore, work is a great place to seek or deliver belonging.

For some, work is their best (and maybe only) option for connection. This partially explains why Michael Scott was so eager to invite his colleagues to an improv show, to hang out after work, or to attend a dinner party. He felt closest to the people that he spent the majority of his waking hours interacting with.

Margaret Heffernan, award-winning business leader and author of the book *Beyond Measure: The Big Impact of Small Changes*, refers to workplace belonging as social capital. She says, "It's the mortar, not just the bricks, that makes a building robust. The mortar, in this con-

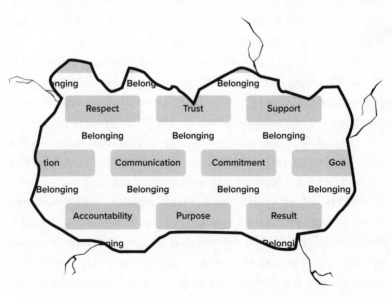

The building blocks of a strong team.

text, is social capital: mutual resilience, an underlying sense of connectedness that builds trust."[3] It's what exists between teammates that strengthens a team.

Heffernan defines social capital as "the trust, knowledge, reciprocity and shared norms that create quality of life and make a group resilient." In her years of running successful businesses, coaching senior executives, and researching the practices of world-class organizations, Heffernan has seen firsthand what investment in social capital can do for the bottom line.

She says, "In any company, you can have a brilliant bunch of individuals, but what prompts them to share ideas and concerns, contribute to one another's thinking, and warn the group about potential risks is their connection to one another. Social capital lies at the heart of just cultures: it is what they depend on and it is what they generate."

A cord of three, four, or five strands is not easily broken. Teams are bursting with the possibility of resilience. In a marketplace in constant flux, social connections hold the key to keeping organizations resilient and thriving through conflict.

Teams who are socially alert to one another's needs are more successful than teams who do not have "social sensitivity." Having empathy and being able to read others' subtle shifts in mood and demeanor is an important element of belongingness at work.

Workplaces that do not foster a sense of belonging unintentionally isolate employees, often causing them to jockey for power, prestige, and individualized gains—gains that might help in the short term but might not necessarily be what's best for the business's sustainability.

Belonging begins when people understand that unity is what allows teams to thrive. In one example, Carol Vallone, CEO of WebCT, a virtual learning technology company that was acquired by Blackboard, explained how her team agreed to yearly budgets.[4] When it came time to draw up the company's annual budget, each department head had to explain their budget so effectively to one of their colleagues that the colleague could defend it at their leadership team meeting. The chief learning officer would argue the case for sales, the head of technology spoke on behalf of operations, customer care explained HR's needs. Everyone had to see the whole company through the eyes of someone else. They felt duty-bound to do the best job possible—if only to ensure their counterpart did likewise. They had to listen to everyone, not just wait their turn.

Belonging is finding comfort among others. Brené Brown, author of *Braving the Wilderness: The Quest for True Belonging and the Courage to Stand Alone*, says "Belonging [is] the innate human desire to be part of something larger than us. One of the biggest surprises in this research was learning that fitting in and belonging are not the same thing. In fact, fitting in is one of the greatest barriers to belonging. Fitting in is about assessing a situation and becoming who you need to be in order to be accepted. Belonging, on the other hand, doesn't require us to change who we are; it requires us to be who we are."

Belonging is not likability. It goes far beyond that. Belonging is being committed to the success of the people around you. Because when people are vested in the success of those they interact with, they become allies, not derailers.

Michael C. Bush, CEO of Great Places to Work, has seen what it takes to become one of the premier organizations in the world. Since 2015, Bush has been involved in choosing the companies that make the very coveted Top Places to Work list. Companies like Cisco, Hilton, Salesforce, and Mars routinely make the list due to the alluring work cultures they possess.

When looking at what the greatest companies do well, as compared to companies that do not make the list, Bush discovered belonging was present within the greatest companies. Bush says, "It is not about ping-pong tables, and massages and pet walking. It's not about the perks. It's all about how people are treated by their leaders, and by the employees that they work with."

Unlocking Higher-Level Working

It's not surprising that belonging was at the top of Deloitte's 2020 Global Human Capital Trends survey as one of the most important human capital issues.[5] According to Deloitte's survey, creating belonging at work embraces three mutually reinforcing attributes: feeling comfortable, being connected, and making a contribution.

Belonging Attribute #1: Feeling Comfortable

Twenty-five percent of global workers identified fostering an environment where workers feel they are treated fairly and can bring their authentic selves to work—comfort—as the biggest driver of belonging.

Having the team at the table is simply not enough; leaders must also "amplify everyone's voices, clear barriers, and appreciate each other for their unique backgrounds" says Rebekah Bastian, former vice president of culture and community at Zillow.[6] Business outcomes often associated with having diverse teams can't be achieved without a sense of belonging. A sense of belonging means that people can bring their full selves to work, and not feel like they're a different person there than at home.

Psychological safety is helpful for creating comfort among a team. Psychological safety creates space where workers feel that they can freely raise concerns, questions, and ideas without repercussion. Psychological safety pays off in increased creativity, trust, and productivity among a team.[7] It is the single most important quality that determines a team's success.[8] More on creating safe spaces like this later in the book.

In addition, to feel comfortable at work, people must feel they are treated fairly and are respected and appreciated by their colleagues.

In 1983, the cofounder of The Ritz-Carlton Hotel Company, Horst Schulze, came up with the company motto, "We are Ladies and Gentlemen serving Ladies and Gentlemen." Schulze challenged the status quo of hospitality, where staff was supposed to be invisible. "Invisibility" makes staff inconsequential as compared to the guests. Schulze constantly communicated that while the staff's job may be to "serve guests," they are in fact not servants; rather they are professionals, when they serve guests with excellence. To this day, the company's motto continues to define their culture of respect and comfort shown to all Ritz-Carlton staff members.

Belonging Attribute #2: Being Connected

Thirty-one percent of global workers said that having a sense of community and identifying with a defined team—connection—was the biggest driver in creating a culture of belonging.[9] Effective connection occurs when workers have strong relationships with their team members, and when they feel connected with the organization's purpose and goals.

Donald Miller, the CEO of Business Made Simple, has a clear and quantifiable mission statement to connect his team to the story and purpose of the organization. Their mission is to have over 100,000 customers using Business Made Simple University within two years because everyone deserves to become a more confident professional. Having a clear and compelling mission unites a team by inviting them into a compelling story.

Workers should feel connected to the people they work with and the teams they are part of.

Belonging Attribute #3: Making a Contribution

Forty-four percent of global workers reported that feeling aligned to the organization's purpose, mission, and values, as well as being valued for their individual contributions was the biggest driver of belonging at work.

Workers receive a sense of contribution when they can see how their individual effort and talent is making a meaningful impact on organizational outcomes and/or advancing the team. In addition, feelings of respect, fairness, and connectedness with colleagues add to the sense of contribution. When asked how creating a sense of belonging supports organizational performance, 63 percent of workers answered that it does so by enhancing alignment between individual and organizational objectives.

Salesforce, the American cloud-based software company, recently found that men and women employees in the same positions were not making the same amounts of money. Upon discovering this, the company immediately calculated the difference and invested $3 million to balance things out. This universal fairness and purpose-driven decision cultivated a sense of connection within the Salesforce organization.

Workers should feel that they contribute to meaningful work outcomes and that their unique strengths are helping their teams and organizations achieve common goals.

A powerful sense of belonging stems from the human desire to utilize one's strengths, gifts, or talents to make a contribution that is valued by the team. Being needed reduces the risk of social abandonment, ultimately freeing people to do higher-level work.

Belonging Is a Boost to Business

The Atlanta United is the greatest soccer team in history. The University of Cambridge is the best university on the planet. Star Wars is the greatest movie franchise ever. Prince is the greatest musician of all time.

Did you have a visceral reaction to any of these statements? You likely did for the reason of . . . affiliation.

You had a reaction to those statements because you have a strong affiliation with or against those entities. For example, you may not like Atlanta United because your affiliation is with the Manchester United Football Club. People have strong affiliations. Look no further than face-painting fans that attend sporting events around the world.

Affiliation is the degree to which people have close social bonds, amicable relationships, and a sense of belonging with others. Sports teams, bands, clubs, and other groups provide a commonality that bonds people together. Why then is there such a lack of affiliation at work, a place where we spend so many of our waking hours interacting with employees who share the same organizational mission?

The energy we bring to our affiliations and the discrepancy between our work team affiliation and other affiliations.

"The need for interpersonal affiliation is an essential element for physical and psychological well-being across the lifespan, including life at work," says John Cacioppo, former director of the Center for Cognitive and Social Neuroscience at the University of Chicago.[10] "Not everybody treats the workplace as an identity making organism, it might not be as important for some people as it is for others, but I think oftentimes that's the dimension of loneliness you are looking to assuage in the workplace. That everybody should find a home here, because home in this sense, means we value your social presence. You matter to us," says Louise Hawkley, PhD principal research scientist at NORC at the University of Chicago.

Isn't it time we cultivate the same all-in affiliation that Star Wars fans have among our work teams? If you follow the upcoming strategies we lay out in Part Three, you can reap the following business benefits of belonging:

▶ **Boosted recruitment.** When employees feel like they belong, they are 167 percent more likely to recommend their organization as a great place to work.[11]

▶ **Boosted performance.** Teams with a strong sense of belonging see a 56 percent increase in job performance.[12]

▶ **Boosted engagement.** Workplace belonging leads to a 75 percent decrease in employee sick days and a 50 percent reduction in turnover risk.[13] Additionally, employees with a best friend at work expend more effort in their job.[14] For example, women who strongly agree that they have a best friend at work are more than twice as likely to be engaged (63 percent) compared with the women who say otherwise (29 percent).

▶ **Boosted collaboration.** Excluded individuals are less willing to work on behalf of the team that excluded them. In fact, a single incidence of "micro-exclusion" can lead to an immediate 25 percent decline in an individual's performance on a team project.[15]

A survey of 1,789 full-time US employees representing a diverse set of industries quantified the impact of belonging in the workplace.[16] For a 10,000-person company, if all workers felt a high degree of belonging, this would correlate with an annual gain of:

▶ Over $52 million from boosts in productivity
▶ An annual savings of $10 million in turnover-related costs
▶ 2,825 fewer sick days being taken during the year, which translates into a productivity gain of nearly $2.5 million

Belonging pays big dividends.

The evidence makes clear that *belonging* must move from a "nice-to-have" buzzword to a business priority. Since work is a profound place for people to create belonging, leaders have an unparalleled opportunity to provide people with a greater sense of acceptance, support, and inclusion that leaves the business boosted.

The Bandit of Belonging

One of the most heated rivalries in all of sports is the New York Yankees versus the Boston Red Sox. Yankees and Red Sox fans do not belong together.

Mina Cikara, assistant professor in the Department of Psychology and director of the Intergroup Neuroscience Lab at Harvard University, has studied the intergroup dynamics of these two teams. "A huge part of conflict escalation is actually a mistake that we make in intergroup contexts, which is that we don't deal with the person in front of us. Instead, what we're doing is we're dealing with some idea, some model, some stereotype of who they are," says Cikara.[17]

Cikara found that Yankees and Red Sox fans became less hostile toward each other when they took a minute to think about what it would be like to grow up in the opposing team's city, cheering for their home team.

Other researchers found that reminding soccer fans about their love for soccer, not just their specific team, increased their likelihood to help someone of a rival team.[18] In a similar study in Australia, reminding students of a common Australian identity increased helping behavior toward indigenous Australians.[19]

The bandit of belonging isn't difference but distance. When someone else's view, perspective, or behavior is unknown, unfamiliar, or unexplored, distance is created. Understanding and empathy grow with proximity. Abraham Lincoln once wisely said, "I don't like that man, I must get to know him better." Distance is the bandit of belonging.

Busyness, distractions, hostility, immaturity, ignorance, efficiency, fear, selfishness, and remote work can all contribute to the distance between people. If less loneliness, increased belonging, and greater inclusion are the goals, then we must close the distance between people. We do this by letting go of our assumptions, pride, and judgments. We must trade certainty for curiosity.

"Personal connection with people who are different from us is so powerful because when you hear their actual perspective, no person can be reduced to a stereotype. People are simply too complicated for that. There are cues, seeing someone's face, hearing their voice. That brings up our human capacity for empathy. Somebody who's different from you, sitting across from you, telling you their story and listening to yours is one of the most powerful antidotes for hatred and disconnection," says Jamil Zaki, professor at Stanford University's Social Neuroscience Lab and the author of *The War for Kindness: Building Empathy in a Fractured World.*[20]

When we extract ourselves from our personal version of the world and enter the version of others, we close the distance between us. This unlocks the ability to empathize with anyone, no matter the differences, ultimately creating belonging.

Arrest the belonging bandit with empathy.

Drivers of Distance at Work

Here are some additional ways belonging is stunted at work.

Too Much Time Communicating Through a Screen

When too much physical distance exists between team members, belonging begins to dissipate. Humans have not evolved to communicate effectively through screens. A physiological barrier exists when people can't be in-person together. Technology can fill the gap when in-person isn't available, but it cannot replace the bond-building and belonging-boosting effects of in-person exposure.

Too Little Recognition

When a gap between effort and recognition exists, belonging suffers. "Being recognized for my accomplishments" was the top activity that made employees feel like they belonged according to LinkedIn's *Inside The Mind of Today's Candidate* report.[21] A lack of timely recognition tanks a team's sense of belonging.

Too Much Conforming

When too much distance is created between employees and their true and whole selves, belonging becomes brittle. The pressure to conform to group norms lingers in the background of any group of people, but conformity isn't true belonging.

Too Little Confidence

When too much distance exists between perceptions and possibility, belonging declines. It's isolating when a capable employee is denied a chance to perform, overlooked, or perceived as incapable by the leader. Discrepancies in abilities and failure to delegate can drive a wedge in belonging.

Too Much Silence

When too much distance exists between what's said and not said, belonging can diminish. The Pulse mass shooting in Orlando, Florida, on June 12, 2016, was one of the most vicious attacks on LGBTQ people anywhere in the world. The next day, James Barr, a member of the LGBTQ community in London, went to work and was surprised that no one checked in to see how he was doing following the tragic news. While his coworkers weren't intending Barr harm, their silence sent a different message. Any comment would have been helpful that day because "at least I know they see me," said Barr.[22]

Humans have an internal drive to build social bonds and mutual caring commitments. When these bonds do not meet expectations, people suffer, including at work.

Winning at Work with Belonging

Eric Lane is the chief human resources officer at Physicians Endoscopy, a company that specializes in the development and management of specialty ASCs (ambulatory surgery centers). With over 60 ASCs and 600 doctors who perform more than 600,000 procedures a year, Physicians Endoscopy is a leading provider of gastrointestinal services in the United States. "Belonging is something that we have absolutely been addressing," says Lane. "We have been focusing on how to build a sense of community, rallying behind our mission, in order to give our employees more of a sense of purpose."

Physicians Endoscopy has done this by having each executive within the organization regularly connect with its key influencers (high-performing men and women who possess a lot of decision-making clout within the company). Each executive connected with 10 influencers from across all departments on a weekly basis, using a one-page life planning guide that steers conversations in meaningful ways. Instead of talking about work, the executive team was coached on how to have conversations that dealt with more personal topics.

Eric says, "the human element cannot be separated from work and life. It is one and the same. Even though mixing personal life with professional life is still a bit of a taboo thing, we are noticing it is becoming less and less. When we outlined the initiative to the executives, we told them to throw the notion that home and work do not mix out the window."

The executives were provided guidelines about how to navigate the conversations and resources to create meaningful dialogues. Coaches followed up regularly with the executives to see how things were going.

After a month of building these relationships with their key influencers, the leaders then had the influencers go out and do the same thing. Each influencer had to connect with 10 people, until eventually all 2,000 people within the organization had become directly involved in this initiative. Eric says, "We sparked belonging, by helping people help each other." Part of the magic from this initiative was making it clear to everyone involved that this was not meant to be about work. It was about demonstrating that people were there for one another.

Six months after rolling out the initiatives, the data was in. Turnover was down from 25 percent to 8 percent. Integrations were noticeably smoother, with increased communication from different parties involved in the process. Employees started asking for the quarterly town halls to be monthly. They were changed to monthly, and the employee engagement during the meetings has never been higher.

Uncomplicate the Complicated

"Good relationships keep us happier and healthier. Period." says psychiatrist and director of the Harvard Study of Adult Development Robert Waldinger. "The people that fared the best were the people that leaned into relationships. The good life is built with good relationships."

Why is this so easy to grasp, yet so easy to ignore? Because we're human. Humans are beautifully complex, and life is wonderfully perplexing. The intricacies of life's relationships run deep, endless, and at times can be extremely exhausting.

But what if it wasn't complicated? What if there was a framework leaders could use to create work environments where relationships flourished? Could the workplace become the blank canvas that all of us need to practice what humanity should be? Could work be a place where lonely, tired, and doubtful individuals find restoration? It should. It can. It will.

Turn the page for the tool that will make it happen.

6

THE LESS LONELINESS FRAMEWORK

I can't change the direction of the wind,
but I can adjust my sails to always reach my destination.

JIMMY DEAN

Tattooing a famous framework, business model, or formula on your body is unusual, unless you live in Philadelphia.

This tattooable diagram is one that is forever immortalized in Philadelphia. No, it's not the infamous business framework, the SWOT Analysis—that's probably the least requested tattoo of all time! However, it's something that proved just as effective.

In the 2018 Super Bowl against the winningest Super Bowl team in history, the New England Patriots, the Philadelphia Eagles had a very slim lead of 15 to 12. The Eagles knew they had to capitalize on every scoring opportunity. So, on the one-yard line of their final play of the second quarter, they took a massive risk.

As the Eagles lined up to take the snap, quarterback Nick Foles began shouting commands at his team over the noise of the crowd. He apparently was calling an audible (an impromptu change of a set play). As Foles walked toward his offensive lineman, in a split second, the ball was hiked, not to the quarterback, but to runningback Corey Clement. Corey then tossed the ball to tight end Trey Burton, who threw it to Nick Foles, who was wide open in the end zone, for the touchdown.

This four-second play is widely considered the turning point of the game, and the catalyst for the Eagles winning Super Bowl 52. This play was called the Philly Special and has since been coined "the boldest trick play in NFL history."

Now this diagram of the Philly Special appears everywhere in Philadelphia: on T-shirts, mugs, hats, wall posters, and even as body art.

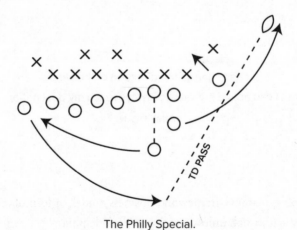

The Philly Special.

Because the Philly Special was clear, practiced, and suitable for the situation, it garnered big results. Those results immortalized the play in Eagles' history, making it a highly desired tattoo. The play not only provided the necessary edge to win but also lifted the confidence of the entire team. Similarly, when business frameworks are clear, tested, and practical they can deliver sizable results as well.

Stephen Covey's time management matrix has helped millions improve their productivity. The food pyramid invented by Anna Britt Agnsäter has helped millions live healthier lifestyles. The Less Loneliness Framework™ introduced in this chapter will help boost belonging at work, creating a more connectable team and workplace.

Just as the Eagles relied on the Philly Special to defeat the Patriots, you can rely on this framework to defeat loneliness.

The rest of the book will dive deep into the specific applications you can take to move your team from isolated to all-in. This short chapter will provide the overview of the Less Loneliness Framework™.

Concurrent Commitments

You're a leader. You're busy. We get it. That's why we've distilled this framework and the applications to simple executable strategies. You don't have time for theoretical and overly complicated processes. In fact, as mentioned in the Introduction, lessening loneliness takes less effort than you might think. Some of the transformational strategies we'll teach take only 0.6, 1, and 5. (As promised, we'll reveal what these numbers mean in the coming chapters and provide a recap at the conclusion of this book.)

The principal reason why these strategies are so transformational is that it only takes you. You don't necessarily need to persuade other leaders, or get buy-in from your team, or overhaul your company culture. There are subtle shifts you can make as a leader to completely change the well-being of your entire team.

The healthiest organizations have found a way to have concurrent commitments to human dignity and performance. They don't sacrifice the well-being of employees for high performance. They also don't sacrifice performance to bend to every need of their employees. They strike a balance. When you utilize this framework to lessen loneliness, it improves employee well-being *and* organizational excellence.

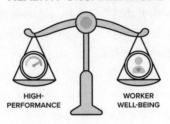

The balance between healthy organizations and teams.

The Less Loneliness Framework™ centers on Link, the most significant need of the 3 Ls of Life™ model we described in Chapter 5. The framework is a four-step process with each step represented by a letter in the word LINK. So rest assured, the actions you decide to take will go toward fulfilling the most important human need of your team. Before covering each step, let's give you some additional context about the framework.

Who Can Use the Framework

Do you have people with a pulse on your team? And do you want them to have better working relationships? Then this framework is for you.

We adopted this framework after the hundreds of client and leader interviews we've conducted over the last several years. The audiences we've helped with this framework have ranged from the C-suite to frontline supervisors and everyone in between.

Where the Framework Works

Our clients and interviewees spanned dozens of industries ranging from manufacturing to software technology to a 40-person law firm. The framework has served Fortune 100 companies and companies with less than 10 people in them. Additionally, each step can be executed virtually or in person, with various strategies that will aid in the process.

What Is the Framework

The framework is a four-step process where each letter of LINK represents a step. The process is to be followed sequentially. Each step has an overarching theme, and we provide multiple strategies that you can choose to enact each step. Some strategies take just a few minutes, while others are more continual.

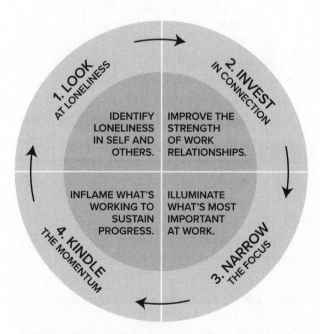

The Less Loneliness Framework™, the four-step process
to lessen loneliness and boost belonging.

Step 1: Look . . . at loneliness.

Identify loneliness in self and others.

- ▶ Look at loneliness.
- ▶ Look inward.
- ▶ Look outward.

Step 2: Invest . . . in connection.

Improve the strength of work relationships.

- ▶ Invest in safe connections.
- ▶ Invest in personal connections.
- ▶ Invest in team connections.

Step 3: Narrow . . . the focus.

Illuminate what's most important at work.

- ▶ Narrow the focus on purpose.
- ▶ Narrow the focus on clear direction.
- ▶ Narrow the focus on growth.

Step 4: Kindle . . . the momentum.

Inflame what's working to sustain progress.

- ▶ Kindle the momentum by re-Looking
- ▶ Kindle the momentum by re-Investing.
- ▶ Kindle the momentum by re-Narrowing.

Look, Invest, Narrow, and Kindle are the LINK from loneliness to belonging.

Why the Framework Works

According to psychologists, the best way to lessen loneliness and limit its effects is by using "prosocial behavior." Prosocial behaviors are actions of comforting, sharing, helping, or cooperating that are backed by a general concern for the feelings, welfare, and rights of other people. Researchers in China found that leaders who show compassion to their employees can mitigate the negative effects of loneliness and thereby boost creativity.[1] Another study of workers at Coca-Cola's Madrid headquarters found leaders were able to reduce feelings of isolation among their team by simply being nice and interacting with others.[2]

Your behavior lessens loneliness. You don't need medication, day-long centering retreats, meditation apps, or to become a certified therapist. You just need to engage in small, intentional, and routine behaviors.

Executing prosocial behaviors every day makes a difference. Woven into the framework are specific prosocial strategies that are proven to work. Those on the receiving end of prosocial behavior were a whopping 278 percent as likely to engage in prosocial behaviors themselves.[3]

Loneliness is contagious, but so are prosocial actions. The ripple effect of lessening loneliness with prosocial behaviors is gigantic. So yes, if your team executes prosocial behaviors, it could ignite similar behaviors throughout your organization and even to the broader world, leading to healthier individuals, stronger families, and more united communities.

Addressing Loneliness the Way Moustaches Address Cancer

Does the term loneliness make you a little uneasy? We get it. While our goal is to normalize the conversation around loneliness and to use the term more openly, we understand that it takes time. For those hesitant to broach the loneliness topic with your team, what if we told you that you can address loneliness without ever talking about loneliness? It's similar to the way prostate cancer can be addressed through the growing of a moustache.

In 2003, two friends (Travis Garone and Luke Slattery) were sharing a beer at the Gypsy Bar in Melbourne, Australia, when they got to talking about moustaches. Inspired by a friend's mother who was fundraising for breast cancer, Travis and Luke decided it would be fun to recruit friends to grow a moustache for 30 days in order to create awareness for men's health while raising money for prostate cancer research.[4] In their first year, they raised over $40,000 for the Prostate Cancer Foundation of Australia, which was the single largest donation the foundation had ever received.[5] The moustache movement was born, and they called it "Movember."

Today over 6 million people have signed up at Movember.com to grow a moustache during the month of November. Participants let their moustaches take the spotlight to start lifesaving conversations. Instead of discussing the intricacies of prostate cancer, Movember participants share their personal fundraising page with friends, family, and colleagues to create the awareness around the important topic.

Since inception, Movember has raised over $1 billion.[6] Today they invest in mental health, suicide prevention, prostate cancer, and testicular cancer initiatives, funding over 1,250 men's health projects in 30 countries. Movember helps millions of men get the physical, emotional, and psychological support they need.

Movember has changed the face of men's health by growing moustaches. No long awkward conversations, personal oversharing, or encroaching in other people's business—just growing an upper-lip accessory. You too can change the face of loneliness by growing belonging-boosting behaviors using the Less Loneliness Framework™ without ever talking about loneliness.

While we'd prefer more open dialogue surrounding loneliness and would encourage you to do so, we're also aware of the sensitivity around the topic. But we don't want anyone to ignore the issue because it's hard to talk about. So, even if you feel the need to avoid the term, don't avoid the problem. In a sense, the solution for less loneliness is right under your nose, in the coming chapters.

Teamwork for the Win

Teamwork is a primary reason for the survival of humanity. What the early humans lacked in size, strength, and speed they made up in communication and collaboration with others. Eventually the communicating of our desires, ideating about a preferred future, and coordinating on a plan to achieve that future has enabled humanity to materialize a world our ancestors could never dream of.

When we foster environments where teams can thrive, big things happen. Our talent is in individuals. Our strength is in numbers. Our hope is in you.

A FLEXIBLE RESOURCE FOR FLEXIBLE WORK

This book and the upcoming chapters are about how to lessen loneliness among a workforce, whether that workforce is in-person, remote, or hybrid. This book is not about remote or hybrid working. However, a remote or hybrid team can be a contributor to worker loneliness; therefore we're keeping a close eye on the evolution of flexible work. The Covid-19 global pandemic forced organizations around the world to embrace new ways of working. And as of this writing, the transition to remote or hybrid work models for many companies and leaders is still very early and unproven. Most of our clients have no idea what to expect in the coming months or how their flexible work policies will change in the future. Since the current situation is so fluid, we wanted to create a flexible resource that we could update as plans for the future of flexibility at work evolve. We'd like to continue to provide resources to you as you champion more connection in a lonely world.

Learn our latest research, thinking, and recommendations on how to create a connectable workforce no matter the distance or structure by visiting LessLonely.com/FlexibleWork.

PART THREE

HOW TO LESSEN LONELINESS AND BOOST BELONGING AT WORK

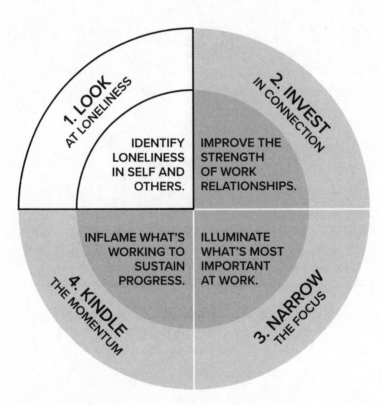

The Less Loneliness Framework™.

CHAPTER

7

LOOK AT LONELINESS

Look at everything as though you were
seeing it for the first time or the last time.
Then your time on earth will be filled with glory.

BETTY SMITH

Would you take a closer look in order to save a life?

On September 25, 2000, Kevin Hines was sitting alone in the back of a bus traveling to the Golden Gate Bridge. While most passengers on the bus were eager tourists, Hines had very different plans. He was making the trip to end his life.

The bus stopped near the bridge. With grave hesitation and as a last-ditch effort to derail his own suicide, Hines sheepishly approached the bus driver, hoping the driver would see the pain he was in and intervene by simply asking, "Are you OK?"

Confused and in shock of his pending actions, Hines was unable to speak up. The bus driver then reacted in the opposite way Hines had hoped—he abruptly shouted at Hines, "Kid, come on. Get off the bus. I got to go."

In one more effort to be seen, Hines turned to a fellow passenger, who pointed at him and said with a smirk, "What the hell is wrong with you, kid?"

That was the moment when Hines thought to himself, "Nobody cares."

Not being seen turned his last bit of doubt into determination. He ran off the bus onto the bridge and threw himself over the railing, plunging 245 feet into the San Francisco Bay.

Like a truck hitting a concrete wall, Hines hit the water at 75 miles per hour, shattering three of his vertebrae, lacerating his lower internal organs, and breaking his legs. After sinking 70 feet, he miraculously surfaced only to find himself unable to stay afloat. While struggling to keep his head above the waves, he noticed a creature beginning to circle underneath him. If he wasn't going to drown, then surely this "shark" would be the death of him.

The creature began to circle faster and faster, and Hines soon discovered it wasn't a hungry shark looking for a meal, but a friendly sea lion helping him stay afloat. The sea lion circling beneath him provided enough lift for Hines to keep his head above water. In a miraculous turn of events, the sea lion saw Hines and saved him from certain death until the Coast Guard arrived.

The Coast Guard informed Hines that he was the first person their unit had pulled out of the water who was alive after jumping from the bridge. Jumping off the bridge holds a near 100 percent fatality rate. It was a miracle.

Hines turned his miracle into a message. Now, as an author and mental health advocate, he shares how he would not have jumped if someone on that bus would have taken a closer look at his situation. Hines also shares a similar true story of a 30-year-old who jumped from the bridge and died. The person's suicide note tragically stated that if just one person had looked at them and smiled while on their way to jump from the bridge, they would not have jumped.

One person. One look. One life saved.

You never know what hangs in the balance of not taking a closer look, especially when looking for loneliness.

Less Loneliness Starts with a Look

Too often leaders unintentionally play the role of the bus driver. In the frenzy of getting to where they need to go, they neglect to truly see the passengers they've been entrusted with.

When passengers (your team members) are on your bus (your team), their well-being becomes your business. While you cannot control what they do outside of the bus, you can control how seen, safe, and engaged they are on your bus. As your team leaves the bus for the evening, weekend, or for greener pastures, how you made them feel while they were on the bus has the potential to impact their off-work behaviors and ripple across the entire community.

We're not asking you to be a therapist or psychologist. You won't be asked to diagnose mental health conditions or heal emotional scars. But rather, look for signs of loneliness and opportunities to create more connection across your team. We're asking you to slow down. Put the bus in park. Get out of your seat. And look . . . really see your team.

Leaders and organizations often neglect to look. A client of ours recently shared that after a 20-year career at one company, she joined a new organization. Ready to begin her new adventure, she showed up for her first day full of excitement. To her dismay, however, the team was more consumed with setting up her computer than connecting with the human who had just joined the organization. She told us that the stark neglect made her think, "Aren't you going to tell me you're excited to see me! Aren't you going to tell me what a great decision I made to come to work here?" The employer squandered a loyalty-enriching moment by not looking at the person.

Take it from a professional looker, Ansel Adams, who is widely considered one of the most influential landscape photographers of the twentieth century, "A photograph is usually looked at, seldom looked into." Go beyond looking *at* and look *into* your team.

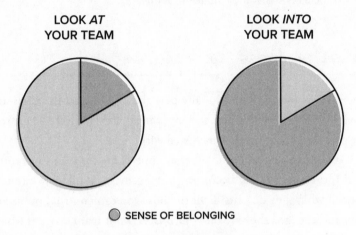

SENSE OF BELONGING

How to create more belonging at work.

In this chapter, we'll provide you the necessary information to look with intentionality to move your team from isolated to all-in.

Looking in Three Simple Steps

Loneliness is an abstract concept that you cannot touch or see. However, most people have an intuitive sense of what loneliness is and feels like because everyone has experienced it to some degree.

To get the best vantage point to look at the full loneliness landscape at work, you must take three steps. These steps will help you see the "unseeable" condition of loneliness.

Step 1: Look at Loneliness

The first step is to look at loneliness. The famous Beatles song "Eleanor Rigby" expresses wonderment at the number of lonely people in the world. This is the type of direct curiosity needed in this initial step. Acknowledge the likelihood that loneliness is present, and then take action to understand it.

It is critical to grasp the importance of loneliness. You do not need to fully understand loneliness like a doctor understands the human genome, but you can understand in the same way a fitness coach assesses individuals. You need to appreciate the health benefits of a strong body and mind, identify unhealthy behaviors in yourself and others, and demonstrate the right activities to promote a healthy lifestyle. You don't need to cure people's ailments (like a doctor), but you can be proactive about easing their condition (like a fitness coach). The previous chapters have hopefully provided you with the necessary knowledge and awareness to tackle loneliness with the respect and vigilance it requires.

As a reminder, lonelier workers quit more often, perform more poorly, and feel less engaged.

The United Kingdom recently appointed a Minister of Loneliness to head up the daunting task of finding solutions to loneliness.[1] The United Kingdom is taking a long and committed look at loneliness, not only because of the negative health impacts to its citizens, but because loneliness is costing employers £2.5 billion[2] ($3.5 billion US). The United Kingdom isn't alone. Loneliness is costing employers around the globe billions every year. Loneliness is silently draining your team's health, their productivity, and your organization's revenue.

Former US surgeon general Vivek Murthy said, "During my years caring for patients, the most common pathology I saw was not heart disease or diabetes; it was loneliness."[3] If the most common ailment among people is loneliness, then it's fair to assume loneliness lingers among your team. The question isn't *if* your team is lonely but *how* lonely they are. To uncover that question, one must take a closer look at loneliness.

It's becoming easier than ever before to look at loneliness, because more people are open to discussing it. The stigma around loneliness is lifting. In 2020, singer and songwriter Justin Bieber released a song titled "Lonely." The song is about how early in his career, Bieber had everything in the world except someone who knew him. Who listened to him. Who saw him. This lack of connection left him extremely lonely.

Bieber's song struck a chord. It was a global hit, rising to number one in Canada, Hungary, Malaysia, and Norway and top 15 in the United States, Switzerland, Singapore, New Zealand, Portugal, Austria, Belgium, Greece, Finland, Germany, Australia, Ireland, Sweden, Netherlands, and Denmark. Ultimately, "Lonely" reached number five on Billboard's Global 200. Clearly people can relate. Additionally, after Bieber vulnerably shared his loneliness story, social media influencers around the world began using the song to share how lonely they actually were.

The world is ready to talk about loneliness.

Getting a grip on the gravity of loneliness is step one in addressing it. Since you're this far in the book, consider this step accomplished!

LOOK EXAMPLE

When Alex Pentland, MIT professor and director of the Connection Science Research Initiative, looked at the communication patterns at a call center, he recommended that coffee breaks be rescheduled so that everyone on the team could take a break at the same time.[4] Providing this one simple opportunity to build social capital among a team yielded the company $15 million in productivity gains, and employee satisfaction increased by 10 percent. Not bad for making a slight change to when people drink their coffee. Alex was able to look and see that his team needed more connection away from their work and provided a solution that instantly had an impact.

Step 2: Look Inward

The next step is to look inward. In order to most effectively help others lessen loneliness, one should understand their personal experience with loneliness and cultivate a healthy relationship with it oneself.

In a 2013 *Saturday Night Live* episode, actors Kristin Wiig and Gerard Butler dressed up as the characters in Disney's *Beauty and the Beast*. Wiig wore the yellow dress worn by Belle in the movie, while Butler in magnificent makeup looked almost identical to the gruesome beast. They danced and sang together, romantically staring into each other's eyes, when Wiig said, "They say true love can break the curse, and I can't imagine a love more true than this." Butler responded, "Oh my darling, I can hardly wait until *your* transformation."

As the live audience laughed, Wiig looked confusedly into the beast's eyes, and her eyebrows went up in disbelief as she asked, "What do you mean *my* transformation?" To which Butler replied, "You know, the curse will be broken, and you can stop being a beast." The two then comedically go back and forth trying to convince the other that they are the one in need of transformation.

Before asking others to make changes or consider a new approach, it's mature and insightful to first take a look in the mirror and observe our own behaviors and beliefs. First looking inward to identify what transformation *you* need to make will give you the perspective and authority to help others transform. Your team can't expect you to help them lessen loneliness if you yourself are blind to its impact in your life.

Remember, loneliness isn't shameful, it's a signal. When you experience loneliness, that means your brain works. Your brain is serving up a reminder that you need community because humans are wired to be social relational beings.

Half of CEOs report experiencing feelings of loneliness in their role, and of this group, 61 percent believe it hinders their performance.[5] Additionally, among first-time CEOs, nearly 70 percent experience loneliness. They report that the feelings of isolation negatively affect their performance.

It's lonely at the top. It's also lonely at the middle and at the bottom. It's lonely everywhere.

According to University of Canterbury's Associate Professor Sarah Wright's research on coping with loneliness at work, "Across all the organizations studied and across all measures, managers are no more or less lonely than their nonmanager counterparts, either in work or more generally. If an effective leader or manager does experience loneliness, the reasons for it are likely to be a complex hybrid of personal, social, and contextual factors rather than seniority alone. Being at the top of the organization's hierarchy is not a predictor of loneliness."[6]

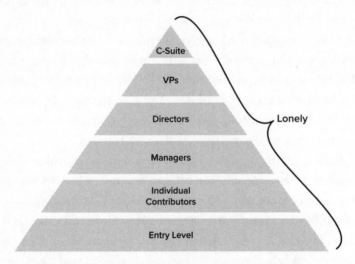

Levels of the organization that experience loneliness.

Leaders owe it to themselves, the team, and the organization to ensure loneliness doesn't impact their effectiveness and get in the way of reducing isolation among the team. Here's how to manage your personal levels of loneliness.

Self-Assess: Look to See What You Currently Can't See

You can't address a problem you don't know exists. Use this short assessment to uncover your loneliness levels. The assessment is adopted from the University of California, Los Angeles (UCLA) Loneliness Scale, which is the most commonly used and widely accepted measure of loneliness.[7]

LONELINESS SELF-ASSESSMENT

How often do you feel the way described below?

Score each statement using the following scale:

1–Never | 2–Rarely | 3–Sometimes | 4–Often

1. Not in tune with people around me.   Never 1 2 3 4 Often

2. Lack companionship.   Never 1 2 3 4 Often

3. Don't have anyone to talk to.   Never 1 2 3 4 Often

4. Don't feel part of a group.   Never 1 2 3 4 Often

5. Not understood by others.   Never 1 2 3 4 Often

6. Starved for company.   Never 1 2 3 4 Often

7. Isolated or excluded by others.   Never 1 2 3 4 Often

8. Social relationships are superficial.   Never 1 2 3 4 Often

9. Interests aren't shared by others.   Never 1 2 3 4 Often

10. Unhappy being withdrawn.   Never 1 2 3 4 Often

Add up each of the 10 scores to get your total.

Total Score	Loneliness Level
10–20	Low Level of Loneliness
21–30	Medium Level of Loneliness
31–40	High Level of Loneliness

Visit LessLonely.com/SelfAssessment to take the digital version of the assessment and receive specific recommendations to improve your loneliness level. Or share the assessment with your team and/or peers.

Schedule Solitude: Look for Opportunities to Be Still

Aloneness can lessen loneliness. As mentioned in Chapter 1, solitude is insurance against loneliness and is leaders' first line of defense in protecting against loneliness in themselves and ultimately their team. When solitude is done right, it helps strengthen the connection with ourselves that in turn equips us to connect more with others.

Solitude is a state of being alone without the negative emotions of loneliness. It is peaceful aloneness created by a state of voluntary isolation. Solitude is found by isolating one's mind from the inputs of other minds in order to freely process or ponder. Essentially, you can experience solitude amid a crowded coffee shop if your thinking is self-directed instead of reacting to the outside environment.

Consider these quotes:

> Pablo Picasso: "Without great solitude, no serious work is possible."
>
> Jane Hirshfield, award-winning poet: "Solitude, whether endured or embraced, is a necessary gateway to original thought."
>
> Albert Einstein: "The monotony and solitude of a quiet life stimulates the creative mind."
>
> Thomas Edison: "The best thinking has been done in solitude."
>
> Paulo Coelho, Brazilian lyricist and author of *The Alchemist*: "If you are never alone, you cannot know yourself."

Solitude provides the necessary margin for leaders to recalibrate, think clearly, prioritize, plan, and recharge. Loneliness will empty a person; solitude, on the other hand, can fill a person up.

The greater the noise, the greater need for solitude. The demands of life and business today are deafening. That's why solitude doesn't come easy. There is always something more urgent and loud that will steal your attention. You have to fight for it.

You may have to get over your fear of being alone with your thoughts, or abandon the feeling that seeking solitude is selfish. There isn't anything selfish about rising above the noise, gaining a grander vision of the future, and leading a team to that preferred destination.

At the writing of this, Ryan has three children five years old and younger. He and his wife, Ashley, often experience the opposite of loneliness. However, as a keynote speaker and author, Ryan has a lot of opportunities to potentially experience loneliness. Twenty percent of his professional time is spent in front of large audiences where he interacts with incredible people around the world. The other 80 percent is spent in hotels, Ubers, airports, and crouched over a laptop writing or creating. If he didn't appreciate the power of solitude, he'd be doomed to a very lonesome career. That's why, as an introvert, he is not antisocial. He's pro-solitude.

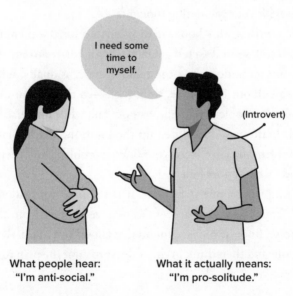

What people hear an introvert say versus reality.

Ryan has made some of his biggest creative strides and break-throughs while in solitude. When his head and heart feel tangled up in something, breaking away from his routine for a day or two can provide the clarity and confidence he needs to make sound decisions.

He is aware of the health concerns, meaninglessness, and limitations loneliness can bring, while appreciating the clarity, creativity, and emotional balance solitude brings. The line between loneliness and solitude is fine, but if you toe the line well, you can reap deep work. Exceptional work requires space to focus. You have important work to do, so seek solitude.

In his experience, the difference between loneliness and solitude is a plan. Having a detailed plan to unpack and dissect an idea, project, or decision while in solitude keeps loneliness at bay.

Solitude can happen in a few moments or a few months. It can also take many forms, such as self-reflection, journaling, meditation, mindfulness exercises, brainstorming, or business strategy sessions. It can even be as simple as taking a few quiet, social-media-free minutes to just be with your wandering thoughts.

When writing this book, if Ryan encountered a mental roadblock, he'd seek solitude. He'd get in his car and drive around Atlanta, without music, podcasts, or the radio on. Occasionally, he'd force himself to talk out loud—yes, to himself—so that his mind stayed focused on the problem at hand. Without fail, while immersed in solitude, his brain would conjured up the solution. The human brain craves problems to solve. Feed your brain a problem, and then give it space to do what it does best.

Seeking time alone is healthy. It is required for leaders to be effective. You owe it to your team to remove yourself from the day-to-day noise, find the higher ground that allows you to clearly see the destination, and then think in the stillness to craft the plan to get the team there.

The benefits of solitude. Rise above the day-to-day noise
to gain a clearer vision of the future.

Speak Up and Speak Out:
Look for the Moments to Share and Be Heard

Acknowledging feelings of loneliness can provide subtle relief. Leaders
can be guilty of denying or burying their emotions in order to save
face or to appear strong for their team. This emotional repression can
be exhausting while sending the wrong signal to a lonely team. The
more emotionally intelligent a leader can be, the easier it becomes to
find support in navigating loneliness and/or dealing with isolation.

By speaking up and being more open about loneliness, we can
set a healthy example for others to speak out as well. Kevin Hines,
the Golden Gate Bridge survivor, says, "A pain shared is a pain
halved." When we share our story, people listen autobiographically,
seeing themselves in our story. Knowing we aren't alone in our loneliness lessens the pain and shame. Discussing loneliness will normalize the topic, destigmatizing it and ultimately alleviating the grip it
has on employees.

"Sometimes you need to be brave enough to be vulnerable," says Shandee Bowman, director of people experience and culture at a 129-year-old supply chain logistics services company. At a recent all-hands meeting, a supervisor named Jerome shared that he had been feeling lonely. This leader let down his guard to admit he was not feeling himself lately. Bowman said that as soon as Jerome mentioned the word "lonely," the entire group unanimously nodded their heads in understanding. One of the women on the call even had tears well up in her eyes. She messaged in the chat forum, "You just described exactly what I have been feeling, but could not articulate." Julius recognized the loneliness he was feeling and acknowledged it to others.

A pain shared is a pain halved. Knowing that we aren't alone in our loneliness lessens the pain and shame.

This has been our experience every time we broach the topic of loneliness with our clients, family, and friends. Because it's a universal human condition, everyone can relate to the feeling and everyone has a story about it. Look for opportunities to talk more openly about loneliness with your team, and you'll likely be surprised with both their receptiveness and the bonding that often follows.

Seek Support: Look for People Who Can Help You Shoulder the Burden

Establishing a trusted advisor who can provide reliable support and/ or journey with you through isolation can be useful in lessening loneliness. This isn't about getting over loneliness; it's about getting *through* loneliness. You don't get over loneliness once and remain free from the emotion thereafter. It's a process. Loneliness is a part of life. You'll never get over loneliness for good. But you can minimize its effects and the frequency with which you experience it. Having someone else on the journey through loneliness can be helpful. Like a good sherpa who helps carry the load when the climb gets tough, a trusted advisor will help you shoulder the burdens of loneliness so that you can keep climbing.

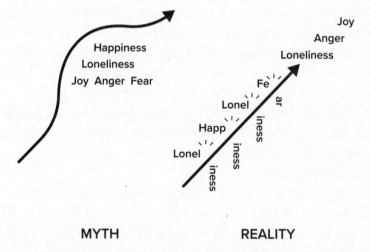

MYTH   **REALITY**

Encountering emotions on the journey of life. We don't get over emotions once and for all. We get through emotions again and again in life.

Support can come from a spouse, board member, or mentor. The space within the collaborative relationship should be safe where you can share your concerns and receive honest, straightforward feedback. Creating a supportive space where you can peel away any layers of ego, brassiness, insensitivity, or skepticism will ultimately strengthen you into a more resilient and capable leader.

Leading is difficult. Trying to conceal your fear, doubt, or insecurities to maintain a false appearance of unshakeable confidence is a fast track to experiencing loneliness, because no one really sees you. They instead see a carefully crafted and unrelatable avatar. No longer can leaders afford to ignore feelings of loneliness. Leaders must proactively work through loneliness so that they can eventually help their teams do the same.

Step 3: Look Outward

The final step is to look outward at your team and assess their loneliness levels. One of Steven's best friends, Brandon, is a special operations Marine sniper. He would routinely ask him the following questions after spending just several minutes at a location together: Who is sitting by the window? How many people are by the front of the building? Where are the exits? On command, and with 100 percent accuracy, Brandon would give him the "intel" he was after. Brandon never misses. When he asked how he is able to do this so well, he simply said, "Easy, I'm a trained observer."

Brandon has spent years becoming a "looker"—someone who pays extra attention to the details of an environment that most of us gloss over. He said, "When you make it a point to pay attention, you see things others don't."

Before we provide you with a list of common indicators of worker loneliness to look for, let's review the populations that are most at risk of experiencing loneliness. Becoming a "looker" is possible with the right intel and practice.

The Workers Most Prone to Loneliness

While the following will provide a more granular understanding of the workers who are most susceptible to loneliness, do not forget that loneliness is a universal condition and is impacting your team whether you see your team represented here or not.

Recently Shawn Achor, the *New York Times* bestselling author of *The Happiness Advantage*,[8] and researchers at his company surveyed 1,624 full-time employees, all of whom were participants in a longitudinal study of 4,000 American workers, to identify employees most at risk for feeling lonely at work.[9] The participants provided details on the degrees of loneliness and social support they experienced on a daily basis, both in and out of the workplace.

The result? America's loneliest workers are single, childless, well-educated, nonreligious, and non-heterosexual.

Legal practice, engineering, and science are the professions with the loneliest workers. And lonely workers are most likely to work for the government or a for-profit company. Occupations with high rates of social interaction, such as social work, marketing, and sales, had the least lonely workers.

People who held a graduate degree reported higher levels of loneliness and less workplace support than those who had completed only undergraduate or high school degrees. In addition, people with law and medical degrees were lonelier than those with a bachelor's degree or PhD.

The following factors had no impact on worker loneliness: geographic location, staying in the same job (tenure), gender, race, and ethnicity. Salary only slightly impacted feelings of loneliness. Workers making $80,000 a year only showed about a 10 percent improvement in loneliness over their counterparts making half that much.

Lonely workers are more likely to be remote workers.[10] And loneliness is the biggest struggle to working remotely.[11] When taking advantage of hybrid work policies, remote workers often feel indebted to their employer, which can lead to working longer hours and neglecting to tend to their personal and professional relationships.

Don't be fooled by extroversion. According to University of Canterbury's Associate Professor Sarah Wright's research on loneliness in the workplace, "A potential difficulty with connecting social skill directly with loneliness is that in certain environments, such as the workplace, social skill may not always act as a buffer against loneliness. For example, interpersonal competence (with leaders, peers, or clients/customers) could account for an individual's rise up an organization's hierarchy, but the individual may still experience loneliness because of professional distance from peers and subordinates, or being marginalized because of status."[12]

Similarly, for some people, success in the workplace may be more prized than closeness to colleagues.[13] Therefore, an individual may discount workplace relationships if achievement at work fulfills his or her primary goals. Taking closer looks to uncover team members' motivations is important.

It's very important to understand that lonely people don't have lower innate social skills, but rather, their preoccupation with their own feelings of loneliness leads to impaired empathy for others and makes them less approachable.

In Achor's survey, nonlonely workers reported higher job satisfaction, more promotions, less frequent job switching, and a lower likelihood of quitting their current job in the next six months. Again, from the employer's perspective, there are big benefits to lessening loneliness and boosting belonging at work.

How to Spot Lonely Workers

Within organizations, leaders and close colleagues are best positioned to spot workers struggling with loneliness. The signs may be subtle, but knowing the risk factors we just highlighted and looking for the indicators listed later in this section will help.

Loneliness is a subjective experience, so there are no hard-and-fast rules about what it looks like. Many people may hide their feelings for fear of embarrassment, or because they don't want to appear weak. This can make loneliness difficult to identify. As a manager, your best approach is to take the time to get to know and really understand your people. This will help you recognize when someone is feeling disconnected or left out by the rest of the team. Be sure to listen to other team members' concerns, too; they might be more aware of their colleague's feelings and emotions than you are.

LOOK EXAMPLE

During a recent conversation with a colleague, Steven could tell immediately something was off. The tone of his colleague's voice was abnormally distraught when he answered Steven's call. Rather than diving into the reason for why he had called, Steven decided to take a closer look at what might be going on by saying, "Hey, Ellis, I can tell something is off—what is going on, my friend?" Ellis began to share how his three-week project in a remote part of Africa was becoming more difficult than expected, how he missed his family, and how he was growing more and more lonely. We spent the next 30 minutes talking about Ellis's feelings of isolation.

Sometimes loneliness can be spotted in an instant. When you take a closer look to get to know people, you're in a better position to spot loneliness and speak into their situation.

Here are 10 common identifiers of lonely workers. As an exercise, think of someone on your team you suspect might be feeling lonely. Which of the following applies to that person?

1. Sloppy Work

Careless behaviors, a decrease in work quality, or irresponsibility from a usually dependable worker is an indicator of potential loneliness. Sloppy work is a key indicator that people are working with a lessened sense of connection to either the team or their work.

Examples:

▶ Missing project deadlines
▶ Makes uncharacteristic mistakes
▶ Takes shortcuts with clients or customers
▶ Delivers incomplete assignments

2. Lack of Learning and Development

Curiosity and a growth mindset are good indicators of employee engagement. When employees are leaning into learning, they show a level of optimism about their future. When they don't, it could be because they are disengaged or disconnected.

Examples:

- ► Limited participation in training
- ► Disdain for extracurricular activities
- ► Doesn't ask questions
- ► Uninterested in career progression

3. Change in Routine

Engaged employees are reliable, with recognizable routines. Reliable employees whose routines change might be an indicator of a growing sense of isolation.

Examples:

- ► Showing up to work late
- ► Taking extra-long lunches
- ► Leaving or logging out early
- ► Working late nights or weekends

4. Stops Offering Input

Feelings of insecurity are associated with loneliness. When workers stop offering suggestions or participating in goal setting, it could be because they do not want to be seen.

Examples:

- ► Lack of eye contact during meetings
- ► Not speaking during meetings
- ► Doesn't ask for feedback
- ► Avoids planning or strategy sessions

5. Skips or Resents Meetings

Lonely people avoid others. Not showing up or arriving routinely late to meetings indicates a disconnected worker. Lonely people can also be hostile to those around them.

Examples:

- ▶ Not apologizing for being late
- ▶ Keeping camera off during video meetings
- ▶ Being disgruntled during meetings
- ▶ Quick to anger while among others

6. Only Talks Work

Lonely workers are often unwilling to talk about non-work-related items. Only talking about work is a signal that someone isn't interested in developing connections.

Examples:

- ▶ Does not talk about hobbies
- ▶ Shies away from discussing personal topics
- ▶ Wary to engage in small talk
- ▶ Deflects any non-work-related questions

7. Limited Interaction with Coworkers

Absent on communication platforms, long delay between communications, or avoiding small work gatherings are indicators that a worker might feel isolated.

Examples:

- ▶ Avoids joining special interest work groups
- ▶ Eats lunch at desk
- ▶ Lack of curiosity in others
- ▶ Short responses during conversations

8. An Apathetic Attitude

An unwillingness to present or defend ideas, fulfill commitments, or be accountable can be a sign of loneliness. Lonely people often demonstrate more negativity.

Examples:

▶ Passive approach to work
▶ Low energy levels
▶ Somber demeanor
▶ Disinterested in serving customers

9. Unkempt Appearance

A disorderly workspace or appearance can be an indication of an indifference to establishing connections with fellow workers.

Examples:

▶ Disheveled clothes
▶ Ungroomed appearance
▶ Messy desk or cluttered workspace
▶ Recurring outfits

10. Excessive Working

Spending too much time working as a way to avoid personal responsibilities can point to an imbalance in social relationships. Taking on too much work can be leveraged as an excuse to avoid professional and personal social interactions.

Examples:

▶ Volunteering for too many projects
▶ Piling up vacation days
▶ Returning emails late at night
▶ Hurrying from meeting to meeting

THE TEAM CONNECTION ASSESSMENT™

The 10 Identifiers of Lonely Workers will help you identify individuals on your team who might be suffering from loneliness. The Team Connection Assessment™ allows you to quantify how connected your team is. It's the first (and only) tool to effectively assess the strength of relationships among a team. It measures the strength and quality of connections teams have with their teammates, manager, and the work itself. It's easy to administer and takes only 15 minutes to complete. After completing the assessment, you will be provided with a team score based on the 4 Levels of Team Connection™ and a custom report providing research-based recommendations to improve the team connection score. Our devices are always informing us how strongly they are connected to Wi-Fi or other networks. It's time workers and leaders have the same connectivity information about their teams.

Take the Team Connection Assessment™ or share it with your team by visiting LessLonely.com/Assessment.

Degrees of Loneliness

When it comes to identifying lonely workers, it's important to understand that loneliness doesn't impact everyone the same.

In 2016, researchers at University of California San Diego School of Medicine conducted the first genome-wide association study for loneliness to determine the degree to which loneliness is a lifelong trait or a temporary state and the degree to which a tendency to loneliness is inherited.[14] They published their results in the publication *Neuropsychopharmacology*. Studying over 10,000 people, they found that the tendency to feel lonely over a lifetime, rather than just occasionally due to circumstance, afflicts between 14 percent to 27 percent of people. In other words, genes do play a role in loneliness, but not as much as environment. The response of loneliness is a complex human cocktail of genetics, personalities, current and past experiences, and culture.

Every person perceives loneliness differently. Like diabetes, people have varying degrees of susceptibility to loneliness. According to Abraham Palmer, professor of psychiatry and vice chair for basic research at UC San Diego School of Medicine, "For two people with the same number of close friends and family, one might see their social structure as adequate while the other doesn't. And that's what we mean by 'genetic predisposition to loneliness'—one person is more likely than another to feel lonely, even in the same situation."[15] For example, you might experience loneliness lightly but frequently, while your coworker experiences it intensely but sparingly. For some it's crippling, and for others it's only a minor agitation.

This loneliness variability has been useful to humans. The degree to which our ancestors experienced loneliness was a natural clue into the role they would play within the tribe. For example, those who were crippled by loneliness would have duties within the village where they connected with other people. Those with low levels of loneliness would be more willing to venture out to hunt, gather, or explore new terrain.

In the context of work, this is important because your experience with loneliness isn't the same as the experience of those you work alongside. Loneliness is universal, yet unique to each person. But no matter how susceptible we are to loneliness, we all need to be known, seen, and heard. Often, the experience of loneliness a person feels at work is unseen by his or her coworkers.

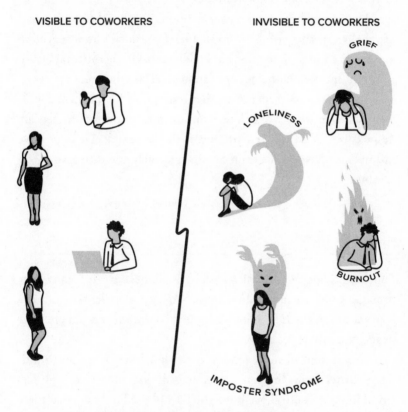

The unseen ailments of today's workers.

Mentally Fit for Duty

Are leaders responsible for the mental health of their employees? No. Are leaders responsible for recognizing shifts in employee behaviors that might indicate they are unfit for duty? Yes.

Consider this scenario: You are a leader at a construction company. Your team operates heavy equipment. What would you do if you noticed that one of your crew members exhibited signs of loneliness over the past few weeks and, on one particular day, she showed up to work really checked out? Would you allow her to operate the machinery that day and potentially put the other crew members in harm's way? No. She is not fit for duty.

Her mental health is not your responsibility, but the physical and psychological safety of the team is. Therefore, today's leaders need to be equipped to look for signs of loneliness and other mental health concerns for the well-being of the individual and the team.

Leaders can't control nor are they responsible for the mental well-being of their team while they're "off the bus." However, leaders are responsible for creating environments that are conducive to positive mental health where the team can operate safely and thrive while "on the bus."

Conclusion

Ducking, dodging, and disregarding loneliness at work can't continue. It's time to address loneliness. We need more leaders to intervene and turn the tide on this crippling condition and to help their teams and businesses thrive.

As you looked more closely at the loneliness levels surrounding your team, maybe you're encouraged, discouraged, or indifferent. However you feel, we hope you'll be pleased to know that there are actionable steps you can take to improve the connectedness and sense of belonging of your team, no matter how dire the situation. You alone have the power to break and reverse the negative cycles of workplace loneliness.

Looking at loneliness, reflecting inward, and observing outward will provide you with the necessary awareness, perspective, and knowledge to begin taking action to lessen loneliness and boost belonging among your team. The next step in the Less Loneliness Framework™ is to Invest in Connection.

We'll provide you with a practical guide to do just that in the next chapter.

LOOK SUMMARY

Look at loneliness to gain awareness, look inward to gain perspective, and look outward to gain understanding of where you can lessen loneliness.

Application 1: Look at Loneliness

Reflective Question:
Are You Curious About Loneliness?

Discuss loneliness as a broad topic with close, nonwork friends or family members. Get their perspective on how they see loneliness showing up at work.

Application 2: Look Inward

Reflective Question:
Do You Have a Healthy Personal Relationship with Loneliness?

1. **Self-Assess: Look to see what you currently can't see.** Take five minutes to complete the "Loneliness Self-Assessment" highlighted in this chapter or visit LessLonely. com/SelfAssessment.
2. **Schedule Solitude: Look for opportunities to be still.** Schedule time to isolate your mind from the inputs of other minds in order to freely process, ponder, and/or plan.
3. **Speak Up and Speak Out: Look for the moments to share and be heard.** Share a story with someone at work about a time you experienced loneliness.
4. **Seek Support: Look for people who can help you shoulder the burden.** Identify a trusted advisor (spouse, board member, mentor, or coach), schedule a 30-minute call, and openly share your loneliness journey.

Application 3: Look Outward

Reflective Question:
Are You Aware How Lonely Your Team Is?

Review the "10 Identifiers of Lonely Workers" and write down the names of any team members who meet a few of the qualities. Want more help benchmarking your team and crafting a custom plan to strengthen their connections? Visit LessLonely.com/Assessment to take the Team Connection Assessment™ and/or share it with your team.

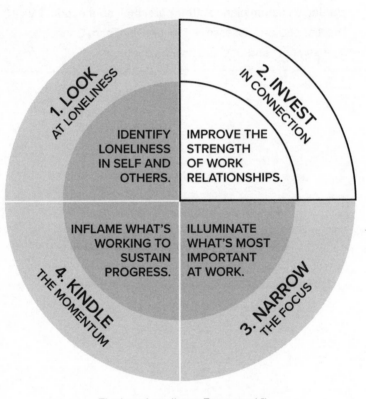

The Less Loneliness Framework™.

CHAPTER

8

INVEST IN CONNECTION

I used to think the worst thing in life
was to end up all alone. It's not.
The worst thing in life is to end up
with people who make you feel all alone.

ROBIN WILLIAMS

How would you feel closing the place that shaped 20 years of your life?

For 20 years, you loyally entered the same building to dutifully fulfill your role on the team. It wasn't a glamorous job, but it gave you great dignity and purpose. Over those years, you shared birthdays, anniversaries, and heartbreak with your coworkers. The halls of the building were filled with memories and milestones of the people you shared life with. Your workplace was your second home.

Then one day it suddenly ended. An unexpected message came down from management that your department was dissolving, the entire team was to be let go, and the building would be closing its doors forever.

Stunned and confused, you searched for someone who had some answers as to why this was happening. No one was there to help.

You felt discarded, worthless, and alone.

To add insult to injury, you were assigned to the team whose job it was to tear down the very place you gave 20 years of your life to. After a few days, still in shock, you begrudgingly began the work to prepare the building for exodus.

While you were preparing the building for closure, you saw an unfamiliar man approach. You heard him say, "This place smells like a milk container left out in the sun," as he walked toward you with an outstretched hand.

"Hi, I'm Rich, the plant's production manager of 20 years," you said. The man responded, "Hi, I'm Hamdi, and I'm considering buying this place."

With pride still in your heart for the plant that meant so much, you generously offered to give Hamdi a tour of the 85-year-old building. Hamdi accepted even though he was growing increasingly hesitant to explore, considering the stench, cracked walls, and peeling paint throughout the factory.

At every corner of the factory, you shared personal stories with Hamdi of the workers who had left for wars, team members who bragged about their children's report cards, and colleagues who proudly reenacted their home runs. The cracked walls and peeling paint started to become an afterthought to Hamdi. He was beginning to see the factory as a place that had built lives. He saw the humanity of the workplace.

During the tour, Hamdi saw the 55 factory workers whose sole job it now was to break apart the plant and close their second home forever. Hamdi couldn't believe that these people weren't angry. Instead, they were silent. They appeared to be feeling dejected, rejected, and forgotten.

Hamdi grew angry toward the factory CEO who had decided to close the plant, a decision based on spreadsheet calculations and made from an ivory tower, far removed from the people who had spent much of their lives working there.

"Spreadsheets are lazy. They don't tell you about people or about communities," said Hamdi.[1]

Driven by a conviction to honor the factory's venerable past and reignite the human spirit, Hamdi made the brave decision to invest in the factory, in its people, and in their future.

He purchased the factory and immediately hired you and three of the factory's original employees. That summer, the four of you painted the walls of the building together. A few months ago, you were disheartened about tearing the place down. Today, you are hopeful as you restore the place that gave so much to you and others. As you paint the walls, you look over your shoulder to see your new fearless leader standing with you, helping you build again.

"In painting those walls, we got to know each other. We got to believe in each other. We got to figure things out together," said Hamdi.

Together, you worked for five years to fix the factory.

In those five years, the new company ended up hiring back most of the original 55 people who had lost their jobs, and then thousands more. The company reinvigorated the entire community of South Edmeston, a small town in upstate New York, with new jobs. Finally, it built a place for people to connect with each other outside of work by constructing a premier Little League baseball field for the children of the community.

All along the way, Hamdi invested in the future of his people. When they built a second plant in Idaho, people said "You're not going to find any trained workers here." "That's OK, we'll teach them," responded Hamdi. He then partnered with a local community college and trained hundreds of people in advanced manufacturing. Hamdi also invested in his employees' future by giving all 2,000 employees shares of the company. According to Hamdi, "The human fundamentals are the ones that matter in business the most. We need a new [business] playbook that sees people again."

This people-first approach to business and the "I've got your back" attitude made Hamdi's company the number one Greek yogurt brand in the United States. He built a category-dominating product line with the same people that the previous owners had given up on and left behind.

An immigrant from Turkey, and once an outsider himself, Hamdi says he "won't let fear stop him . . . even the fear of being lonely."[2] And he's made big investments to boost belonging among others who feel like outsiders. Thirty percent of his company consists of refugees and immigrants. To date, he has had a hand in helping more than 25 million refugees around the world move from isolated to engaged through his nonprofit organization, Tent Partnership for Refugees, a coalition of businesses that have committed to take action to help refugees in need.[3]

Hamdi is a person who cares for others and has created a company that protects its people and their community. It's fitting then that Hamdi Ulukaya named his yogurt company Chobani, which in Turkish means "shepherd," one who protects, guides, and cares for a group.

Hamdi, a caring, connected, paint-the-walls-with-the-team leader, did what the disconnected make-decisions-from-an-ivory-tower leader couldn't do. At times, a new team isn't needed, just a new way of leading. Are you an ivory tower leader or a paint-the-walls leader? Are you investing in the team you have or looking for the next opportunity?

Like Hamdi, you can produce more with the team you have if you lead like a shepherd.

Introducing Invest in Connection

Leaders are shepherds. You watch carefully over your team, tending to their needs, protecting them from harm, and guiding them to a better future. Shepherds are invested in their flock because the flock is tied to their financial and social livelihood.

What does your flock need most? Connection. As a leader, by definition, you go first. You must go first in making the proper investments for connection to occur among your team.

Connections don't build themselves.

Hamdi's story provides us with a map on how to invest in connection. He first invested in fixing the factory (the place connection occurs); he then invested in building relationships by painting the factory walls with his team; and then he invested in team connection where people built bonds together at the community college or baseball stadium he built.

Now that you have grasped the importance of understanding loneliness by looking closely at your team members, the second step in the Less Loneliness Framework™ is to Invest in Connection with your team. When it comes to lonely workers, the thing they need most is connection. Here are the three ways leaders need to invest in connection.

Invest in . . .

- ▶ Safe connections
- ▶ Personal connections
- ▶ Team connections

This chapter will provide you with the tools to successfully invest in connection with your team. The investing won't cost you anything. But with a little bit of time and effort, you'll reap the benefits of less loneliness and more belonging.

Like anything worthwhile or meaningful, establishing and building meaningful connections with other people takes time. Investing in relationships is a complex and ever-evolving process. With that said, there is a lot of ground to cover in this chapter, which is why we have segmented it into three micro chapters to give you actionable strategies in each of the Invest in Connections categories: safe, personal, and team.

MICRO CHAPTER #1
INVEST IN SAFE CONNECTIONS

The first step to Invest in Connection is to ensure that a connectable environment exists where the team feels comfortable to connect. You need to first "fix the factory." This step goes well beyond physical safety, which we're going to assume is already present among your team.

Unfortunately, today's workers are more stressed and anxious than ever before as they battle unmanageable workloads, struggle to meet performance standards, and tackle tedious tasks. And with remote work on the rise, the lack of in-person connection is causing workers to feel voiceless and isolated. All of this is taking a mighty toll on workers' mental health. And as the following research highlights, employees are not confident that their leaders have the skills required to help.

According to a study of 12,000 employees, managers, HR leaders, and C-level executives across 11 countries, 82 percent of workers believe robots can support their mental health better than humans can, and 68 percent would prefer to talk to a robot over their manager about stress and anxiety at work.[4] And 76 percent of workers believe their company should be doing more to protect their mental health and that of their fellow workers.

This preference for robots over relationships is concentrated among the emerging generations. Gen Z workers are 105 percent more likely than other generations to prefer robots over humans to help with mental health support. And 93 percent of Gen Zers have demanded more tech-based solutions at work. In addition, Gen Z, Millennials, and LGBTQ+ people are more likely to experience mental health symptoms for longer durations and are also more open to diagnosis, treatment, and talking about mental health issues at work.[5]

Why are workers wanting to talk to robots instead of confiding in a human?

▶ Robots offer a judgment free zone (34 percent)

▶ Robots are unbiased (30 percent)
▶ Robots provide quick answers to health questions
   (29 percent)

For these benefits, workers are turning to virtual mental health services like VideoAmp that offers coaching, therapy, meditation, and other resources.

Workers are clearly struggling with their mental health. In fact, 80 percent of people will suffer from a mental health condition in their lifetime.[6] And yet, today's relationships at work don't appear to be safe enough to warrant conversations. People prefer machines over mankind.

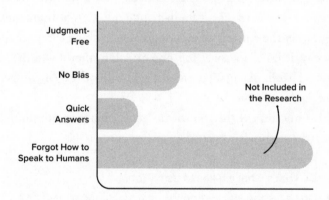

WHY DO WORKERS PREFER TALKING TO ROBOTS INSTEAD OF CONFIDING IN A HUMAN ABOUT THEIR MENTAL HEALTH (TRUE DATA)

Judgment-Free

No Bias

Not Included in the Research

Quick Answers

Forgot How to Speak to Humans

We might be out of shape socially.

An overdependence on technology is a leading cause of loneliness; therefore we should not rely solely on AI-based tech solutions to address mental health at work. It's a job best suited for a compassionate human. A shepherd.

Yet many leaders are either ignorant, ignoring, or ill-equipped to support the mental health of their team.

As the late great Vince Lombardi once said, "Most people fail not because of a lack of desire but because of a lack of commitment." You have a desire to help your team (otherwise you wouldn't be reading this), so let's focus on commitment.

Think of yourself as a loneliness "first responder" who—like an emergency medical technician (EMT) is aware of the imminent dangers, trained to act, and committed to help—is now aware, knowledgeable, and committed to help, ready to spring into action at the first sign of loneliness, disengagement, or distrust.

Along with training and clearer information about where to go or who to ask for support, the mental health resource workers want most is a more open and accepting culture.[7] That you can do. Turn on the siren, you're on your way.

The #1 Question of Humanity

In your gut, down your spinal column, and in the deepest recesses of your mind lingers the most fundamental question of humanity. It's the question the entire human population is asking every second of every day. If leaders answer this one question, they'll win the head, heart, and hands of employees resulting in better engagement, performance, and retention.

This question is the root of the most common questions that workers ask themselves every day, such as . . .

- ► Do I have what it takes to do my job?
- ► Do I have the knowledge to speak up during a meeting?
- ► Do I have enough money to provide for my family?
- ► Do I have the confidence to ask for a promotion?
- ► Do I have the wisdom to lead my team effectively?
- ► Do I have the sensibility to lead a diverse team?

The question behind the above questions—and most other questions we ask ourselves—is the much simpler question that drives human behavior: Am I safe? No matter age, role, or status, all humans are unconsciously and repeatedly asking themselves this one question. "Am I safe" is the cornerstone of each of the 3 Ls of Life™: Live, Learn, and Link.

For the Live need, humans ask, "Am I fed, hydrated, and protected?" Satisfying these primary human needs leads directly to safety.

For the Learn need, humans ask, "Am I growing into my full potential?" The reason humans are interested in learning is because it's critical for our safety. We must learn how to walk, communicate our needs and wants, and contribute our gifts. If we aren't learning and growing, we run the risk of not contributing meaningfully to the tribe and thus becoming vulnerable to being cast out.

Humans derive a sense of safety from being able to deliver a valuable skill that will help the tribe to thrive while sustaining a fruitful career for the individual. Learning keeps us informed on how to adjust to our surroundings in order to remain safe. Additionally, by striving toward our full potential, humans are seeking safety from regret. Regret for not living life fully and doing what we were called to do.

For the Link need, humans ask, "Am I contributing, connected, and valued?" As we've covered throughout this book, there is safety in numbers. We have a desire to belong because it's safe. We desire to link to others and establish connections because we can watch each other's back, we can leverage each other's strengths, and ultimately we can achieve more. Community protects us.

How can leaders move team members beyond safety seeking?

By creating psychological safety.

Psychological safety is a place "where one feels that one's voice is welcome with bad news, questions, concerns, half-baked ideas, and even mistakes," says Amy Edmondson, author of *The Fearless Organization: Creating Psychological Safety in the Workplace for Learning, Innovation and Growth*. When psychological safety is absent, people stifle their ideas and experience a number of negative emotions.

Much like hunger or thirst, fulfill the human need of psychological safety, and the mind and body are freed to focus on loftier goals.

What happens in meetings without psychological safety.

When psychological safety is created, people are free to ask questions, raise concerns, and pitch ideas without unnecessary repercussions. Psychological safety is invaluable for today's organizations, as they deal with issues of equality and building allyship, as well as reducing loneliness among workers.

When workers feel psychologically secure and protected, their need for belonging is fulfilled and thus loneliness is lessened. Leaders who create psychological safety among a team also reap:

- ▶ 12 percent increase in productivity
- ▶ 27 percent reduction in turnover
- ▶ 40 percent reduction in safety incidents[8]

Google recently spent two years studying 180 teams to discover what made teams successful. The study, called Project Aristotle, analyzed over 250 different team attributes and discovered that psychological safety was the single most important quality that determines a team's success.[9] Psychological safety improves a team's confidence, creativity, trust, and capacity for innovation.[10]

In a world where black swans lurk around every corner, it's critical a team feels safe enough to show up without a playbook and challenge the status quo. Psychological safety allows the team to take action, freely admit mistakes, and talk through errors—which then enables fast learning and quick iteration.

The absence of psychological safety represses innovation, stunts engagement, slows performance, and decreases the strength of connections needed to support mental health among a team.

Psychological safety is the wellspring workplaces need to repair and refresh workers who are struggling with their mental health. One of the most integral aspects of leadership is the ability to satisfy a team's deep desire to feel safe. Creating psychological safety came easy for Hamdi Ulukaya because he grew up in a family where he "felt safe, enough, and complete."[11] Most leaders will need to invest a little more time and energy to create the psychological safety that allows connections to grow.

Leaders should serve as "normalizers-in-chief" when it comes to mental health challenges like loneliness. Workers want a more open and accepting culture, and leaders must be the "first responders" to sound the alarm and address the issue. Nick Tzitzon, executive vice president of marketing and communications at SAP, recently told *Harvard Business Review*, "When SAP CEO Bill McDermott goes out of his way to champion wellness and mindfulness, it sends an unmistakable signal to 100,000 colleagues that we're serious about building a culture of psychological safety."[12]

Psychological Safety Building Blocks

Teams can be lonely places. People can feel vulnerable and exposed if they believe their teammates don't support their ideas or appreciate their work. These interpersonal struggles intensify for remote workers who lack the support of a nodding ally across the table.

It's challenging for leaders to create psychological safety because by virtue of their role they have power, and power is a barrier to psychological safety. To counterbalance the weight of their powerful role, leaders have to go out of their way to intentionally and strategically build psychological safety.

Listen to Unlock

Active listening is a hallmark trait of psychological safety. Too often leaders selectively listen for information that reinforces their view. Other times, they only listen to the extent that they can address the immediate issue while ignoring the full picture. Here are the three styles of listening. Which one are you most prone to using?

- ▶ **Are you listening to win?** This listening style is used when you are trying to convince someone of something and get your way. You listen only to pick up what you can refute or discredit. You're not listening to understand, you're listening to tear down.
- ▶ **Are you listening to fix?** This listening style is used when you are interested in providing direction. You listen for the specific problem that needs addressing, ignoring any other information. You're not listening to fully understand; you're listening to provide advice.
- ▶ **Are you listening to unlock?** This listening style is used when you are fully focused on understanding and unlocking a new perspective. You listen to understand from where individuals are speaking and why they have the opinion they have. You're not listening to win or fix but to comprehend—to fully see the situation and empathize with the individual.

Consider prefacing a conversation by asking these three questions to know which listening style to take:

▶ Do you want me to share? (Listening to win)
▶ Do you want me to fix? (Listening to fix)
▶ Do you want me to understand? (Listening to unlock)

While each listening style has its benefits, listening to unlock has the greatest benefits in boosting belonging. And if psychological safety is your goal, cultivating a culture of listening to unlock is pivotal.

Speak Last

When asked, "Where did you learn to be a great leader?" Nelson Mandela, former president of South Africa, explained that he learned how to be a great leader from his father.[13] His father was a tribal chief. When Nelson was young, he would go with his father to tribal meetings, where he remembered two things. The first was that his father always had his tribal council sit in a circle. The second was that his father was always the last to speak.

When leaders share their thoughts about a topic and then ask for the team's opinion, it's too late. By speaking first, leaders undermine the dialogue and thwart creativity because the team will be less likely to volunteer any ideas that conflict with the leader's.

The skill of holding your opinion to yourself until everyone has spoken provides leaders with the authentic and unbiased thoughts of the team, and it provides team members with the feeling that they are heard and valued contributors.

How to effectively speak last:

▶ Craft open-ended, nonbiased question(s).
▶ Get comfortable sitting in silence as the team processes thoughts, ideas, or concerns.
▶ Address responses in a neutral manner, such as, "Thank you, that was an insightful observation."

▶ Trade comments for clarification. Resist providing any
    commentary, and seek more clarity by stating phrases like,
    "Tell me more."

Once leaders start speaking last, they create more space for their
team to have a voice. Teams where a manager spoke 80 percent of
the time or more were less successful than teams who practiced turn-
taking during discussions.[14] Psychological safety exists when team
members feel they have the opportunity to speak in roughly equal
proportions to their peers.

Speaking last creates space for individuals to speak up allowing
proportional conversations to occur. When the expectation is for each
team member to share before the leader does, team members have
equal opportunity to have their voice heard during a meeting.

Here are some ideas for conducting proportional conversation
during meetings.

▶ Prepare and share the meeting agenda ahead of time to give
    people the opportunity to gather their thoughts beforehand.
▶ Assign different team members to run the meeting and rotate
    weekly. (This is especially helpful for hybrid teams. Assigning a
    remote team member to run the meeting pulls them more into
    the in-person meeting.)
▶ For hybrid meetings, encourage remote team members to
    contribute first to involve them fully and not have them fall into
    the background.
▶ Consider smaller or one-on-one settings to continue the
    conversation with quieter individuals.

Stop Asking and Start Giving

Steven's wife Jen lost her mom in 2020 after a two-year battle with
cancer. As the primary caretaker of her mother, Jen witnessed the sad
decline of a once vibrant woman who knew how to steal the spotlight

at a party. The crushing experience left Jen feeling exhausted, emotionally incapacitated, and drained.

Friends and family would routinely ask, "What can I do to help?" to which Jen defaulted to the standard answer, "nothing." Even though the gesture of asking what could be done to help was courteous, it did not make Jen feel better. It did not help make her life easier or aid in her ability to recover.

It was those who did not ask Jen how she was doing, but instead sent over food, letters, flowers, keepsakes, and pictures that allowed Jen to feel a sense of relief. When people actually did something proactively that they thought would be helpful, they made a difference. These unasked-for gestures made Jen feel provided for, appreciated, and loved. It did not matter what dish was made or what picture was sent; the proactive gesture had the biggest impact.

Similarly at work, asking employees what they need will often garner a response similar to Jen's "nothing" or "I'm good." On the other hand, thinking about how you can help places you in the shoes of the person needing help, support, or encouragement. In other words, it expresses empathy. Belonging isn't always about pushing people together; it can also occur by pulling people in. Proactive gestures at work might include:

▶ Writing them (or their family member) a letter to share your appreciation for their contributions.

▶ Buying someone a book that you think he'd enjoy.

▶ Scheduling a lunch after someone's proposal got rejected.

▶ Giving someone the day off following a family incident.

Stop asking if others need help and start giving unprompted, proactive assistance. When it comes to loneliness, based on the numbers (72 percent of global workers feel lonely at least monthly, with 55 percent saying at least weekly), you can safely assume your team wrestles with loneliness and is longing for more belonging.

Allow your thoughtful and proactive actions to speak louder than your words to make people feel valued and included.

Scale Support with Psychological Safety

Psychological safety encourages an entire team to Look for Loneliness. It scales leaders' ability to provide and care for their team. For example, in Chapter 5 we covered how "Too Much Silence" was a driver of distance at work by sharing the example of James Barr, a member of the LGBTQ community, who felt unseen when no one at work asked how he was feeling after the Pulse mass shooting. Without psychological safety, the responsibility to support individuals falls squarely on the shoulders of leaders. So, if the leader didn't hear the news that day, his silence could be interpreted as not showing up for the individual.

A culture where psychological safety exists creates a shared burden among the team. A team that is committed to offering support can proactively look for who might need help, and it provides a safe place where individuals can speak up. An up-front investment in safe connections by leaders can save them from the impossible task of always knowing how and when to show up for people.

INVEST EXAMPLE

Stewart Butterfield, CEO of the team-messaging application Slack, holds a welcome meeting for all new hires. He shares the following about building trust through psychological safety:

"Raise your hand if you've ever treated someone you love in a way that you later regretted." Of course, everyone puts up their hand. And then I tell them that if we act in ways that we regret in the relationships that matter most to us—with spouses, parents, children, close friends—we're going to do it here at work, too. We're going to step on each other's toes, and—intentionally or not—we're going to insult one another and challenge and provoke one another in all kinds of ways. In order to get things done, everyone has to bring a certain level of trust and assumption of good intentions to work. Because it's a downward spiral if you don't."[15]

Everyone plays a critical role in cultivating a culture of trust and safety.

With a psychologically safe work environment, connections can really flourish. The second step to Invest in Connection is to spend time building relationships. The following section provides some powerful ways to promote stronger personal connections at work.

MICRO CHAPTER #2
INVEST IN PERSONAL CONNECTIONS

Ryan recently had an experience that made him hyperaware of the sinister role technology plays in eroding the human connection. Recently, he and his wife, Ashley, were watching an emotionally charged episode of the NBC hit TV series *This Is Us*.

Halfway through the episode, Ryan turned part of his attention to his phone to casually scroll his Instagram feed. A few minutes passed, and he returned his full attention to the program and his wife, only to discover that Ashley was in tears over something that had happened. Where a lump in Ryan's throat usually correlates with Ashley's tears, this time he was left completely emotionless.

He was able to follow the storyline of the episode while engrossed in his phone, but his split attention robbed him of any emotional connection to the characters in the story. This was an enlightening and humbling moment for him, a tech-appreciating multi-device-wielding Millennial.

What's at stake when you check a device? Emotional intelligence.

Want to instantly boost your emotional intelligence? Resist dividing your attention.

This emotional disconnect can happen anytime you are not completely present with the people around you. Whether it's checking a social feed during a TV show, checking email during a conference call, checking texts during a meeting, or scanning news headlines during training, as your attention fractures so does your ability to connect emotionally.

Allow your valuable attention to deviate from the person in front of you, and it will hinder your ability to . . .

- ► Connect and serve a customer
- ► Fully understand someone's perspective
- ► Build trust with coworkers
- ► Influence a team

The onslaught of distractions will continue to be a high-risk factor for disrupting and undercutting human connections. As technology evolves and becomes even more pervasive at work and in our personal lives, we must be vigilant about putting tech in check. We never know what hangs in the balance for our frustrated staff, anxious coworkers, or irritated customers if we aren't fully present with them.

ME: TIME TO GO THROUGH MY WORK EMAIL.

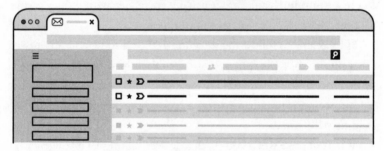

ME: 5 MINUTES LATER.

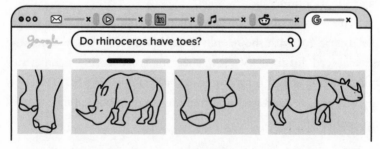

How quickly and easily technology can distract us from our priorities.

Guarding against technology robbing your attention not only heightens your emotional intelligence, but it also enhances creativity and innovation.

Constant engagement thwarts creativity. The conscious human brain has access to the equivalent of about two feet of information around us.[16] But the subconscious brain has access to the equivalent of about 11 acres of information around us, which includes every book read, movie watched, or conversation had.

Intentionally disengaging from technology can unlock the vast knowledge of the subconscious brain to solve a complex problem or show up fully for the person in front of us. Once we know what hangs in the balance of our attention, why would we ever intentionally choose scrolling over connecting?

Improve Your Smartphone Etiquette

Ninety-two percent of Americans believe smartphone addiction is real, but most underestimate just how much they use their smartphone. Sixty percent of people think they touch their phone 100 times or less per day; however, typical users tap, touch, or swipe their phone 2,617 times per day.[17] Yes, you read that right!

In our opinion, smartphones offer more benefits than risks. GPS, camera, transportation (Uber and Bird), education (podcasts and audiobooks), note-taking, and search are just a few of the benefits we wouldn't want to live without. But we also don't want to live without giving our work and family our full focus. Always available translates to being never fully available.

If the risks of smartphones remain unchecked, the devices can encroach on our relationships and productivity in the workplace and at home. The mishandling of smartphones can result in:

▶ **Stress.** Employees tally an average of eight hours a week answering work-related emails after leaving the office.[18]

▶ **Disengagement.** 80 percent of workers think it's wrong to check phones during meetings, but 50 percent do it anyway.[19]

▶ **Unproductivity.** 95 percent of people are interrupted more than five times per hour.[20]

Whether at work or home, these tips will ensure your smartphone (or other devices) don't sever the connections in your life:

▶ **Curb your checking.** Resist the urge to check your phone every time it dings, pings, or rings. Ride the arc of the craving to check and consciously choose not to check. Every time you successfully beat the urge to check your phone, you strengthen your resolve of resisting your phone. Dishes aren't washed every time a single plate is dirtied. Dishes are done in batches. In the same way, batch your responses to ensure you don't lose focus. Manage the tech—don't let tech manage you.

▶ **Announce your activity.** When someone checks her phone during a conversation, both parties are immediately and momentarily disconnected from one another. This can cause resentment on one side and mental (and sometimes emotional) detachment on the other side. Instead, if you must check your phone, announce your activity and narrate out loud why you're checking your phone during the conversation, such as "let me check my calendar to see if I'm available," or "allow me to check my flight departure time." Announcing your activity keeps both parties actively engaged in the conversation. If you don't have a good reason to narrate your phone activity, then keep your phone away. This will also help curb your checking.

▶ **Accentuate your alternatives.** Emotion drives attention. This is why it's so easy to slip into the mindless scrolling of social feeds, because it inserts us into the lives of those we care about. To make checking your phone less appealing, engage yourself through a better alternative. Find ways to attach emotion and meaning to the work and tasks you do every day.

Fully Human at Work

When you put tech in check, it expands your capacity for emotional intelligence. An investment in raising your emotional intelligence is an investment in your personal connections. A better awareness of your emotions expands your capacity to recognize emotions in others, enabling you to connect with empathy.

However, there is still a pervasive myth that needs to be overcome. This myth stifles well-being and performance at work. The myth is that emotions don't belong at work. That workers can flip a switch and shed all of their fear, joy, sorrow, hope, and loneliness at the door of work. This myth leads many to act cold and stoical throughout their professional lives.

Not only is feeling feelings part of being human, but research shows that when coworkers drop their polished professional presence, those around them experience a boost in trust, kindness, performance, and connection.[21] Divorcing ourselves from our personal lives is not only unfortunate, it's bad business.

HOW EMOTIONS AT WORK APPEAR TO MANY PEOPLE

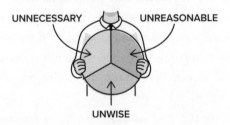

WHAT EMOTIONS AT WORK ARE

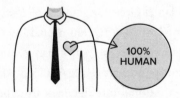

Emotions belong at work because humans belong at work.

According to Liz Fosslien, coauthor of the *Wall Street Journal* bestseller *No Hard Feelings: The Secret Power of Embracing Emotions at Work*, "In the moments when our colleagues drop their glossy professional presentation, we are much more likely to believe what they are telling us. We feel connected to the people around us. We try harder. Perform better. And we are just generally kinder. So, it's about time we learn how to embrace emotion at work."

To further emphasize the benefits of embracing emotions at work, Google's study of 180 teams, Project Aristotle, found that high "social sensitivity" is a top attribute of a high-performing team member.[22] Social sensitivity is defined as the ability to identify, understand, and respect the feelings of others. Social sensitivity requires emotional intelligence.

Emotional intelligence will be a hallmark of the most successful leaders and organizations of the future. The ability to identify and manage one's personal emotions and the emotions of others will be an advantageous skill for leaders as loneliness and other mental health concerns continue to rise in the modern workforce.

If leaders can't get comfortable wading into emotional waters, they run the risk of never fully solving the problems of their team or customers because empathy, a core pillar of emotional intelligence, is required to fully solve problems. As Bill Gates stated in his 2014 Stanford University commencement speech, "If we have optimism, but we don't have empathy, then it doesn't matter how much we master the secrets of science. We're not really solving problems; we're just working on puzzles."[23]

Emotions aren't a problem to solve but a tension to manage. How leaders successfully manage that daily tension is with emotional intelligence.

According to Daniel Goleman, author of *Emotional Intelligence: Why It Can Matter More Than IQ*, emotional intelligence is a better predictor of academic success, job performance, and life success than someone's intelligence quotient (IQ). And, unlike with IQ, people can increase their emotional intelligence throughout life. Here are three steps and questions to lead with greater emotional intelligence.

Find Balance on the Emotional Spectrum

A line exists between sharing feelings that build trust and oversharing, which can erode trust. Oversharing can undermine influence, elicit discomfort in others, and demonstrate a lack of self-awareness.

Most people either let their emotions drive the car of their life or they lock their emotion out of the car. Neither is ideal. Emotions help us navigate the world. They shouldn't be driving or locked out, but rather in the passenger seat where they are visible, included, and used for guidance.

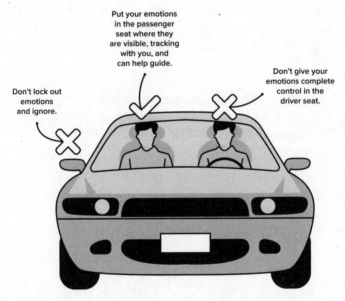

Put your emotions in the passenger seat where they are visible, tracking with you, and can help guide.

Don't give your emotions complete control in the driver seat.

Don't lock out emotions and ignore.

Where should emotions ride in the car of life? Riding shotgun.

Emotional expression is a wide spectrum. At one extreme are under-emoters, people who prefer just the facts or have a hard time accessing their feelings. At the other extreme are over-emoters, people who are constantly sharing their feelings. Neither of these extremes is healthy. If you are prone to oversharing, consider editing. If you are more reserved, look for moments to open up and be more vulnerable or relatable.

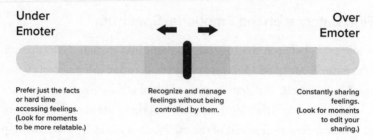

Under Emoter		Over Emoter
Prefer just the facts or hard time accessing feelings. (Look for moments to be more relatable.)	Recognize and manage feelings without being controlled by them.	Constantly sharing feelings. (Look for moments to edit your sharing.)

What emotional expression do you bring to work each day?

Emotional intelligence is about finding a balance on this spectrum. Recognize and manage feelings without being controlled by them. What emotional expression do you bring to work each day?

Not sure if you under-emote, over-emote, or strike the right balance? Take this emotional intelligence audit.

THE EMOTIONAL INTELLIGENCE AUDIT

Score yourself on the following statements.

Score each statement using the following scale:
        1–Difficult | 2–Somewhat Difficult | 3–Neutral |
        4–Somewhat Easy | 5–Easy

1. Recognizing emotions in myself is . . .

                        Difficult 1 2 3 4 5 Easy

2. Recognizing emotions in others is . . .

                        Difficult 1 2 3 4 5 Easy

3. Pausing before speaking is . . .

                        Difficult 1 2 3 4 5 Easy

4. Controlling my thoughts is . . .

                        Difficult 1 2 3 4 5 Easy

5. Accepting criticism is . . .

                        Difficult 1 2 3 4 5 Easy

6. Displaying authenticity is . . .

                        Difficult 1 2 3 4 5 Easy

7. Demonstrating empathy is . . .

Difficult 1 2 3 4 5 Easy

8. Extending praise toward others is . . .

Difficult 1 2 3 4 5 Easy

9. Delivering constructive feedback is . . .

Difficult 1 2 3 4 5 Easy

10. Offering an apology is . . .

Difficult 1 2 3 4 5 Easy

11. Letting go of resentment is . . .

Difficult 1 2 3 4 5 Easy

12. Honoring commitments is . . .

Difficult 1 2 3 4 5 Easy

13. Providing help to others is . . .

Difficult 1 2 3 4 5 Easy

14. Keeping cool under pressure is . . .

Difficult 1 2 3 4 5 Easy

15. Protecting myself from toxic people is . . .

Difficult 1 2 3 4 5 Easy

Add up each of the 15 scores to get your total.

Total Score	EQ Level
15–34	Low Emotional Intelligence (often under- or over-emoting)
35–55	Average Emotional Intelligence (occasionally under- or over-emoting)
56–75	High Emotional Intelligence (rarely under- or over-emoting)

Consider Relatability Over Vulnerability

Brené Brown, an author and professor who has spent the past two decades studying courage, vulnerability, shame, and empathy, recently found herself at a US Air Force base talking to a very serious group of fighter pilots. She shared this with the group: "Care and connection are irreducible needs when we lead. We have to care for and be connected to those we lead otherwise we cannot lead effectively."[24] Many pushed back on her comments, stating, "That's bulls*#t. I'm not here to like you, I'm here to lead you." Then a general turned to Brown and said, "From the highest ranks of the United States Air Force, we believe you cannot lead people that you do not feel affection for. If someone can't find a way to feel affection for the people they lead, we need to move them on."

As a leader, if you're unable to create a caring connection with your team, you create a culture of concealment. People hold back, walk on eggshells, and are constantly in their head—wondering, questioning, second-guessing, and not producing useful work.

If leaders fail to share clearly what they are experiencing at work, it sends the message to the team that certain topics are off-limits. This creates eggshells for the team to walk on because the leader is not being explicit about what is on or off-limits. The team is left to assume it's all off-limits because the leader is not communicating clearly and transparently. When you fully compartmentalize work and life, you send the signal that everyone has to compartmentalize and those who don't compartmentalize aren't safe.

Also, when you don't share, people might begin to wonder if they are as close to you as they thought, thinking that if they were, you would have shared something. Or if they have something to share, they won't do it. Thus, quality connections are stunted.

Emotional intelligence seems to be inextricably linked to vulnerability. While vulnerability can be a valuable tool, too often—for leaders especially—it can position someone as weak and erode confidence among a team. Leaders should instead strive for relatability.

By definition, being relatable establishes a social or sympathetic relationship with others. Asking, "Am I relatable?" or "What's it like to be on the other side of me?" forces you to consider the circumstances of the person you're interacting with, which creates an opportunity to empathize.

Here are three ways others can relate to you as a person, not just a professional:

- ▶ **Tell your story.** Replace the polished professional presence with relatable stories of discomfort, doubts, or delight in a way that is authentic and in service of others. People listen autobiographically to storytellers. So when you tell a personal story, others are listening through the lens of their own life. Share where you've been, where you are, and where you're going in order to become more relatable.

- ▶ **Ask to hear a story.** People long to be seen, heard, and belong. Ask thoughtful and open-ended questions of the people you serve; that will allow them to respond in story. Often the stories we ask to hear are much better than the stories we tell.

- ▶ **Selectively share.** Address your emotions at work by selecting appropriate information that you are comfortable sharing. If a feeling is non-work-related or isn't associated with an individual or team, then flag the feeling without going into detail by telling the individual or team that you are having a tough day and it has nothing to do with work or them. Or consider being transparent about what support looks like for you.

Brown provides a great example of what relatability through selective sharing sounds like for leaders communicating to their team about a hardship they are experiencing:

I'm really struggling right now. I've got some stuff going on with my mom and it's hard. And I wanted you to know. I wanted you to know what support looks like for me during this time. I'll check in with you if I need something from you. I may take some time off. Support for me is sharing this with you now and bringing it up when it's helpful for me but not having to field a lot of questions about it. I appreciate being able to tell you. I appreciate we approach things different when we have hard things going on in our lives. This is what I need right now.

This type of selective sharing sends the clear signal to the team that life impacts work and that it's OK to talk about it. And it lets team members know how they can help because support looks different for everyone.

Not only does relatability grow when leaders become vulnerable like this, it also opens the door for everyone on the team to share, which creates a ripe environment for better connections to occur.

FIRST IMPRESSION

AFTER SHARING A PERSONAL ANECDOTE

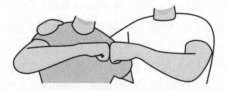

Sharing strengthens social connections.

INVEST EXAMPLE

Zack Rubinstein, the head of global inclusion learning at Expedia Group, shared how his company is using relatability as a way to cultivate connections across the organization. Expedia has been gathering relatable moments from employees, across the organization, and sharing them companywide. Expedia has been encouraging employees to embrace vulnerability when sharing their stories. The goal has been to use vulnerability as the vehicle that allows team members to be seen, understood, appreciated, valued, and applauded.

Rubinstein says, "Vulnerability is contagious. When we had our C-suite, specifically our CEO, share vulnerable stories, it opened up hundreds of doors for other people to do the same. Now our entire leadership team shares their stories regularly. They find ways to infuse relatability. Which is a great way to transform culture!"

Hundreds of these stories are shared across the organization as videos, blog posts, podcasts, and as a part of the digital learning series. Not only have the stories made it easier for employees to connect with their relatable leaders, but it's cultivated a culture where teams are encouraged to share stories, relate to each other, and ultimately build trust across the organization.

In the past, the employer-employee relationship was very transactional. Punch in, punch out, and collect a check. But in today's always-on work culture, the boundaries of the employee-employer relationship are expanding. And considering work is the activity people spend the most time engaged with after sleep, employees are expecting more from the workplace.[25]

More and more employers are leaning into the highly emotional aspects of their employees' lives. For example, Hilton offers an adoption assistance program that reimburses team members for qualified adoption expenses up to $10,000 per child, with no limit to the number of adoptions.[26] Facebook offers employees up to 20 days of bereavement leave in the event of a family member's death.[27]

As employees seek more from their employers, moving from employing to empowering will serve employers well.

Are emotions messy? Yes. Are emotions inescapable? Yes. The choice to sweep them under the rug or to recognize and honor them in employees is up to leaders.

Connect Like Oprah

Putting tech in check and embracing emotional intelligence positions you well to really connect with others on your team to develop deep and meaningful relationships.

To strengthen your personal connections with your team, operate like Oprah. Oprah has an uncanny ability to draw out the most from people she converses with. She is able to establish strong connections with people and cultivate a comfort level where people can be completely vulnerable with her.

Stronger connection lurks under the surface. Small talk is a gateway to deeper connection. Don't stay small. Dive deeper.

Think of the best boss you ever had. Chances are the person you are thinking of was someone who drew the best out of you, got you to see things in yourself you didn't know were there, and truly cared for you.

We don't remember the leaders who stay on the surface, who keep things fully professional, who want emotions left at the entrance to work. We remember the leaders who are willing to show us they care and actively try to establish meaningful connections.

Here's how Oprah establishes strong connections and how you can too:

1. **Share the space.** Unlike many TV hosts who sit behind a desk, she is often on the same couch or sitting in the same kind of chair, making the exchange devoid of power dynamics. She leans in to people, she walks the aisle getting close to her audience. She knows how to create a welcoming environment, ripe for connection. Ask yourself: *Do you create the right physical environment to connect with your team?*

2. **Establish eye contact.** Oprah strikes a healthy balance when it comes to eye contact with her guests. Strive to maintain eye contact 60 to 70 percent of the time during a conversation. One hundred percent eye contact is perceived as aggressive and creepy. Not enough eye contact is perceived as disinterested, embarrassed, or shy. If you are going to truly see someone, what better place to look than into their eyes, the "window to the soul." Ask yourself: *Do you provide your people with your undivided attention, making eye contact so they know you are genuinely interested?*

3. **Reiterate what was said.** Oprah masterfully summarizes what her guests say. She shortly debriefs the most important information, demonstrating that she listened and understood. Simply stating, "What I'm hearing you say is (insert statement summary)" helps lift any miscommunication and leaves the other person feeling heard. Ask yourself: *Do you reiterate what others say so they know you are listening?*

4. **Search for similarities.** Oprah often uses phrases like, "I was so thrilled to realize how you and I are alike in that . . ." to highlight a similarity between herself and the other person. When you identify that you share similar upbringings, interest in music, or disdain for snakes, a deeper connection is formed. Ask yourself: *Do you search for similarities among your team?*

5. **Lean into emotion.** Oprah doesn't diffuse or dilute the emotional responses of others. You know she doesn't lean into the emotion because it's good TV, she often reciprocates by getting emotional herself. Comforting, celebrating, or just sitting in the emotion helps build a bond. Ask yourself: *Do you lean into emotion when it surfaces, embracing the moment?*

To see Oprah's connectable genius in action, search "Oprah Can Make Anyone Cry, Including James" on YouTube.

INVEST EXAMPLE

Catherine Mattice, CEO and cofounder of Civility Partners, a leading consultancy specializing in workplace bullying, says that her team keeps their video communications platform open throughout the day. The team is able to see one another work, similar to if they were in the office together. Catherine's team loves the approach because they all get to provide banter, updates, and acknowledgments in real time. The team gets to have lots more touch points with each other throughout the day, helping strengthen their relationships.

Make It Your Job to Invest in Others

The former chief marketing officer of Chick-fil-A, David Salyers, shared in our interview how he approached final interviews with job candidates.[28] Salyers's approach is a master class in investing in personal connections at work.

Chick-fil-A is known for delivering "second-mile service." First-mile service is delivering what customers expect such as quality food, quick service, and a clean restaurant. Second-mile service is delivering more than what customers expect, such as escorting customers to their car with an umbrella on a rainy day or carrying heavy food trays for parents with small children. As a leader at Chick-fil-A, Salyers extended second-mile service to his employees.

After candidates had been interviewed by every person they would be working with, Salyers would meet with the potential hire for a final interview and communicate the following:

> We have come to the conclusion; we cannot imagine another day without you in this organization. Truett Cathy [the founder of Chick-fil-A] taught me that we become like those we surround ourselves with for better or worse. When I'm around you, I feel like I'm getting better by the day. And I want that influence in my life and we want to be that influence for you. Collectively we want to work together to create value that results in a big paycheck. However, I want your paycheck to be the least important thing you ever get from Chick-fil-A.

Salyers would then grab a pad of paper and ask the candidate:

> For your paycheck to be the least remarkable thing in your life, what would make that true? Tell me about your bucket list items. Who do you want to become in life because of working here? What will be important for your family?

Salyers would take copious notes about what the candidate's remarkable future needs to look like. Salyers said those notes become his "job description."

Most leaders provide employees with a job description. That's expected. Other leaders make supporting and developing employees their job description. That's unexpected. That's second-mile leadership. Chick-fil-A's 97 percent employee retention rate is a result of leaders like Salyers who make it their job to invest in personal connections with their team.[29]

Protect Your Team's Connections

Your team members have other connections outside of work. They are connected to children, bandmates, partners, moviegoers, volunteers, spouses, fanatics, and classmates.

While creating stronger personal connections with your team, don't forget to make margin for them to maintain strong connections with their personal connections outside of work. Engagement is important. At times, what's equally important is disengagement. Ensuring your team members' other connections remain strong—by giving them the guilt-free and uninterrupted time to tend to those connections—is important to keep loneliness sidelined.

Between April 5 and 9, 2021, LinkedIn surprised all employees by giving them a week off to avoid burnout. Michael Susi, director of global wellness at LinkedIn, said this about their RestUp! Well-Being Week Off: "It's a one-time, global paid week off for employees. It's an opportunity for us to take care of ourselves and put our well-being first."

Other than allowing employees to disconnect early or take the day off, here's how a few companies are finding ways to protect their employee's connections outside of work. Basecamp, a web application company based in Chicago, pays for employees' hobbies. Mattel, Inc., the toy manufacturing company, offers employees up to 16 paid hours off to participate in their kids' school events. Airbnb, the community-driven hospitality company, provides employees with $2,000 a year to spend on Airbnb properties anywhere in the world. Burton, a snowboarding outfitter, provides employees the day off to hit the slopes if two feet of snow falls in 24 hours. REI, the retail and outdoor recreation services company, offers an employee challenge grant where employees get $300 in products for an outdoor activity, as long as it's a challenge like backpacking in the High Sierras or running a marathon in Thailand.

With investments in safe connections and personal connections, it's time to focus on creating opportunities for the team to connect with each other. It's easy to categorize loneliness as an individual problem, but it's actually a systemic problem that affects the entire team. Getting the team to team up against loneliness will help evict it and ensure it stays banished.

A psychologically safe environment led by an emotionally intelligent leader provides the best chance of effectively working with your team. In the following section, we provide solutions to improving team connections.

MICRO CHAPTER #3
INVEST IN TEAM CONNECTIONS

Has this ever happened to you? You get the sense that your team is disconnected. You believe the culprit is that they are not socially connected with each other. The obvious and easy solution? Happy hour!

You know you have enough money in your social budget, so you decide to send an email to the entire team stating that there will be a happy hour at The Tin Roof Restaurant and Bar from 5 to 7 p.m. The happy hour starts, and the team sporadically begins to show up. Outside of the usual compliant-and-gossip conversations, the team *seems* to have a good time. However, the next day not only are they still not connected, but now they are also exhausted and behind on work.

You correctly identified the problem (disconnection), you had noble intentions in addressing it (happy hour), but the solution missed the mark (the team was already overwhelmed, and another commitment wasn't ideal).

Don't Rely on Outings and Activities

Team outings and activities are awkward at best and alienating at worst. Mandatory workplace mixers, team-building retreats, and embarrassing holiday parties are the butt of countless movie and TV jokes.

Happy hours (and similar events) are filled with good intentions, yet they continuously fall short from creating the connections needed to rid your team of loneliness. Beyond the superficiality and senseless-ness of such team activities, their ability to cultivate meaningful social connection fails because of the following issues.

Issue 1: Competing Commitments

Social activities usually intrude into the already overscheduled cal-endar of many employees. Team dinners and happy hours that occur outside of normal business hours especially overstep. Hosting weekly team lunches might also encroach on the personal time employees

Why a minor hourlong commitment can feel so daunting.

need to check out by checking in on their family, their favorite sports team, or the latest celebrity gossip.

Solution: Turn a standing weekly meeting into an impromptu social event. The team already has the time allocated, so it won't impede their progress on other projects or infringe on other work or personal commitments.

Issue 2: Clashing Relationship Types

Attempting to move a colleague from a workmate to a friend can be complicated. Nonwork relationships are typically communal and are formed on the basis of common or shared needs. You establish a relationship with your neighbor because you share the same community. Work relationships are usually exchange based, formed on the basis of give-and-take—you give Sam the expense report, Sam takes it and processes it.

Mixing exchange and communal relationships can get confusing and uncomfortable. When one worker prematurely attempts to switch an exchange relationship into a communal one by oversharing personal vulnerabilities, it can create more awkwardness than connectedness. To avoid this awkwardness and manage additional relationship commitments, workers keep things surface-level and ultimately will decline the social event.

Solution: Create psychological safety where there is collective commitment that the team is a safe place to share vulnerabilities and ask for emotional support.

Issue 3: Gravitation Toward Work

Groups have a tendency to discuss information that they all have in common. Researchers call this the "common information effect."[30] What do workers on the same team have in common? Work. Therefore, most discussions during social activities gravitate toward work, leaving connections shallow.

Solution: Have a theme to an event or prepared activities that stretch team members to discuss more than just work-related items. Implement a swear jar, but for conversations that drift toward work. Instead of putting money in a jar, they have to Venmo someone money or buy the next drink of the person they are conversing with.

Gravitate Toward Work
(leaves connections shallow)

It's work to get workers to discuss nonwork topics.

Issue 4: People Are Drawn to Similarities

Similar to gravitating toward common information, people are drawn to common likeness. Just as birds of a feather flock together, people flock to others who are similar to them in age, race, stage of life, profession, department, and so on. In fact, Paul Ingram and Michael Morris, professors at Columbia, studied 100 business executives at a social event and discovered that most attendees associated with people they already knew even though the purpose of the event was to meet new people.[31] Additionally, most attendees joined groups that contained at least one member of their own race.

Solution: Be intentional about drawing people to differences. Here's an example of how one company gets different people interacting. Southern Company Gas, a Fortune 500 energy services company, uses an activity called "speed dating" during their corporate training events to cultivate connections. The team splits into two groups and forms an inner circle and an outer circle with people facing each other. The group has a few minutes to ask prepared personal questions of the person standing in front of them. After a few minutes, the inner circle rotates one person to their left and asks the same questions again, this time to a completely different individual. The fun and formal structure of the exercise ensures that the team members are interacting with everyone, not just those they find the most similarities with.

**Drawn to Similarities
(new connections don't form)**

Workers of a feather flock together.

Socialize Smarter

Look for the opportunities to create more team connection, and then get creative with the ways in which people connect. Here are some examples of team social activities that encourage and solidify connections:

▶ Some UK companies have created connection spaces, such as a "Chatty Table" or "Friendly Bench," where the expectation is for people to connect when present in those spaces.

▶ Other organizations have created micro-communities where people connect based on similar interests, such as running before work or salsa dancing.

▶ Recently, our company helped The Home Depot create an onboarding scavenger hunt where new hires were not only oriented to the work and workspace but also to the people inside the organization.

▶ At Kohl's, a leading retailer in the United States, our company helped introduce an activity called "Show & Tell." It's exactly what you think. During each weekly meeting, one team member brings an item from home (or presents it virtually) that means something special to him or her. The person then tells the story behind the item. Rachel Tringali-Pesden, a senior manager at Kohl's, said, "The team loves the activity, we all look forward to it every week!"

INVEST EXAMPLE

Felicia White, VP, global operations training and development at Church's Chicken, invests in team connection by hosting non-typical social experiences where team members have fun with one another.

One event was designed around a virtual karaoke experience, where team members got to play their favorite song or, if they were feeling courageous, sing it. Other events included virtual charades, a clean version of "Never Have I Ever," and a family night where team members introduced their kids, spouses, roommates, and pets and provided a virtual tour of their office or home. Additionally, each week Church's Chicken's learning and development team led Facebook Live sessions for everyone within the organization to attend.

> When asked how they kept the team connected during the 2020 pandemic, White said, "When events happen that impact the team on a personal level, you have to start connecting with your team on a personal level."

Peer Coaching Is a Social Feast

What happens when we don't have a healthy and filling meal? We snack. Snacking provides less nourishment, but it satisfies enough. If we snacked all the time, our body would lack the nutrition to stay strong and healthy. The same is true socially. If we don't have healthy and filling conversations, we snack.

"Social snacking" activities are described by psychologists as browsing through other people's social media profiles or reading comments without contributing anything to the digital dialogue or connecting only over email, text, or chat.[32] Social snacking only provides the illusion of social sustenance. It temporarily masks loneliness. What people need is real, nourishing conversations.

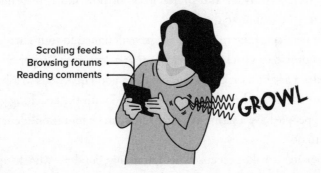

Without healthy and nourishing conversations, we socially snack.

We are snacking too often. When researchers recently asked Americans, "How many confidants do you have?" two decades ago, the most common response was "three." The most common response today was "zero."[33] Cue the heartbreak! We need less snacking and more sharing.

Peer coaching to the rescue! Peer coaching can help replace "social snacking" with purposeful conversation, establish trusted confidants, cultivate a culture of psychological safety, and drive deeper connections among a team.

Peer coaching consists of two peers who take turns coaching one another. It's a reciprocal, nonevaluative process in which colleagues work together to gain new perspectives and to keep each other accountable for follow-through. The goal is to create a network of allies who can provide positive support and encourage better performance. Those involved in peer coaching garner feelings of trust and connection that lessen loneliness.

Peer coaching involves at least two peers where one person shares something about work in the context of their whole life. The other peer listens intently focused on understanding and asks thoughtful, useful, and open-ended questions. They recap what was shared and switch roles.

According to Stewart Friedman, an organizational psychologist at the Wharton School who has provided peer-to-peer coaching opportunities in his Wharton courses and in all kinds of organizations, the most important ground rule is, "You choose what you want to disclose. Respect privacy and preferences for how much information members are willing to disclose."[34]

In peer coaching initiatives we have designed for our clients, we always provide a coaching check sheet as a part of the experience. It provides a few best practices to remember, good questions to ask, and a list of the defined expectations associated with the coaching goals. When people have a script to follow, they can be more confident with what to do.

Be sure to make peer coaching opt-in only. For those who do opt in, have them consider scheduling their sessions over lunch. Not only is it a natural way to converse about non-work-related items, but sharing a meal has been proven to increase trust and cooperation.[35]

Because there is no pressure to impress, peer coaching creates opportunities to lessen loneliness more effectively than social events where people often hold back from sharing their genuine thoughts, experiences, and challenges.

Peer coaching humanizes work. When vulnerable, thoughtful, and encouraging conversations are happening at work, people view work as a place of nourishment.

Loneliness takes a hike among teams where individuals have a sense that everyone is committed to their success and focused on helping each other along the way. Giving and receiving help is a very tangible way to experience the connections that exist between people. The leaders that invest in building peer coaching networks signal to their teams that talking candidly about life with colleagues in an inquisitive and supportive way is welcome at work.

Get your teams' hands out of the social snacking jar!

INVEST EXAMPLE

Ernst & Young, better known as EY, is a leading professional services firm with over 200,000 global employees. Routinely awarded as one of the top places to work, EY takes investing in team connections seriously. One of its flagship programs revolves around its "Counseling Families." Each new employee is placed in a partner-led counseling family. The family is designed to be a support network detached from participant's boss, department, or peers. Each family has around 30 members who meet on a monthly basis. Social budgets are provided for each family by an appointed social chair who coordinates events. Nicos Marcou, associate director—people consultant, said, "Because our business model is based on recruiting so many people straight out of college, we have to have these types of programs, because we are recruiting people who want the social component at work."

See the Human Behind the Job

Many teams operate with efficiency, respect, and friendliness, but team members are still craving to know more about their colleagues. Being oblivious to the rich life experience that each person brings to a team keeps the door to loneliness wide open. To shut the door on loneliness, create opportunities for individuals to share aspects of their personal lives. Allow team members to see the human behind the job.

To bring his team closer, Vivek Murthy, the former US surgeon general, created the "Inside Scoop" exercise where his team devoted five minutes during weekly all-hands meeting to allowing one person to share pictures of anything they wanted as long as it wasn't related to their job.[36] One researcher on Murthy's team was perceived as very detailed oriented and "nerdy" by her colleagues, but that changed once they saw the pictures of her marathon training and heard about how she qualified for the US Olympic team. She saw herself as an athlete, not just a researcher, and now her colleagues saw that too.

Through this simple exercise, the team members discovered that they were working alongside a decorated Army nurse, a woman who had spent years providing medical care to prison inmates, an accomplished pianist and preacher, and several team members who had struggled with addiction in their family. They had no idea how gifted, caring, and real their team members were.

In response to the effect of sharing more, Murthy said:

> The impact was immediate. Presenting was an opportunity for each of us to share more of who we were; listening was an opportunity to recognize our colleagues in the way they wished to be seen. These sessions quickly became many people's favorite time of the week, and they were more enthusiastic about participating at staff meetings. People felt more valued by the team after seeing their colleagues' genuine reactions to their stories. Team members who had traditionally been quiet during discussions began speaking up. Many began taking on tasks outside their traditional roles. They appeared less stressed at work. And most of them told me how much more connected they felt to their colleagues and the mission they served.[37]

A simple exercise like the "Inside Scoop" can help uncover interesting aspects of team members' lives away from work and pave the way for deeper connections among team members.

Another way to prompt personal sharing is to place a jar in your office or meeting room. Fill it with "get to know you" questions like, "What was your favorite vacation" or "When have you felt most alive?" Pull one question before the meeting and discuss for a few minutes.

Add a New KPI

The usual key performance indicators (KPI) that businesses use to track the performance of their team are important. Hopefully, by now you grasp the significance that safe, personal, and collective connection plays in the success and longevity of a team.

A new KPI that you should weave into your current KPIs is "Keep people invested" metrics. Start to measure the social connections of your team.

Sample metrics:

- ▶ Number of "social" engagements
- ▶ Number of times colleagues meet up outside of work
- ▶ Number of team members involved in coaching sessions

Start with adding just one metric so that the same attention and importance you've traditionally placed on net sales, revenue growth, social views, order fulfillment, and so on can now be placed on team connections.

Conclusion

Remote workers who work in the office at least once per week are the happiest, according to a Gallup poll of 9,917 employed US adults.[38] These same workers were more likely to say they had a best friend at work. Getting together in person matters. Face-to-face connection builds stronger relationships, accelerates trust, and improves communication. We need each other.

Teams disconnected by time zones, busyness, or a lack of purpose can begin to unite when a leader invests in connection. Leaders who prioritize people, like Hamdi Ulukaya did, and serve as shepherds protecting the space where people connect, caring for their emotional connection needs, and guiding their team interactions will be rewarded by higher performance, satisfaction, and loyalty.

The solutions covered in this chapter aren't the cure for loneliness, but they can make a sizable dent. Short steps, subtle suggestions, and small signals compounded over time can create a wave of connection that loneliness can't escape.

This chapter started with a quote by famous actor and comedian Robin Williams: "I used to think the worst thing in life was to end up all alone. It's not. The worst thing in life is to end up with people who make you feel all alone."

Feeling alone on a team is tragic but understandable considering how much of the world wants to steal our sense of belonging. Feeling alone on a team because of a leader's neglect to invest in connections is even more tragic. It's inexcusable, because it intensifies loneliness. As the shepherd of those who have been entrusted to your care, you must care for them by investing in connections. Leadership isn't for the faint of heart—it's for those who want to touch a heart.

Investing in connections that are safe, personal, and teamwide will create a belongingness forcefield that loneliness can't easily penetrate.

The next step in the Less Loneliness Framework™ is to Narrow the Focus, where you'll discover the nonnegotiables every leader must focus on to sustain a less lonely team.

INVEST SUMMARY

Invest in connections that are safe, personal, and teamwide so that workers feel connected to their leader and teammates.

Application 1: Invest in Safe Connections

Reflective Question:
Does Psychological Safety Exist on Your Team?

Start creating more psychological safety among your team members by conducting proportional conversations where every team member has equal opportunity to speak. And in every meeting you attend this week, practice speaking last.

Application 2: Invest in Personal Connections

Reflective Question:
Do You Demonstrate Emotional Intelligence During Conversations with Employees?

Strive to be relatable to your team by sharing your story and asking to hear a story. Consistently, ask yourself or a trusted advisor, *Am I relatable? What's it like to be on the other side of me?*

Application 3: Invest in Team Connections

Reflective Question:
Are You Actively Facilitating Opportunities for Your Team to Connect with Each Other?

Create more opportunities for the team to see the human behind the job. Have a "bring your kids or parents to work" day, provide a virtual tour of your home office, or carve out five minutes each meeting to have someone share a personal anecdote.

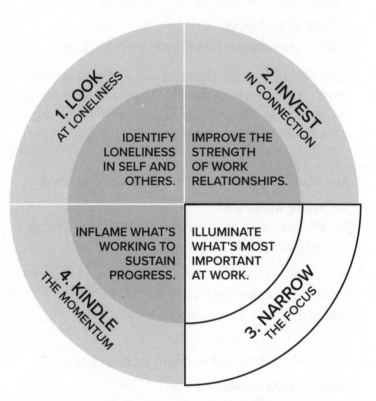

The Less Loneliness Framework™.

9

NARROW THE FOCUS

Concentrate all of your focus
on the important work at hand.
The sun's rays do not burn
until brought to a focus.

ALEXANDER GRAHAM BELL

Can you imagine being trapped in the same location for over 300 days, where all communication is remote, and you can't go outside without the right equipment? To make matters more challenging, can you also imagine having a personal space the size of a phone booth, being 254 miles away from civilization, and traveling at 17,500 miles per hour?

Unless you are one of the 242 astronauts who have ever boarded the International Space Station, then it's difficult to imagine how anyone can deal with such extreme isolation. If you or your team experience isolation due to remote work, then take note of how the most isolated people in the universe cope with it.

American engineer and class of 2013 NASA astronaut Christina Koch is all too familiar with remote isolation. On February 6, 2020, Christina Koch returned from the International Space Station after breaking the record for the longest continuous time in space by a woman. She was in space for 328 days,[1] circling earth 5,097 times. Koch likened the International Space Station to living in a five-bedroom house, where your personal space is the size of a phone booth, and where you only see a total of 11 different people over a period of 328 days.

Before her record-breaking space voyage, Koch experienced other intense remote isolation. She spent multiple winter seasons at Summit Station in Greenland where the population is five and the temperature can be as extreme as minus 31 degrees Fahrenheit. Starting in 2004, she spent three-and-a-half years traveling the Arctic and Antarctic regions where she spent a winter at the Amundsen–Scott South Pole Station. This station is in Antarctica at the southernmost part of Earth, where temperatures often fall beneath minus 100 degrees Fahrenheit. Barren, brutal, and brrrr come to mind. Interestingly, some of the research stations in Antarctica are more than 370 miles away from the nearest humans, making them even more remote than the International Space Station.[2] On numerous occasions, Koch has been one of the most isolated humans in the solar system.

Even with regular check-ins with psychologists to make sure her mental health remained stable during the extreme isolation, Koch still described her time in the South Pole as mentally and physically challenging. "[This] means going months without seeing the sun, with the same crew, and without shipments of mail or fresh food. The isolation, absence of family and friends, and lack of new sensory inputs are all conditions that you must find a strategy to thrive within," says Koch.[3]

In a cruel twist of fate, to further stress test her expert ability to handle isolation, upon her return to Earth in early 2020, Koch had to trade the isolation of outer space for the isolation of inner home. Imagine being removed from all of life's normality for 328 days, longing for the day to hug your family, share a drink with friends, and eat at your favorite restaurant (where anything that wasn't freeze dried and floating in the air would suffice)—and then have it all ripped away for another year after you return home. The things that got you through the toughest seasons of your life were suddenly locked just out of arm's reach when you needed them most. Gut-wrenching. To say Koch knows how to handle isolation would be an understatement. In response to self-isolating due to the pandemic, Koch said, "What you can control is how you react to the situation. What you can control is whether you let yourself go down a bad mental path or not."[4]

How did Koch overcome isolation, prevent loneliness, and accomplish her mission so masterfully that she made *Time* magazine's 100 Most Influential People of 2020?

She narrowed the focus.

PERCENT OF DAYS YOU'VE SURVIVED FEELINGS
OF ISOLATION AND LONELINESS

A reminder to whomever may need it.

Introducing Narrow the Focus

If Koch and other astronauts can remain engaged, productive, and grounded while orbiting Earth 254 miles away, then your team can, too, no matter how remote, disconnected, or disengaged they might be. It just takes some intentional focus to illuminate what matters most at work.

Loneliness is lessened when a team narrows their focus on:

▶ Purpose
▶ Clear direction
▶ Growth

As you'll discover in this chapter, astronauts utilize these three elements to thrive in isolation. We'll provide you with practical strategies for each category that you can enact among your team to lessen loneliness and boost belonging.

Look was about connecting to loneliness. Invest was about connecting to others. Narrow is about connecting to the work.

Narrow the Focus on Purpose

Common purpose creates camaraderie.

Purpose is critical for astronauts before, during, and after their missions. "We go to the space station, not just to hang out, but with an intent, trying to get something done," says Canadian astronaut Chris Hadfield.[5] "Having a sense of purpose is really important to maintain your psychological well-being. How do you stay productive and psychologically healthy amongst disruption and a feeling of derailed helplessness? Focus on a common purpose."[6]

Purpose seems inherent when you are an astronaut. You are exploring and understanding the future frontiers of humanity, conducting research that provides benefits to people on Earth. Astronauts also get to experience a unique sense of perspective, one out of the commonality of the human experience, by looking down on Earth. However, purpose can be fleeting for astronauts. And they, too, just like us grounded folks, must repeatedly narrow their focus and the focus of their team on a purpose.

For example, while in space and isolated aboard the space station, the thought of seeing family members, her dog and walking on the beach gave Koch enough purpose to fend off the creeping loneliness.

After experiencing the weightlessness of space and returning to Earth, astronauts can struggle with standing, walking, and moving their limbs. Sixty-day-long rehabilitation programs are common among astronauts to readjust to Earth's gravity. Some even struggle reintegrating into everyday life after accomplishing such a lofty goal as traveling to space.

To ensure Koch sustained her physical and mental health, she leaned into her existing goal of walking on the beach.[7] Her desire to see the water again and regain her strength to walk kept her motivated. A week after landing, Koch tweeted a picture of herself standing on the beach with her arms triumphantly outstretched, looking up into the sky. You can't help but get the sense that purpose helped her conquer both space and surface.

Now that she is back on Earth, her new purpose is to inspire others who had the same dream she did as a child of going into space. On February 6, 2020, Koch tweeted: "This journey has been everyone's journey. Thank you to all involved in the success of our mission, and for giving me the opportunity to carry everyone's dreams into space."

Purpose Is a Premier Loneliness Suppressant

Nothing squashes loneliness quite like contributing to a worthwhile goal and feeling a part of something bigger than oneself. As mentioned previously, a powerful sense of belonging stems from the human desire to utilize one's strengths, gifts, or talents to make a contribution that is valued by the team. Being needed reduces the risk of social abandonment, ultimately freeing people to do higher-level work.

Purpose gives meaning to people's efforts, and a shared purpose builds togetherness. Leaders can counter the energy-sapping effects of loneliness by getting teams engaged in the wider impact of their work.

The most impactful leadership behavior to counteract loneliness is to create shared meaning among a team.

Researchers trying to identify key drivers of social cohesion among thousands of employees recently discovered that creating opportunities to build shared meaning with colleagues had the biggest effect on moving teams from disconnected to connected.[8] Workers in the study who reported having high levels of social support and a strong sense of shared meaning with colleagues were 30 percent more likely to get a raise for superior work. Intent to quit fell by 24 percent. According to other research, Gen Z workers are 2.5 times more likely to stay with their employer for five or more years if they feel their skills are fully utilized with challenging, meaningful work.[9]

Communicate the meaning of the team's collective work so that a sense of purpose, not necessarily passion, can be instilled. Purpose trumps passion. Passion can energize employees, but it also isolates because passions can be individualistic. Purpose, on the other hand, is shared. Purpose knits teams and organizations together.

Purpose Delivered in Five Whys

How can leaders provide purpose to their team? Identify the beneficiaries of the labor. Identify the specific person(s) who benefit from the collective labor of the team. When team members understand how their work improves the lives of other people, it provides them with more meaning and purpose at work, thus lessening loneliness and boosting belonging.

For example, research found that fundraisers who were attempting to secure scholarship donations felt more motivated when they had contact with scholarship recipients.[10] Lifeguards were more vigilant after reading stories about people whose lives have been saved by other lifeguards.[11] Similarly, in another study, cooks were more motivated and worked harder when they saw the people who would be eating their food.[12] Lastly, other studies have shown that x-ray scanning accuracy increases when radiologists are shown a picture of the patient.

Workers who are connected to the people benefiting from their labor perform better, experience less loneliness, and demonstrate "above and beyond" behaviors.

Workers are seeking more than a paycheck. And Gen Z leads the way in this desire, with 74 percent of Gen Z believing jobs should have greater meaning, compared to 70 percent of Millennials and

69 percent of older generations.[13] In addition, 30 percent of Gen Z would take a 10 to 20 percent pay cut to work for a company with a mission they deeply care about.[14]

How do you identify the beneficiary of the labor? Ask why repeatedly.

In the 1930s, Sakichi Toyoda, the Japanese industrialist, inventor, and founder of Toyota Industries, discovered that asking "why" five times was generally sufficient to understand the root cause of something.[15] It was so useful that Toyota Motor Corporation still uses his "5 Whys" technique today over 80 years later.[16]

Take an interrogative approach to understand who exactly is benefiting from the work a team does. Ask why they do the work, and each answer forms the basis of the next four "why" questions.

Here's how the 5 Whys can be applied to identifying the beneficiaries of the labor if you were talking to a team that cleans hotel rooms.

▶ Why do you clean hotel rooms? "It's our job."
▶ Why is it your job? "We were hired to do it."
▶ Why were you hired to do it? "Hotel rooms get dirty."
▶ Why clean dirty rooms? "Clean rooms are safe, sanitary, and pleasant."
▶ Why does safe, sanitary, and pleasant matter? "It provides a place for weary travelers to rest and rejuvenate."

This technique was recently applied to a company that provides portable toilets to construction sites. Not a sexy job to say the least. After asking why enough times, their team discovered the beneficiaries of their labor. While providing convenience and comfort to construction workers, their labor also enabled speedier work, ultimately giving a neighborhood family faster access to the school being built. They weren't just delivering portable toilets to construction sites but helping build stronger communities.

When workers can draw a straight line from the work they do to the person(s) benefiting from their labor, purpose follows. And a shared purpose sheds loneliness.

Narrow the Focus on Clear Direction

Confusion spurs alienation. Kick confusion to the curb with clarity.

Astronauts avoid loneliness by having clarity in their direction. While the direction of their overarching mission is clear: safely up and then safely down; creating clarity in their roles, tasks, and daily routines is important.

They achieve clarity in the following ways:

- ▶ Know the duration of each mission.
- ▶ Know what resources they will have.
- ▶ Know what is required of them every day.

Astronauts have 12-hour workdays that are scheduled down to five-minute increments. Koch says, "Regimentation is not a problem on the space station. Having a sense of purpose every single minute of your day is one of the things that helps us get through those long periods of isolation. Regimentation can really help."[17]

If Koch would start to find herself beginning to experience loneliness, she would "Identify a specific problem, and come up with a specific solution."[18]

Without a clear path, we're susceptible to wander. Wandering leads to being lost. Being lost is lonesome. Carter Cast, professor at Northwestern and author of the book *The Right—and Wrong—Stuff: How Brilliant Careers Are Made and Unmade*, said, "the loneliest I have ever been was when I was managing at scale and I just did not know if I was doing it right. I did not know who I could talk to."

Cast, the former CEO of Walmart.com and a senior leader at both PepsiCo and Electronic Arts, has seen firsthand how a lack of direction can lead people adrift. In an interview, he discussed how when people face a problem with a lot of unknowns, they often pull back, isolating themselves rather than seeking the advice they need. "People get scared and retreat."

Having clarity around what your team does and the tasks at hand every day will help get them engaged.

Narrowing Is Natural

Humans have a built-in mechanism for making sense of the world; it's called "perceptual narrowing." Perceptual narrowing is a developmental process during which the brain uses environmental experiences to shape perceptual abilities.[19] This process improves the perception of things that people experience often and causes them to experience a decline in the ability to perceive some things to which they are not often exposed. For example, human infants are born with the ability to sense a wide variety of stimuli, and as they age, they begin to selectively narrow these perceptions by categorizing them in a more socially relevant way.

By three months old, infants start to favor faces of their family and the language they hear in their tribe. Even though infants begin life being attentive to anyone and have the potential to learn any language, they naturally narrow their focus on the people they know and trust to keep them safe. They begin to facially discriminate people outside their immediate caretakers.

The brain naturally narrows on what's important. Unless the direction you're trying to give to your team is a physical sign that flashes, rings, or moves, then you'll have to put extra emphasis on the direction you want your team's brains to narrow upon. A lack of clarity will confuse the brain and default it to focusing on the most urgent items, not necessarily the important ones.

According to neuroscience research, the brain craves certainty.[20] The slightest bit of ambiguity or uncertainty creates tension in the brain and inhibits our ability to think clearly. Obscurity causes hesitation. It creates inaction where people don't buy into products, people, plans, or priorities. To be unclear is to be unkind.

Leadership expert and author Andy Stanley helps his team members create a "one-sentence responsibility statement." The responsibility statement goes well beyond a job description and provides individuals with extreme clarity on their primary responsibility at work. It's as if team members' one-sentence responsibility statements are stored safely in the "break glass in case of emergency" containers and are relied upon when things get overwhelming, confusing, or chaotic.

Work Is Full of Loneliness Lifelines

"Lonely people's brainstems are saying, 'I need to be ready to be hurt. I need to be vigilant for people taking advantage of me. I need to watch out and take care of myself. I need to let people in only gradually so they don't do what they have done before,'" says Steve Cole, a leading researcher on loneliness and a professor of medicine, psychiatry and biobehavioral sciences at UCLA.

Lonely people lack trust in people around them. They are apprehensive to let others in, and they keep a wide distance in social settings. They put up an imaginary barrier to keep people at a distance. Like the Great Wall of China, the barrier snakes around their entire emotional response system, creating a blockade that is difficult to penetrate. The longer someone experiences loneliness, the higher and stronger the walls.

Fortunately, according to Cole, researchers have discovered a strategy that works as a "secret door," allowing someone to get past the wall undetected. The usual workplace response to loneliness is

The secret door to get past a lonely person's guarded walls.

to avoid it or hope the individual gets help on his personal time—but that doesn't serve the individual, the leader, or the team. The better approach is to make the lonely worker feel he is contributing to a worthy mission that is advancing the team toward its purpose.

Cole suggests, "Go to lonely people and essentially say, 'I need your help. We have this big problem over here that requires your ability to do X.' People need to feel strong, valuable, and contributory. Biologically, we love to help other human beings, even if we tend to mistrust them. This idea of coalescing around values, aspirations, and goals, to gradually overcome the mistrust, is a rekindling that allows us to have a renewed sense of community. Work gives us an unbelievable opportunity to do this."

Loneliness lifelines are abundant at work. Work can provide purpose, routine, learning, and meaningful relationships. Other than priests, workplace leaders have the best opportunity to throw these lifelines into the ocean of lonely workers. It's all about giving lonely people something meaningful to strive for. Says Cole:

> There are fundamentally different brain circuits for moving toward stuff and for running away from stuff. The threat circuitry is what lonely people are running all the time. But what's interesting is that this wanting, hoping, seeking system in the brain that runs on dopamine, is what gets us climbing and searching and seeking. It is one of the few systems in the brain that can veto threat biology.
>
> If you are going after something that matters, like there is a burning building and your child is inside, you run toward the building, even though the default threat response is to run away from it. The brain structure shows that if you care enough, you can overcome some of the most fundamental tenets of self-preservation and threat and insecurity.

Rather than wading into the tricky waters of psychoanalyzing your lonely workers, instead narrow their focus on the meaningful contributions they can make to help the team.

Context, Not Control

An effective way to narrow the focus of a team is to lead with context, not control.

If mistrust is a big component of loneliness, then building trust is important in making a team less lonely. One way to build trust is to use context. Control is the opposite of trust. Little trust is present among a team where a leader controls every employee's action and decision. Context on the other hand is providing the team with the necessary information so that they can act and decide on their own.

At Netflix, one of their mantras is "lead with context and not control." The company believes that "high performance people will do better work if they understand the context."[21]

Reed Hastings, the cofounder of Netflix, shared an example of the importance of context in his book *No Rules Rules: Netflix and the Culture of Reinvention*. After one of Reed's managers made a poor decision, Reed sat down with the manager and asked why he had made the decision. As the manager shared his thought process for making the decision, Reed realized it was a reasonable decision based on the limited information the manager had. The costly decision could have been avoided if Reed had shared more context about the situation, thus enabling the manager to make the best decision.

According to Steve Urban, a remote engineering leader at Netflix:

> Executives share extensive documentation from each quarterly business review with every employee, at all levels in the company. Major decisions are communicated, along with supporting information which gives insight into the factors and alternatives that were considered through memos, open FAQs, and presentations. In cases where we do need to adopt a new tool, or change the way we work, the reasons are well thought out and clearly communicated to all affected. Thanks to this level of transparency, each team understands the environment in which they operate and the high-level business goals they, and every other team, are striving to support.[22]

If you don't trust your team to take the right actions and make the right decisions after giving the appropriate context, you likely have a hiring problem.

Context builds trust. Trust erodes loneliness.

Quick Tips to Create Clear Direction

1. **Break up goals.** Leaders should break big goals down into smaller, achievable ones, so they can better track the progress employees are experiencing.
2. **Include pertinent information.** Highlight the what, who, when, how, and the priority level of the task or request.
3. **Create very specific "finish lines."** Ambiguity stalls action and inhibits progress. Replace broad goals like, "Complete the project" with specific goals like, "Send a one-page project overview to Landon by this Friday at noon." If an employee's goals are clear and specific, it enables them to track and celebrate their own progress, which creates a more independent, productive, and engaged worker.
4. **Meet regularly.** Employees are 3.5 times more likely to be engaged at work when given meaningful weekly feedback.[23] Weekly meetings can provide leaders with a better pulse on where and when an employee is progressing (or stalling).
5. **Get confirmation.** After providing direction, confirm the individual understood the intended message by asking, "To ensure I communicated clearly, share with me your next steps?"

United We Don't Crack

Could a carton of 12 eggs support your body weight?

It can. To the shock of many workshop attendees over the years, we have demonstrated this amazing feat. Brave attendees of all sizes have set aside their fear of a yolk-soaked foot and have stood barefoot on top of a full carton of eggs without a single one cracking. The carton of eggs can absorb all of the weight because it is evenly distributed across each egg. A solo egg is easily crushed; a group of eggs is uncrushable.

When a team has clarity in their positions and roles, collectively they can bear big pressure and support big goals.

NARROW EXAMPLE

Shari Perez-Conway, a senior director of people at Southwest Airlines, said that informational transparency was one of Southwest's strategies to prevent loneliness during the Covid-19 pandemic. When there was a lot of uncertainty regarding traveling restrictions, Southwest's CEO Gary Kelly scheduled all leader meetings and posted three to four videos a week on Southwest's intranet so every employee knew exactly what was going on.

Shari said, "People did not have the opportunity to fill in the gaps on their own, because they were included in all of the communication." Total transparency was present throughout the organization. Even though times were getting tough, everyone had the opportunity to be aware of what was happening and why.

Transparent communication is caring. It is saying, I value you enough to let you know what I know. I value you so much that I do not want you to feel out of the loop. Making people feel informed shows you care. It points them in a direction and gives them confidence to keep moving forward. It is hard to feel lonely when everyone is in it together, when everyone knows the same things, and everyone is moving in the same direction.

Narrow the Focus on Growth

Learning starves loneliness.

While in extreme isolation, astronauts sidestepped loneliness by continuously learning. Some of the learning was built into the job, and some learning was happenstance, like trying to get a good night sleep in zero gravity. But they also had to get creative, pushing themselves to find new opportunities for learning. Astronaut Chris Hadfield, famous for his Space Oddity music video that he recorded in the International Space Station that eventually was seen by millions of people around the world, found many ways to learn and be creative while confined inside a single structure.

Hadfield viewed the space station as an "old attic" where he explored and discovered new ways to stimulate his mind. He found an old Japanese bell and became fascinated with how the sound would float through the station. He found a gorilla suit that a previous crew member had left behind. He made it a priority to narrow his focus on growth by starting "fresh projects and learning new skills."[24]

Importance of Learning and Development

It's difficult, if not impossible, to be angry when you are grateful. If your brain is searching for possibilities, generosity, and value (gratitude), then it's not searching for what's unfair, missing, or wrong (anger). Similarly, it's difficult to be angry when learning. When our brain is enraptured in learning something new, loneliness is absent.

The brain doesn't want to be confused, so feed it something that it can try to make sense of. As highlighted in Chapter 5, "learn" is one of the 3 Ls of Life™. The intrinsic question we ask ourselves is: *Am I growing into my full potential?* Learning is important because it gives us hope. Albert Einstein famously said, "Once you stop learning, you start dying." Learning gives us a sense that tomorrow can be better than today. As speakers and consultants, we have experienced firsthand how learning lifts the human spirit.

Has this ever happened to you? A new problem surfaces during a meeting and the entire team turns to you because you have the unique skill required to tackle the problem. They look to you with eyes that say, "Hurry, save us!" What did you feel in that moment? Like a hero.

Acquiring in-demand skills makes us feel strong, superhuman, and confident. Like Liam Neeson–level confidence from the movie *Taken*, when he said: "If you are looking for ransom, I can tell you I don't have money. But what I do have are a very particular set of skills. Skills I have acquired over a very long career. Skills that make me a nightmare for [problems] like you."

Survival is another reason learning is important. If you haven't learned a skill or perspective that is valuable to the tribe, then you are at risk of being excluded. Freeloaders create a drag on the tribe. Learning provides reassurance to individuals that they can or will contribute value. And learning provides reassurance to the tribe that you are improving yourself for the benefit of the group.

Also, learning leads to social connection. When you learn something, you often share what you learned with someone else. We learn to play an instrument so that one day we can share a song with an audience. We learn a new joke to bring a smile to a friend. We learn how to communicate more effectively to deepen our connection with a spouse. We learn about workplace loneliness to move a team from isolated to all in. After we learn something, we are often eager to share it with the world.

Solo activities that can lessen loneliness.

Learning Teams Are Cohesive Teams

Despite the importance of learning, there's a disconnect between what employers believe they are doing to promote learning and the experiences of employees. Seventy percent of managers report that their companies always or very often invest in employee development.[25] Yet only 47 percent of employees report the same. It's time to end that misalignment, especially considering 66 percent of organizations that view learning and development as critical to their success had a stronger market position than their competitors.[26]

While conducting his thesis for his master of science in organizational development at Pepperdine University, Steven discovered just how monumental learning can be in unifying a team.

Steven built and analyzed a comprehensive training program that required frontline supervisors to spend three consecutive weeks training on-site through the guidance and support of the management team. Each cohort had representatives from across all departments come together to learn, grow, and build meaningful connections. The strategy was to have each cohort learn in the morning, then go out in the afternoon and apply their lessons in real time. This meant that throughout the year the initiative was run, there were leaders out in the field almost every day executing assignments with all employees at the site, assignments focused on active listening, positive reinforcement, strategic planning, and morale boosting.

Employees of the supervisors who attended the training cited a 67 percent increase in better communication, 50 percent increase in workplace standards, 67 percent increase in cross-functional collaboration, 45 percent increase in positive recognition, and 40 percent increase in time spent with their leader in the field.

This led to an overall increase in team morale of 57 percent. Production increased, injuries decreased, regulatory compliance improved, retention went up, and all other major metrics for site performance were enhanced the year the initiative was implemented. Most importantly, however, from the interviews conducted with the leaders who attended the initiative and the employees of those leaders, the most consistent feedback was "we feel more connected."

Teams that learn together, grow together.

Be Development-Focused

Ryan recently spoke to an executive of a billion-dollar fast-food company. The leader shared with him, "If you were to ask any of our 2,000 operators, 'What business are you in?' You won't hear any of them say, 'We are in the fast-food business.' You're more likely going to hear this response, 'We are a leadership development academy masquerading as a fast-food restaurant.'"

Team members of this fast-food chain aren't in the food business. They are in the human development business. They use food to fund their leadership development academies (aka their restaurants). Operators and managers are not only running a business that serves customers and provides employment opportunities, but they are preparing the next generation with the skills needed to contribute to society meaningfully and effectively.

With a narrow focus on the growth of their people, it's not surprising that this restaurant chain is the most beloved brand in its category, make more per unit than its competitors, and experiencing a 96 percent retention rate among operators.[27]

Ways to Grow Your Team

Now that you understand the critical role of learning to lessen loneliness, let's provide you with some ideas on how to better focus on the development and growth of your team by modeling, encouraging, scheduling, building, and scaling learning.

Model Learning

Learning and training get shoved to the bottom of most teams' to-do list. To make sure training gets prioritized and to begin creating a culture of learning, leaders must set the example. As a leader, you go first. You have to model what learning looks like. Grant permission to your team to explore more by sharing with your team a book you're reading, a video you found fascinating, a podcast that reframed your perspective, or a conference you're excited to attend.

Encourage Learning

Pamay Bassey, chief learning officer at Kraft Heinz, told us that she recently launched a daily learning challenge as a corporate initiative. The challenge encouraged employees to take risks and proactively look for ways to learn. More than 1,000 employees have committed to learning one new thing per day.

Learning opportunities abound when you're looking for them. Look for small ways to delegate new tasks and encourage more learning. Consider having a team member:

- ► Run a meeting
- ► Attend an industry conference
- ► Train a coworker
- ► Shadow a colleague
- ► Lead a presentation

Schedule Learning

Schedule time to experience learning together. Training creates opportunities for workers to develop skills, gain knowledge, and deepen relationships with their colleagues. Timely and well-designed training instills confidence, injects energy, and infers a sense of belonging. Training sends the message, "We are investing in you because we value you. We see your potential."

Build Learning

Building custom training, digital courses, or other learning initiatives allows for the learning to be very relevant to the team. This option requires the most time, effort, and money, but the payoff (if done right) is worth it.

Harvard Business Publishing's "State of Leadership Development Report" identified the top three reasons learning and development programs fail: (1) poor content, (2) not enough external thinking and expertise, and (3) no application to on-the-job requirements.[28]

Therefore, if you want learning and development programs to succeed, you must: (1) deliver relevant and accessible content, (2) harness expertise from external sources, and (3) make it applicable.

This is obviously much easier said than done. If you're serious about building learning experiences that your team uses, enjoys, and applies, then consider partnering with an experienced learning and development team. If you have a dedicated team internally, fantastic! If not, learning and development consultancies like SyncLX.com can help.

Emilie Schouten, the VP of HR at Coeur Mining, worked with Sync Learning Experiences (LX) to create a comprehensive learning program that delivered relevant content in the form of singing karaoke (building resiliency), scrapbooking (story sharing), bike building (practicing psychological safety), and giving back to charity (making an impact). Second, they harnessed the expertise of SyncLX by having them lead weeklong sessions in tandem with their internal human resource leaders. Last, the company made the learning applicable by using site mentors who meet monthly with participants to track their progress and guide them through their learning goals. Schouten made a commitment to grow Coeur's leaders the right way. Which is why Coeur Mining continues to be an industry leader.

Scale Learning

Scale your learning efforts by empowering your team to teach others. Everyone has something to teach someone.

Astronauts are always learning. During Hadfield's mission, he took his learning one step further. While aboard the International Space Station for five months, he made over 100 videos and shared them on YouTube. His goal was to share what it's like to live in space and help others learn.

Evernote, the note-taking and task management application company, encourages anyone to teach anything as part of their Evernote Academy program. Its head of security ironically taught a class on how to pick a lock. Another employee taught how to build the Evernote logo out of Legos. Someone else led a class about how to draw Disney characters. Other classes are meant to be profound learning experiences like how to talk to people about difficult problems. In response to teaching a class, an Evernote employee said, "I've always feared public speaking, so I love having the opportunity to work on my presentation skills in an environment where I feel supported."

Similar to Evernote, the cloud computing company Nutanix allows any of its 6,100 employees to teach courses about topics they are passionate about. They even opened up their learning library to the families of their employees, thereby encouraging learning away from work. The children of Nutanix employees can sign up to learn from other employees how to play guitar or bake cupcakes.

Learning is a powerful lever to unify a team. While the mind feeds, loneliness starves.

NARROW EXAMPLE

Joseph Loch, brand president at College Nannies and Sitters, has a goal to provide best-in-class learning at any level throughout the organization. College Nannies and Sitters provides flexible, in-home childcare solutions to families across the United States.

The company recently surveyed its caregivers and discovered they "felt detached from the organization," said Loch. To connect their caregivers, company leaders turned to training. They invested in a new and innovative learning management system that created a community where caregivers could connect with other learners inside the organization and develop professionally.

They now offer certifications where caregivers can earn badges that increase their visibility and confidence among the families they serve. By narrowing their focus on learning, College Nannies and Sitters made Glassdoor's coveted list of Employee's Choice Best Places to Work in 2020.

Conclusion

Work provides a plethora of lifelines to lessen loneliness. While working as the most isolated humans in our solar system, astronauts use purpose, clear direction, and growth opportunities to protect them from loneliness. A shared purpose sheds loneliness. Clarity and context build trust, which erodes loneliness. And learning starves loneliness.

Loneliness stands no chance when leaders narrow the team's focus on what's most important at work.

Now that you've Looked at loneliness, Invested in connections, and Narrowed the focus, the next chapter will equip you to Kindle this momentum to ensure loneliness remains isolated from your team.

NARROW SUMMARY

Narrow the focus on purpose, provide clear direction, and encourage growth so that worker engagement overpowers loneliness.

Application 1: Narrow the Team's Focus on Purpose

Reflective Question:
Does Your Team Know the Impact of Their Work?

Identify the beneficiaries of the labor of each team member. Take an interrogative approach to understand who exactly is benefiting from the team's work by asking "Why?" five times.

Application 2: Narrow the Team's Focus on Clear Direction

Reflective Question:
Does Your Team Have Clarity to Act Swiftly?

Lead using context, not control. Provide your team with the necessary information so that they can act and decide on their own.

Application 3: Narrow the Focus on Growth

Reflective Question:
Is Your Team Actively Learning and Developing?

Encourage on-the-job learning by delegating tasks. Have team members run a meeting, lead a presentation, or train a new hire in order to experience new learning and starve loneliness.

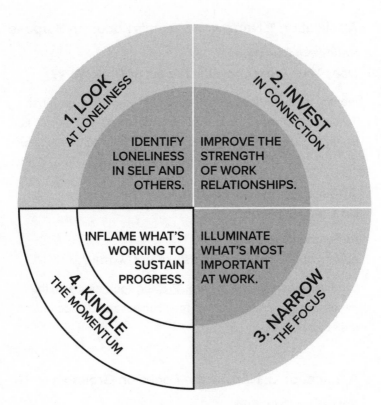

The Less Loneliness Framework™.

10

KINDLE THE MOMENTUM

The mind is not a vessel to be filled
but a fire to be kindled.

PLUTARCH

Do you know who created the world's first social network? It wasn't Zuckerberg, Dorsey, or Tom from MySpace.

It was a young brave.

Many generations ago when the land was still young, people were cold, wet, hungry, and afraid. Then one day, according to Native American legend, a great thunderbird flew over the land and sent down a flash of lightning, hitting an old oak tree. Hot embers formed in the tree trunk.

After the thunderbird flew away, a young Native American Indian warrior, or brave, came across the embers. As he looked closer, the ember spoke to him in a whisper, saying, "Feed me." "What should I feed you?" said the young brave. "Kindling. Twigs, straw, and sticks," said the small ember.

The young brave did as the ember said, placing it on the ground and putting small sticks, straw, and twigs upon it. To his surprise a flame emerged and began to grow. The flames began to dance and speak to the young brave, instructing him to continue to kindle the fire. The young brave obeyed, feeding it more fuel. Before long the fire's loud crackling, billowing smoke, and beautiful orange glow attracted others in the village toward it. Soon everyone was gathered around basking in the warmth of the flames.

The young brave had created the worlds' first social network. A fire.

The discovery of fire changed everything. Fire became a cornerstone of human survival. It was instrumental in protecting the village from predators, cooking food, and providing light in the dark. And it transformed how people connected. The light from a fire extended the day, giving humans more time to connect and providing warmth that wondrously enabled relationships to deepen like never before.

A recent study of the Ju/'hoan hunter-gatherers of the southern African countries of Namibia and Botswana found major differences between firelit talk and nonfirelit talk.[1] When the Ju/'hoan weren't around a fire, their conversations centered on "practicalities and sanctioning gossip." Firelit conversations, however, "evoked the imagination, helped people remember and understand others in their external networks, healed rifts of the day, and conveyed information about cultural institutions that generate regularity of behavior and corresponding trust."

Fireside conversations put people on the same emotional wavelength, elicited understanding, and elevated trust and empathy, ultimately strengthening people's social networks. It is also common for the Ju/'hoan to sing while sitting around a fire. To this day, the comfort and security we feel when we sit by an open fire can be traced to our ancient ancestors who utilized fire as a social and survival essential.

What else provides this sense of security, source of light, and setting for socializing? Work.

Introducing Kindle the Momentum

Much like fire, work can deliver security through a paycheck, light that illuminates a brighter future, and socializing among team members.

Looking at Loneliness, Investing in Connections, and Narrowing the Focus will create a small fire that begins to draw people together. For that small fire to grow into a roaring blaze of belonging, it needs to be kindled, stirred up, and continually stoked.

A team that is an ember has potential, but without the proper kindling, will eventually burn out. A team that is ablaze contributes to the raging fire, creating protection, warmth, and community for all involved. Moving from an ember to a blaze takes a leader who will protect and tend to the flame.

After Native Americans learned to control fire, they appointed a keeper of the fire, who was often called the "flametender." Because the open flame played a central role in basic human survival, those tending to the flame held a sacred role in the tribe.[2] The perpetual or eternal flame provided hot embers for the kindling of other fires in the tribe. One fire served as the impetus for all the fires across the tribe.

Leaders must play the sacred role of "flametender" for their team. Leaders must tend to the flames of belonging that they've created by Looking, Investing, and Narrowing. The next and final step in the Less Loneliness Framework™ four-step LINK process is to Kindle the Momentum. Kindle—amplify and sustain—the momentum you've generated toward lessening loneliness among your team.

Inflame what's working to sustain progress.

Starting is easy, sustaining is hard. Sparking a fire is simple. Sustaining that fire day and night through wind and rain is difficult. But when the fire is essential to you and your tribe's survival, you push through and find a way.

Kindle the momentum by:

- ▶ Re-Looking
- ▶ Re-Investing
- ▶ Re-Narrowing

These actions are critical for turning the ember of belonging into a raging fire that will have loneliness running for the hills.

Kindle the Momentum by Re-Looking

On January 3, 1864, a ship named the *Grafton* was sunk by a hurricane on the southern end of Auckland Island, a part of the New Zealand subantarctic area.[3] Four months later, another ship, the *Invercauld*, was astonishingly sunk by a violent storm on the opposite end of Auckland Island. Two different ships, just a few months apart, sunk near the same island on opposing coasts.

Both crews made it to shore, but not to safety, as Auckland Island is one of the most inhospitable places on earth. Freezing rain, howling winds, and little to eat year-round makes Auckland Island a miserable place to be. Both crews spent more than a year on the island unaware of each other's presence.

Unknown to these crews, fate had orchestrated an interesting experiment in teamwork. The threats to survival were similar for both groups, but the results were very different. The *Grafton* and *Invercauld* captains and crews developed different governance structures and group norms when confronted with the new island conditions that would likely mean death for solitary individuals.

The *Invercauld* crew retained the formal hierarchy used on the boat and did not devise a new team structure to survive on land. The lack of structure to fit their new circumstances led crew members to focus on their self-interests and behave with little regard for each other. As a result, the crew splintered and fought, descended into cannibalism, and only 3 of the 19 crew members survived. Their rescue was by chance when another ship sprung a leak, sent a boat ashore to seek assistance, and found the remaining three crew members.

The *Grafton* crew, on the other hand, *relooked* at their existing governance structures and group norms and decided to abandon formalities from the past. Instead, they adopted a new structure of group consultation, decision making, and problem solving to fit their new and dire circumstances. They created a culture in which everyone's survival was tied to the survival of each other. This structure encouraged individuals to work for the good of the group rather than for themselves at the expense of the group. They worked together to build shelters, gather food and water, and eventually to construct a vessel that the crew used to sail out to sea where they were eventually rescued.

Both crews felt the pain of isolation, but the *Grafton* crew succeeded because of the team structure that fostered collaboration and connection. Humanity's remarkable accomplishments are not attributable to our individual might, but our collective efforts.

The winds of a pandemic and the changing tides of technology have crashed today's workplace ship onto the treacherous shores of an Auckland Island–like environment, where unfamiliar threats like loneliness, burnout, and depression await. These threats can snatch the well-being away from any unsuspecting team. These new and growing workplace challenges require new structures to support the wellness and performance of workers. We must adapt, devise a new plan, and execute, because too much hangs in the balance of our teams, communities, and future generations.

After leaders Look at Loneliness to gain awareness, perspective, and understanding of the challenges facing their team, they can kindle the momentum by creating structures (systems, plans, or programs) that continuously relook for loneliness and proactively address any growing concerns. Structures are the kindling that can inflame the progress toward identifying loneliness and replacing it with belonging.

The First Responders of Mental Health

One company has created a structure that continuously looks to root out loneliness and improve the overall mental health of its employees.

"In 2019, we had two employee suicides. They were both so devastating to our employees," said Donna Kimmel, chief people officer at Citrix, an American multinational company with more than 11,000 employees that provides digital workplace technologies to more than 400,000 organizations around the world. Unfortunately, the alarming rise of suicides across the globe makes this type of team devastation increasingly likely.

According to a 2019 Centers for Disease Control report, suicide is the tenth leading cause of death in the United States.[4] There were an estimated 1.8 million suicide attempts in 2019 alone, with 47,511 American's dying by suicide that year. Globally, nearly 800,000 people die by suicide each year, which is roughly one death every 40 seconds. Suicide is the second leading cause of death in the world for those 15 to 24 years old. Since the year 2000, suicides have increased by 35 percent in the United States.

The two suicides at Citrix left employees across the organization with lots of questions. Kimmel explained that employees started to ask, "What could we have done? How could we have known? What's next for our team?"

Feeling the gravity of the situation, Kimmel and her team expanded the company's efforts to fundamentally shift how mental health concerns are addressed across the organization. Following guidelines from Mental Health First Aid International, Citrix established its peer-based mental health support initiative—Mental Health First Aiders.

Kimmel's team realized that staff suffering from depression or loneliness would be keener to seek out help from a peer than from a manager. "Reaching out to peers is much easier because people fear if their boss knew they were anything short of perfect, it would hinder their trajectory," said Kate Stemle, senior well-being manager at Citrix.

After a successful pilot with its Cambridge, UK, team and with support from leaders across the organization, Citrix asked for volunteers companywide to join the new initiative. The goals were to create permission to talk about these important issues in the work culture and to make conversations about mental health easier for individuals. To have broad reach, Citrix worked to ensure every department and level had representation in the program. People from engineering, legal, human resources, sales, and many other departments signed up for the initiative, which officially launched in 2020.

Once vetted and approved, the first aiders attended workshops delivered by experts in the mental health industry. They learned what signs to look for, how to navigate difficult conversations, and what resources are available through Citrix's HR team or directly including benefits like its EAP, employee accommodations, or leaves of absence. For Mental Health Awareness Month in May 2021, Citrix launched the program. It was so successful in the initial launch cities that Citrix is making it a global program.

Citrix is rethinking what it means to provide mental health resources. Instead of leaning solely on traditional tools like EAPs, they are preparing their staff to help peers across the organization get connected to care or other resources. Citrix's bold plan and structure is kindling its momentum toward extinguishing loneliness and other mental health concerns.

While Looking at loneliness (and mental health) is the appropriate and necessary first step, a structure and plan is the kindling needed to ensure the efforts and benefits are sustained for maximum and long-term impact.

A Plan for Social Fitness

Another example of an organization that looked at the problem and then created a structure—or plan—to fight off loneliness was the US Army.

"We don't assume people can shoot when they come into the Army, so we teach them how to load weapons and how to aim," says Brigadier General (retired) Rhonda Cornum, former director of the Comprehensive Soldier Fitness program. "We need to attend to psychological fitness the same way we do physical performance."[5]

A 2011 large-scale study confirmed that many returning soldiers struggled with loneliness and found that those who committed suicide had reported being lonelier and more depressed than soldiers who did not commit suicide.[6] The Army needed some structure to kindle more belonging.

The US Army committed to a new structure and rolled out its Comprehensive Soldier Fitness program to 1.1 million active-duty soldiers, reservists, and members of the National Guard to enhance soldiers' ability to cope with the mental rigors of life.[7] Just as soldiers were training physically to gain strength, agility, and stamina; they began training to enhance their social fitness as well. Fifty social fitness exercises were developed to help soldiers learn techniques for establishing, maintaining, and strengthening their connections. Participants were also given tools to help others who were feeling lonely.

Soldiers tending to their social fitness reduced their loneliness and improved their overall well-being. They also developed social resilience, which is the capacity to foster, engage, and sustain positive relationships and to endure and recover from life stressors like social isolation.

A master sergeant who participated in the training applied what he learned at home with his spouse, who in turn responded, "What has the army done to you? And why haven't they done this sooner?"

Re-Looking to Reconnect with Humanity

Just like a healthy body requires exercise regimens, so does a healthy social life. Better well-being, improved mental health, and less loneliness can be the result when we practice social fitness. As the US Army proved, social exercises can reverse the negative effects of loneliness at work and at home. Additionally, because loneliness is contagious (as discussed in Chapter 2), the benefits of replacing negative behaviors with positive ones will also spread. Remember, because loneliness is rising, it means it's malleable and thus can also decline.

To provide working professionals with the same level of social fitness success that the US Army experienced, the Connect Deck™ was created. The Connect Deck™ is 30 custom playing cards with simple and fun daily challenges that are proven to reconnect people with their team and kindle their connections with humanity.

Every day for 30 days someone picks a new card and completes the two- to five-minute evidence-based activity described. Here are a few examples of the daily card challenges.

▶ **Slow Down a Bit.** Busyness is leaving us with less time to connect, making us feel more lonely. Slow your roll. Spend the day saying "After you" in social settings. Whether you're exiting a crowded elevator, speaking at the same time as a colleague during a meeting, or simultaneously entering the coffee shop as someone else, simply say "After you" to allow others to go first.

▶ **Insert an Emoji.** Insert an emoji into your next digital message. Research indicates that the same part of the brain that processes human faces also processes emojis. If the person can't see your face, use an emoji to communicate your emotional intent.

▶ **Smile at a Stranger.** Briefly make eye contact with a stranger today and smile. That's it!

▶ **Scroll Down Memory Lane.** Look back through the photos on your phone to see who you were with one year, week, or month ago today. Send a text to the person in the photo, include the photo and a short message about that memory. #TimeFlies

▶ **Arrive Extra Early.** Plan to arrive 10–15 minutes early to your next meeting, appointment, or social meetup. Research proves that time constraints severely limit our willingness to engage with others. If you are constantly rushing from one thing to the next, you constrain the opportunity to connect with someone along the way. Don't let busyness blind you to the needs and presence of others around you. Create more margin to create more connection.

The Connect Deck™ provides a structure to reconnect with those around you, while boosting your well-being in the process.

The social fitness of humanity has been one of the greatest (if not *the* greatest) contributors to the longevity of our species. A human can't outrun a lion, or overpower a rhinoceros, or outswim a shark. Humans don't have natural armor, can't fly, and don't have sharp teeth. What makes humanity so dominating is our social skills—our ability to work, learn, and communicate together. We watch each other's back, identify mutual threats, establish cultural norms, support one another, and form alliances.

The ability to work together has humans on top of the food chain.

Loneliness and isolation run counter to the very thing that makes us the most spectacular species on the planet. Loneliness directly conflicts with being human. Social creatures have a social muscle that requires social fitness. And the good news is every person has the power to improve theirs.

Maybe you were one of the many people who experienced an atrophy in social muscle coming out of the pandemic lockdown. The months of no social gatherings and distanced conversations caused many people to have a weak social muscle that made it difficult to connect with others like they did prepandemic. The Connect Deck™ is the protein-packed workout shake for your social muscle. Grab a deck for yourself or team at LessLonely.com/Deck.

Flametenders had structures and plans in place to keep the fire burning for their tribe. They knew how to combat any weather that threatened to douse their flame. They typically positioned the fire in

An example of social muscle atrophy. Too much tech has us out of touch.

the middle of the tribe so the flametender could quickly kindle a fire for anyone who needed it.

What structures can you create that will re-look at loneliness to keep the fire of belonging burning strong?

Kindle the Momentum by Re-Investing

The Magic Castle Hotel is the second highest rated hotel in all of Los Angeles, based on thousands of reviews on TripAdvisor. It even outranks the Four Seasons at Beverly Hills. The Magic Castle isn't nearly as beautiful as the Four Seasons. Nor are the amenities as nice. Nor is the location as desirable. So, what does the Magic Castle have that the Four Seasons doesn't? A standout moment maker.

Located by the pool at the Magic Castle is a cherry red phone called the popsicle hotline. When a guest picks up the phone, someone at the other end of the line answers, "Popsicle hotline, what kind of popsicle would you like?" Then a popsicle delivery attendant dressed in a fancy butler's outfit with white gloves delivers the guest's popsicle on a silver platter. The moment is unforgettable.

A study of hotel reviews on TripAdvisor found that when guests reported experiencing a "delightful surprise," an astonishing 94 percent of them expressed an unconditional willingness to recommend the hotel, compared with only 60 percent of guests who were "very satisfied."[8]

Listen to a true crime podcast and you'll hear reporters, law enforcement officers, and attorneys alike continuously harp on just how unreliable people's memories are. We tend to color the past with a multitude of colors, never quite fully remembering exactly how things happened. Famed poet and civil rights activist Maya Angelou gives us a good perspective on what people really remember when she said, "People will forget what you said, people will forget what you did, but people will never forget how you made them feel." The moments that make us feel something are remembered: the love you felt on your wedding day, the pride you felt during your daughter's graduation, or the satisfaction you felt when your first customer walked through the door.

Magic Castle guests may not remember every detail of their stay, but they'll never forget the feeling of joy and wonder when a popsicle was delivered on a silver platter just for them. Feelings can anchor us in a specific moment in time. Moments time stamp a place and feeling in our soul that binds us to those we experience the moment with.

After leaders Invest in safe, personal, and teamwide connections, they can kindle the momentum by reinvesting in relationships using meaningful moments. Moments are the kindle that can inflame relationships into roaring fires of belonging.

Firsts Are Fertile Ground for Moments

There are many milestone days in a person's life. Graduations, weddings, and retirements are examples of days that deserve punctuation. Another milestone day is starting a new job. The combination of new work, new people, and new places creates an opportune window for leaders to create a lasting and impactful moment for new employees.

What better time to demonstrate what inclusion should look and feel like among a team than when a new hire starts? But unfortunately, leaders too often trade memorability for familiarity. They let the busyness of the business blind them to the prime connection opportunity in front of them.

The first-day experience for new hires often starts like this: New hires arrive without clear direction of where to park or whom to meet. When they finally connect with someone who vaguely remembers hearing that someone was starting today, they are ushered to a random empty desk and instructed to "get settled in." For the leader, a huge opportunity was wasted.

First-day experiences should be filled with remarkable moments, not bureaucratic activities. After their first day, new employees should leave thinking:

1. I belong here.
2. My work matters.
3. I'm important to them.

We recently worked with The Home Depot to help leaders weave some of these elements into employees' first-day experience.

1. **I belong here.** New hires at the corporate office are given orange aprons.
2. **The work matters.** They are then engaged in a campus-wide scavenger hunt where they work in teams to familiarize themselves with the amenities of their new work environment, meet important team members, and learn the history of the company. They learn the impact they are making in the community by visiting the onsite company museum.
3. **I matter to them.** At the end of their first day, each hire learns the company story and values by receiving a copy of the book *Built from Scratch: How a Couple of Regular Guys Grew The Home Depot from Nothing to $30 Billion*. The book serves as a symbol of how the company will invest in them.

Research shows people's most vivid memories are drawn from when they were 16 to 25 years old. Psychologists call this phenomenon the "reminiscence bump."[9] The reason we remember our youth so well is because it's a time of firsts: a first romantic relationship, first time traveling without parents, first paycheck, and so on.

Not sure where to look for meaningful moments? Find the firsts. Turn a first sale, a first work anniversary, a first promotion, or a first million-dollar quarter into a moment when the team can come together to celebrate. Leaders are trained to solve problems, not to make moments. Keeping an eye out for the moments that need punctuation will take intentionality but will kindle a boost in belonging.

A Moment with Massive Impact

While it was his last, it was also his first.

On the last day at a previous job, Steven experienced a moment he'll never forget. All the senior leaders at the organization got together to share a very special and unexpected gift with him. The gift was passed from one person to the next, each sharing a heartfelt story about his work at the company and thanking him for his service. Once every person in the room had the chance to share, Steven was handed the gift.

It was an explosives container with personalized messages about how big of an *impact* he had made—very fitting coming from the mining company he worked for.

Like any employee, Steven had his ups and downs working for this employer. But what he remembers most about his time at the company is his last day. The day where he, experienced warmth from his team like he had never felt before. Steven is forever connected with those people in that moment.

Also, truth be told, Steven might not have been so anxious to leave the company if he had got to experience this moving moment sooner. So word to the wise, don't let the last day be the first time you create a meaningful moment for someone. Look for the moments on the first and last day and every day in between to reinvest in connections.

Drumming Up Powerful Moments

Another reason moments are so belonging-boosting is that they make people feel seen.

As a 10-year-old, Clint Pulver tapped everything. Like other high-energy kids, Pulver would tap his toes on the ground, tap his pencil on desks, and tap his fingers on any available surface. A quiet classroom was no place for tapping, so Pulver would get scolded regularly. Trips to the principal's office and other punishments couldn't stop his tapping.

One day Pulver's teacher, Mr. Jensen, asked him to stay after class ended.

"I've always believed a single moment can change a person's life. And this was one of those moments for me," said now 34-year-old Pulver about the moment he approached Mr. Jensen's desk.[10]

Instead of scolding Pulver, Mr. Jensen opened his desk drawer, reached in, and pulled out what would be Pulver's very first pair of drumsticks. Mr. Jensen then said, "You're not a problem; I think you're a drummer."

Since that moment, Pulver hasn't put down those sticks. He has been a professional drummer for over 20 years—touring, recording, and playing drums all over the world. He even used drumming to pay for his college education. All from a single moment when a teacher took the time to see the potential in front of him. The two are still connected all these years later. Imagine the strength of the connection that Pulver has with Mr. Jensen. Moments matter when they speak to who someone is.

As the flametender of your team, the flame is your key to spark opportunities for people to gather and experience meaningful moments together.

What moments can you create to reinvest in the connections with your team?

FREE PASS

To NOT Connect With Others

★ ★ ★ ★ ★ ★ ★ ★ ★ ★

Not valid for anyone at any age,
community, status, stage of life,
or work role.

If connecting with others had a free pass. There is no point in life
(age, stage, status) that exempts us from the need to connect with others.

Kindle the Momentum by Re-Narrowing

The sales of chewing gum have been mysteriously plunging for years.
In the last decade, sales have fallen by double digits.[11] Is poor marketing, health consciousness, or a bad economy to blame? No.

Smartphones are the culprit.

Impulse buys aren't happening as often in the checkout lines at
stores because people are distracted by their devices. Magazine sales
are also on the decline for the same reason.[12] One study found that 62
percent of people pulled out a device while waiting in line, and more
than 80 percent of those people whipped that device out in less than
20 seconds.[13]

With just a few seconds to spare, people will focus their attention
on their smartphone. When the alternative is less appealing, people
are turning to their devices. While not ideal or healthy, this is the new
reality and is likely impacting your team as well.

After leaders Narrow their team's focus on purpose, clear direction, and growth, they can kindle the momentum by using captivation to direct the team's attention on what's most important at work.
Captivation can inflame focus on the benefits of belonging.

Re-Narrowing on Purpose

For over 10 years, Ryan has had the pleasure of speaking to thousands of audience members around the globe. Every time he takes the stage, he is instantly competing with hundreds of emails, texts, news alerts, sports scores, social media notifications, and Candy Crush for their attention. However, never once has he asked an audience to turn off or put away their devices.

Why? Because it's his responsibility as a communicator to earn their attention. His content has to be more gripping than the next post from their favorite Instagram presenter. His delivery has to be more dynamic than a sports highlight.

Attention can no longer be expected, it must be earned. How can you earn it? Storytelling.

People still have strong attention spans. In fact, the top three highest grossing movies of all time (*Avatar*, *Avengers: Endgame*, and *Titanic*) have an average run time of three hours. A well-crafted story captivates.

In Chapter 9, we discussed the importance of narrowing your team's focus on purpose because a shared purpose sheds loneliness. To kindle the momentum of a purpose-driven team, invite your team into a compelling story.

Stories compel people. Teams disengage when they are invited into a narrative void of unclear direction. Whenever a void exists, a good or bad leader will rise to fill it. If leaders don't lead their people somewhere desirable and prosperous, then someone might lead them somewhere undesirable and unfortunate. Leaders stand in the gap between success and failure.

How do leaders invite their team into a compelling story? Answer the three burning questions every follower secretly asks of a leader:

1. What are we doing?
2. Why are we doing it?
3. How do I fit in?

The answers to questions 1 and 2 should be the same across the team. However, the answer to question 3 needs to be unique and specific to each individual. Leaders should help each team member script their role in the story.

A leader's role is to be the guide, not the hero of the story. Leaders play the role of Luke Skywalker's guide, Yoda. Or Katniss Everdeen's guide, Haymitch Abernathy. When leaders remove themselves as the hero, it creates room to invite the team member to be a part of the story. In their own eyes, all individuals are the hero of their own life story and are looking for guides (leaders) to help them pursue worthwhile goals.

Inviting your team into a compelling story isn't a one-time event. It's a weekly (if not daily) task. There is so much distracting noise clamoring to captivate your team's attention. It's the job of a leader to turn down that noise and captivate using truthful and meaningful stories. One of the many hats effective leaders must wear is the "Chief Reminding Officer" hat. Consistently and continuously remind the team of the compelling story they are a part of and that they each have a unique and valuable role to play. When you think the team has heard the story enough times, keep reminding. This will kindle momentum toward lessening loneliness.

KINDLE EXAMPLE

Kroger, the largest supermarket company in the United States, has a very clear purpose: "Feed the human spirit by uplifting each other, our customers, and our communities." As a way of re-narrowing the organization's focus on purpose, Kroger has turned its purpose statement into an emblem that is used on name badges, aprons, and banners throughout the organization. Chelsea Cubero, district manager of Fred Meyer, a division of Kroger, starts every meeting with an "uplift story" about great customer service, a community connection, or an employee's twentieth wedding anniversary. In fact, every meeting at Kroger starts with an uplifting story as a way to reemphasize the purpose of the organization. When asked how purpose has kindled belonging at Kroger, Cubero said, "The purpose and culture of connection motivated me to get my Masters in Food Industry Leadership to further the impact Kroger is making in communities." No surprise that Cubero herself was uplifted by Kroger's Feed Your Future education benefit.

Meandering Minds Are a Menace

The average person has over 150 undone tasks on his or her mind at any given time.[14] From small tasks like needing to do the dishes to more major tasks like finding time to discuss a sensitive topic with a work colleague, these undone tasks are like open files in our brain.

With so many open files, it's overwhelming and extremely difficult to know what to focus on. Without focus, our minds will wander. Wandering minds make people unhappy and unproductive. According to Matt Killingsworth's, senior fellow at The Wharton School, University of Pennsylvania, Track Your Happiness project, our minds wander 47 percent of the time, but they almost always wander to negative thoughts and get stuck in rumination.[15] Ruminating and overwhelmed minds increase stress, decrease focus, and ultimately tank productivity.

A wandering mind isn't all bad, but an always wandering mind is concerning. Wandering too far leads to someone being lost. When people are lost, they become alienated, and loneliness soon follows.

To keep your team's minds from wandering too far off track and to kindle the momentum by re-narrowing their focus, let's turn to the worlds of Super Mario and Zelda.

Progress Spells Game Over for Loneliness

Video games are extremely captivating. Consider these staggering numbers:

▶ 2.81 billion video gamers are active worldwide and will likely grow to 3.07 billion by 2023.[16]

▶ 53 percent of 23- to 36-year-olds pay for gaming services, outpacing those who pay for cable TV (51 percent).[17]

▶ 8.8 billion hours (or over 334,855 years) of video game live streams were watched in the first quarter of 2021;[18] up from 3.6 billion hours two years previously.

Wouldn't you want this type of captivation and engagement from your team? Of course you would.

Why is gaming so captivating? It provides a sense of progress.

Gaming elements—like the progress bar or the story completion percentage—clearly inform players of where they started, how far they've come, and what's left to accomplish. The improvement of a game character's skills or gear enhancements also contribute to a gamer's sense of progress. You don't get a sense of progress from watching television.

Nearly 12,000 diary entries provided by 238 employees from seven different companies were rigorously analyzed by Teresa Amabile for her book *The Progress Principle: Using Small Wins to Ignite Joy, Engagement, and Creativity at Work*. Amabile discovered that what had the strongest impact on employee engagement was "Progress in meaningful work."

Conversely, the number one event that diminishes employee engagement is having setbacks and experiencing a feeling of moving backward in their work. The negative effect of setbacks at work can be two to three times greater than the positive effect of progress.

Amabile's research discovered that it's the everyday actions of managers (and coworkers) that can make the difference in catalyzing or inhibiting progress. Yet, when Amabile surveyed 600 managers about what has the strongest impact on employee engagement, they ranked "progress" last.

Leaders should search for progress. "Create a climate of attention, where everyone is looking for opportunities to support one another's progress and nourish the people who are making it," recommends

Amabile. And then acknowledge forward movement. Whether it's accomplishing a small win, overcoming an obstacle, learning a new skill, achieving a breakthrough, or completing a goal, leaders should recognize and reflect back to teams or individuals on their progress.

Acknowledge people's progress. This isn't an exotic concept, but it's too often underestimated and overlooked. We quickly categorize worker progress in the "part of the job" or "what they get paid for" bucket and move on to more pressing items. Progress is an abundant opportunity to kindle belonging, yet it is too often overlooked. That should end now, especially if your goal is to make people feel seen.

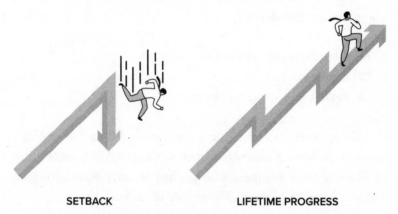

SETBACK   **LIFETIME PROGRESS**

Put setbacks in perspective. The valuable perspective of acknowledging lifetime progress.

The Top Employee Motivator for over 46 Years

Captivation follows appreciation.

After reviewing four similar studies of employee motivation conducted in 1946, 1980, 1986, and 1992, Carolyn Wiley, the department chair for Management, Leadership, and Human Resources at Roosevelt University, uncovered top responses such as "interesting work," "job security," "good wages," and "feeling of being in on things."[19] Yet over the 46 years of studies, only one answer was cited every time among the top two motivators:

"Full appreciation of work done."

According to Wiley, "More than 80 percent of supervisors claim they frequently express appreciation to their subordinates, while less than 20 percent of the employees report that their supervisors express appreciation more than occasionally." There is a massive appreciation gap at work.

In the past, the expectations surrounding recognition were yearly, quarterly, or at best, monthly—hence the popularity of "employee of the month" programs. Strive to extend appreciation on the fly; don't limit it to once a month, quarter, or year.

When extending appreciation for work done, leaders should communicate the following:

1. I recognize your good work.
2. I value you.
3. We're going places together.

During a recent client visit, a leader named Daniel shared how he overcame one of his most challenging management issues. One of Daniel's team members, George, had recently been testing his patience by being "defiant, difficult, and disrespectful."

Then an opportunity presented itself. To Daniel's surprise, George had successfully completed a special safety project where his work exceeded expectations. Rather than letting his resentment lead to inaction, Daniel made it a point to highlight the good work.

Daniel wrote George a letter. In the letter, Daniel highlighted George's specific actions that led to the project's success (1. I recognize your good work.). Then Daniel expressed how George served as a lynchpin in the project's success (2. I value you.). And then he shared the compelling story the company was working toward and how together they would make it reality (3. We're going places together.).

Not long after Daniel delivered the letter, George came into Daniel's office, closed the door, held up the letter, and said, "This is the single nicest thing anyone has ever done for me." Daniel's words of appreciation captivated George's head, heart, and hands. George's attitude, demeanor, focus, and overall engagement shifted significantly. Thrilled to see George transform in such a positive way, Daniel now makes it a priority to express appreciation for the work done by his entire team. Fill the air of your organization with appreciation and be rewarded with a captivated and all-in team.

With a torch in hand, flametenders can continue to illuminate what's important at work by re-narrowing the focus of the team. Flametenders have the power to bring light (purpose, vision, and hope) to once dark places. Light the way, leaders.

What will you use to captivate the team's attention and then re-narrow their focus on what's most important?

Conclusion

The reason the flametender is such a sacred role is because if the flame ever went out, the whole tribe would become vulnerable and suffer. The tribe relies on the flame being consistently lit.

Similarly for leaders, you must ensure the fire of your team remains lit and tend to it often to provide security, light, and connection. The upside of healthy, driven, and committed team members is worth the effort.

The trait of consistency is typically only talked about when it's lacking. Most people don't find themselves overly grateful that the train is consistently on time. But the one time it's inconsistent, it's the worst thing ever. Consistency isn't sexy, but it's central to long-term, healthy connections.

Which people in your life do you hold in high regard? It's likely the people who demonstrate consistency in their life. They can be counted on to return a phone call, show up when you need them, or follow through on their commitments.

Assurance, trust, comfort, and dependability all rest at the feet of consistency. When you know you can count on your next-door neighbor to check if you closed the garage door; your insurance company to cover damages; your Uber driver to get you to your destination; or a Coca-Cola to taste the same whether you're in Atlanta or Abu Dhabi, there is peace of mind.

Athletes, actors, musicians, business owners, parents, students, or anyone operating in the top echelon of their respective field got there by consistently executing behaviors that drive high performance. Are there any worthwhile achievements in life that don't require consistency? We can't think of any.

The embers you have created in the Look, Invest, and Narrow stages will require you to consistently Kindle them in order to generate the momentum necessary to keep loneliness suppressed.

Keep consistently stoking the fire of belonging, and soon it will be big enough that everyone will want to come and watch it burn.

KINDLE SUMMARY

Kindle the Momentum by re-Looking, re-Investing, and re-Narrowing so that progress can be maintained toward boosted belonging.

Application 1: Kindle the Momentum by Re-Looking

Reflective Question:
Is There a Structure in Place to Foster Continued Connection?

Adopt a structure like Citrix's Mental Health First Aiders or the US Army's Comprehensive Fitness Program or purchase the Connect Deck™ for your team at LessLonely.com/Deck.

Application 2: Narrow the Momentum by Re-Investing

Reflective Question:
What Moments Can You Punctuate in Order to Reinvest in Relationships?

Search for the "first" milestones of your team and create unique and memorable moments to punctuate them and unify the team.

Application 3: Kindle the Momentum by Re-Narrowing

Reflective Question:
How Can You Captivate and Re-Narrow Your Team's Attention?

Invite your team into a compelling narrative by answering the following questions: (1) What are we doing? (2) Why are we doing it? (3) How do I fit in? Then acknowledge progress and appreciate their work advancing that story.

11

BE INTERRUPTIBLE

All relationships have one law:
Never make someone feel alone,
especially when you're with them.

UNKNOWN

In March 2017, Robert Kelly became the original parent who was interrupted by his child while working from home. His interruption happened live on national television and has now been viewed hundreds of millions of times. It was the interruption seen around the world.

During a Skype interview, professor Robert Kelly was talking live to the BBC about the intricacies of politics on the Korean peninsula from his home in South Korea when his two young children walked in on the interview. Kelly's wife then came sliding into the frame (literally because she was sprinting down the hallway in her at-home socks), quickly grabbing the children to try to reduce the distraction, salvage the interview, and prevent any further live video bombing.

Talk show host Ellen DeGeneres said after watching the video, "I've never laughed so hard over a video about North Korea in my life."

Throughout the live interview clip, Kelly repeatedly says "my apologies" while closing his eyes as if to try to wish himself out of this extremely awkward moment. Following the interview, Kelly and his wife were embarrassed, frustrated, and devastated that they might never be asked back on the BBC. When asked if the BBC could share the video clip, Kelly responded via Twitter stating, "Is this the kinda thing that goes 'viral' and gets weird?"

It wasn't weird. In fact, most people found it wonderful.

The video of the interruption indeed went viral. So many people found themselves chuckling and empathizing with Kelly. Little did the world know that family interruptions during video calls would be the new normal in 2020 and beyond.

As we saw in Nicholas Epley's research earlier in the book, connecting with others—even strangers—makes us feel good whether we're the initiator or the receiver—and no matter if we're an introvert or extrovert. Most people wrongly predict that engaging with others won't be pleasant. Our brain misleads us because the research shows we have the most positive experiences when connecting with others.

Like Epley's research and much like Kelly's experience, people wrongly predict how restorative and positive an interruption can be and just how welcoming receivers of an interruption often are.

As the line between work and life continues to blur, we'll be met with more interruptions—more home interruptions at work and more work interruptions at home.

A Most Valuable Resource

The cost of interruptions is paid using one of the world's most precious resources. What is this most precious resource? Some might say time, money, or oil.

Those are indeed valuable resources; however, the resource we'll discuss in this chapter is even more valuable, and it's the key to getting the most of what you want out of work and life.

Let's set some context. One of the most valuable resources on the planet is oil. For centuries millions of people have dedicated their livelihoods to discovering it from the most remote parts of the globe. The two biggest oil companies in the United States are Chevron and Exxon Mobil. At the time of this writing, Chevron's market cap is around $210 billion and Exxon Mobil's is around $258 billion.

There is another company that mines something entirely different from oil that has an $897 billion dollar market cap. This highly sought-after and precious resource is in your possession. Right now. In fact, you're generously expending it as you read this book.

The world's most valuable resource is attention. Facebook, which has the $897 billion market cap, is in the attention-grabbing business, a business that is valued more than Chevron, Exxon Mobil, and the rest of the top eight oil and gas companies in the United States combined!

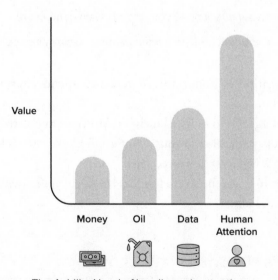

The Achilles' heel of loneliness is attention.

Extracting oil and natural gas is big business, but extracting attention from humans is an even more prolific endeavor. Attention is the new oil in today's economy. If attention is the most coveted resource, then someone who controls this resource would maintain great wealth and power.

What do wise people with access to the world's greatest resource do? Barter. They don't carelessly give away the resource. They trade it for other valuable items.

Similarly, to use your resource of attention wisely, protect it and trade it only for things of equal or greater value.

> Give your attention to a coworker. Gain trust.
>
> Give your attention to a stranger. Gain empathy.
>
> Give your attention to a task. Gain progress.
>
> Give your attention to work. Gain experience.
>
> Give your attention to a customer. Gain loyalty.
>
> Give your attention to learning. Gain knowledge.
>
> Give your attention to your breath. Gain composure.
>
> Give your attention to a team member. Gain influence.

Your attention is important. Where you spend your attention defines you.

If your goal is to move a lonely workforce from isolated to all in, you must pay attention to your attention. Because when is loneliness lessened? When attention is received.

Want to make the world less lonely? Wield your attention well. Undivided. Fully.

Today's Unfortunate Dichotomy

Attention seems to be at the crux of today's new age dichotomy. The dichotomy between being excessively busy—allowing our attention to be grabbed by the slightest of dings, pings, or rings, and being painstakingly bored—where we allow our attention to divert to anything that makes us forget we're idle.

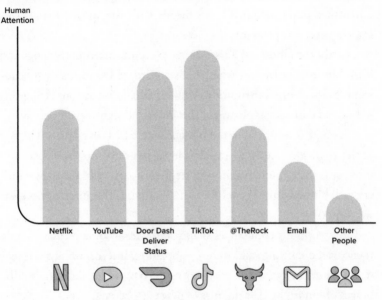

What has people's attention. Pay attention to what has your attention.

Have you considered allowing the unexpected and the unpredicted to collide with your busy life, welcoming it with open arms?

This is the art of interruptibility.

Interruptibility is the ability to be interrupted.

The timeless classic, *A Christmas Carol* by Charles Dickens, provides a glimpse into the transformational power of interruptibility.

The story opens with Ebenezer Scrooge sitting in his counting-house where he angrily shouts "Bah! Humbug!" at his nephew who drops by. This interruption was unexpected.

Later that evening, Scrooge is interrupted by the ghost of his dead partner, Jacob Marley, who informs Scrooge that three spirits will be visiting him. This interruption was startling.

Next the Ghost of Christmas Past interrupts Scrooge and escorts him on a journey where he relives the moment his former fiancé,

Belle, leaves him because his desire for money outweighs his ability to love another. This interruption was tragic.

The Ghost of Christmas Present interrupts Scrooge next to unveil what Christmas will look like that year. Scrooge finds his nephew's Christmas party delightful and pleads with the spirit to stay. This interruption was pleasant.

Lastly, the Ghost of Christmas Yet to Come interrupts Scrooge and leads him to a graveyard where he is confronted with his own headstone. Scrooge urges the spirit to alter his fate, promising to change his selfish and curmudgeonly ways. This interruption was eye-opening.

Scrooge is returned to the present where he is overcome with joy at the chance to redeem himself. He rushes out into the streets and interrupts the Cratchit family, his nephew's party, and other bystanders with his newfound generosity and kindness. This interruption was welcomed by all.

Interruptions come in all shapes and sizes—some pleasant, some tragic, some startling, and some eye-opening. Interruptions often represent a turning point in a great story. The basis of breakthroughs. The hinges of hindsight. The premise of new perspectives.

Avoiding the interruptions of life can turn the most well-intended person into a recluse and isolated from those around him or her by not seeming approachable.

The margin between a task at hand and an interruption is narrow yet bursting with opportunity. The margin holds potential to get mad, frustrated, or irritated. The margin also holds potential for character building, direction defining, enrichment of well-being, and belonging for all parties.

Scrooge filled his margin with "Bah! Humbugs!" until he finally realized that most of life is about people. People he decided to create more space for. Creating the space for others is interruptibility.

Healthy and happy leaders are interruptible. They don't let tasks and deadlines override their relationships. They have the necessary margin and self-permission to say no to the urgent and lean into the important. If you wish to be a memorable and impactful leader of people, the discipline of being interruptible is a must.

A Swift Blow to Loneliness

The Less Loneliness Framework™ solutions covered in the previous four chapters are the formula to boost belonging and sustain a lower level of loneliness among your team. However, we decided to include this "Be Interruptible" chapter at the end because it's something you can commit to today, practice routinely, and hopefully maintain throughout your less loneliness journey. It's more of a mindset shift than a tactical strategy. It's something that will serve you well at work and at home.

Considering that business is a leading modern cause of loneliness, practicing interruptibility will deliver a swift blow to loneliness. The decrease in loneliness is immediate for yourself because you're present and connecting with the person or situation in front of you, engaging more deeply with your sense of humanity. And it's immediately beneficial for the other party because people sense your presence and connection to them in the moment.

When asked, "What's the one thing I can do to lessen loneliness?" our answer is: be interruptible.

Don't Lose Focus of Focus

Interruptions mostly get a bad rap. And for good, research-based reasons.

According to the *International Journal of Stress Management*, employees who experienced frequent interruptions reported 9 percent higher rates of exhaustion and a 4 percent increase in physical ailments such as migraines or backaches.[1] A *Journal of Experimental Psychology* study found that people make twice as many errors after a brief interruption of about 2.8 seconds.[2] According to University of California Irvine research, it takes an average of 23 minutes and 15 seconds to get back to a task after an interruption.[3]

Interruptions are costly. Interruptions can also be stressful, but so is busyness. Assuming your to-do list is more important than what your team needs from you is a fast track to a lonely workforce.

Interruptibility doesn't mean throwing focus, productivity, and priorities out the window. It actually means the opposite. Being interruptible is about intentionally placing your focus, productivity, and priority in the right place and on the organization's number one asset, people. Parting with your most precious resource, your attention, makes others feel seen, appreciated, and included. Productivity is not about squeezing people, but about showing up for them.

Leadership focused on people requires a willingness to be interrupted. Leave never drifting off task to the robots. Drifting off task and wading into the lives of others is best suited for a strong leader like you.

The Plight of Interruption for Leaders

Leaders are the least interruptible workers, and yet they are the ones who need to be interrupted most. The more important and serious you consider yourself, the less open you are to detours and interruptions.

Three in four employees see effective communication as the number one leadership attribute.[4] Yet, less than one in three employees feel like their leaders communicate efficiently.

Breaking our attention from the email inbox and directing it toward people to really hear what they are trying to convey is interruptibility. This discipline strengthens our relationship with others and helps us to communicate more effectively because we are fully receiving the information, both said and unsaid.

Leaders are often seduced by the perception of "having it all together." They are tempted by the allure of "having all the answers." Leaders place these unwarranted obligations on their own shoulders. The unnecessary pressure to be everything to the team causes well-intended leaders to not listen, dominate conversations, downplay nonurgent employee issues, lock themselves in an office, or hide behind back-to-back meetings. All these actions communicate that leaders are not interruptible.

If you're wrestling with the idea of being interruptible, you may be placing your reputation over what your team actually needs from you: your presence.

Measuring Your Level of Interruptibility

During a conversation, not maintaining eye contact, not listening (or only thinking about what you're going to say next), not making the conversation about the other person, or consistently using phrases like "I'm too busy" are all telltale and easily recognized signs of not being interruptible.

A more important and much more difficult question that leaders must ask themselves to uncover their interruptibility is: Am I growing more or less irritable? How irritable are you when you are interrupted? Your reaction the moment you feel your attention being drawn away from the task at hand is revealing. What you feel in that split second is your gateway into understanding your interruptibility.

When interrupted, is your urge to build up your defenses, mentally shout "Bah! Humbug!" or quickly scan your brain for an excuse that will get you back to the task at hand? If so, you are not interruptible. When interrupted, if your urge is to lean into the interruption with anticipation and genuine curiosity, you are interruptible.

Pay attention to the irritability of your interruptions.

In college, Steven's favorite professor was Dr. Robert Husband. His teaching style was untraditional. Instead of sitting in rows of desks, his students sat in a circle of chairs. Instead of having midterm and final exams, students had comprehensive projects. And instead of having defined office hours, he had an open-door policy.

During Steven's senior year, a bit unsure of what his plan was after college, he went to see Dr. Husband. Because he was no longer his student, Steven wasn't sure if he would be open to making the time to chat. His door was open, so he decided to interrupt. He peeked in, and with a big smile Dr. Husband said, "Steven, great to see you, my friend." He closed the book he was reading, swung his chair away from the computer monitor on his desk, and told Steven to have a seat. It took him less than a second to usher Steven into his office with open arms, ready to chat about whatever was on Steven's mind.

Two years after college Steven had a work trip that required him to visit his alma mater. Having irregularly stayed in touch with Dr. Husband, Steven was not a stranger, but by no means a close friend. Out of the blue Steven decided to call him. He left a message letting Dr. Husband know that he was going to be in town and was eager to grab a cup of coffee with him, if, of course, he had the time. It wasn't five minutes later that Dr. Husband called back so they could arrange a meeting.

Over coffee they spent two hours chatting about all the professional activities Steven was focused on at the time. He asked Steven lots of questions, shared lots of perspective, and challenged Steven to rethink the professional journey he was on. He told Steven that he did not seem enthusiastic about the work he was doing and recommended a different path. He told Steven about a grad school program that he should consider, saying, "It would be the best next step in your promising career." That very grad school program eventually changed Steven's life.

Dr. Husband put his students first. He welcomed interruptions with open arms and was a beloved professor for it.

How fast does your chair swivel in the direction of an interruption? How quick are you to answer or return a phone call? How fast do your headphones come off when someone needs you? Your answers to these questions are insightful indicators of just how interruptible you currently are.

Welcome the Outside

Leaders should point their people to a better future. But identifying "better" is difficult because it's subjective and "better" can be quickly outdone in today's fast-moving marketplace.

Every industry has shared assumptions that fuel the prevailing model of how things have always been done. Today a "this is how we've always done it" mindset is a slippery slope to irrelevance. Right now, somewhere in the world, someone is messing with the rules of your industry's prevailing model. Someone is pioneering new approaches under the safe canopy of anonymity, getting ready to strike with an improved product or service and completely interrupt your world.

Mobile technology and ubiquitous connectivity have enabled accelerated disruption. The 33-year average tenure of companies on the S&P 500 in 1965 narrowed to 20 years in 1990 and is forecast to shrink to 14 years by 2026.[5] At the current churn rate, about half of today's S&P 500 firms will be replaced over the next 10 years. Now more than ever, the prevailing model causes leaders to get complacent, industries to get stuck, and companies to go under.

The benefits of interruptibility extend beyond lessening loneliness and boosting belonging among a team. Interruptibility allows leaders to find the necessary innovation to stay relevant in today's high-flux marketplace.

According to Al Ries, author of *Focus: The Future of Your Company Depends on It*, "The next generation product [idea or solution] almost never comes from the previous generations." Fresh eyes often bring the best ideas. Our natural human tendency is to deny our ignorance and focus on the familiar and comprehensible things we can control. But effective leaders face their ignorance in order to discover the uniquely better solutions that will keep their company unstuck.

An effective way to face your ignorance and discover uniquely better solutions is by listening to outsiders. Listen to those outside of your organization, industry, and generation. Outsiders aren't bound by the same assumptions and prevailing models that are likely to hold your organization or industry back.

You know what's full of outsider-ness? Interruptions. Interruptions are literally something unexpected from the outside that disrupts your current reality. A new hire dropping by your office with a novel idea to impact the business is the type of unexpected interruption that reveals to a leader the prevailing model that can be holding back the team or organization.

Interruptions from uniformity, work routines, and thinking patterns can bring the much-needed perspective to stay cutting-edge in today's fast-evolving marketplace. And that same interruption can provide enough of a break from the interrupted task that you revisit the task with refreshed eyes. Research proves the benefits of stepping away from a project or task to then reengage later with greater focus, energy, and perspective.

A coupon valid anytime, anywhere, for anyone.

Interruptions are a free ticket to a renewed perspective, an uncovered blind spot, and possibly a better future. So, the next time you are interrupted in the middle of a task, a routine, or a thought—smile and know this could lead you to your next big breakthrough.

How to Be Interruptible

To reiterate, interruptibility is the ability to be interrupted. Here are some suggestions on how to be gracefully, genuinely, and strategically interruptible.

Ensure people feel safe. As discussed in Chapter 8, psychological safety allows people to freely ask questions, raise concerns, and pitch ideas without unnecessary repercussions. A key to being interruptible is to make sure the team feels safe to interrupt without consequence.

Set expectations. Identify any absolute distraction-free times and communicate those to the team. Set the expectation with yourself that interruptions will occur every day. Consider leaving extra margin at the end of the day or week to tackle any priorities that got rescheduled due to interruptions.

Transition well. If the task at hand requires you to complete your thought, ask the interrupter (with a smile) for a moment to transition your full attention. Knowing they are about to receive your undivided attention will help people to wait patiently. Consider making a quick note to yourself about where you need to pick back up so you can mentally transition fully to the situation in front of you. If you absolutely can't be bothered, present a clear path to the interrupter to circle back with you such as "email me" or "let's meet before tomorrow morning's meeting."

Provide a preview. Model for others the posture you take with interruptions. Examples include:

▶ Asking good questions, responding positively when people speak up, or actively bringing people into the conversation during a meeting all suggest you welcome new ideas.

▶ Speaking little or last during conversations or meetings suggests you are much more interested in hearing from others than in dominating conversations.

▶ Be wary of your body language. Frantically typing on your computer, rushing to and from the break room, and constantly wearing headphones are subtle indicators to others that you are not to be interrupted.

Clarify your role. To gain clarity during an interruption, start by clarifying the role the interrupter would like you to play. Simply ask, "Would you like me to share, fix, or understand?"

- ▶ Share: Listen to share your advice or opinion.
- ▶ Fix: Listen to get to the root of the issue and then provide a fix.
- ▶ Understand: Listen to understand the situation, empathize with the individual, and unlock a new perspective.

Knowing your role during the interruption provides helpful guardrails for how you are to engage in the unexpected situation. For more info on each listening style, revisit Chapter 8 where we cover each more in depth.

Know when to cut it short. If you either get the sense that the interruption topic requires more time than you have or if the interrupter cannot clarify what exactly she needs from you, then graciously end the interruption. To ensure you conclude graciously, use the term "Forgive me." This implies you wish you could help or give your full attention but the current circumstances don't allow for it. An example might be, "Forgive me. I must get back to my prep work for tomorrow's presentation. Contact my assistant with what you specifically need from me."

If interruptions are negatively impacting more people than you, such as in a large group setting, don't stand for the interruptions. Address interrupters in private, quickly, following the incident.

Leaders are susceptible to not being willing to take certain actions for one employee unless they can do it for the whole team. Don't let that perfectionist mindset hold you back from showing up for those who need you. At times you'll have to do for one what you wish you could do for all. Don't get stalled by the lie that you have to be available for everyone. Just be ready, today and tomorrow, to be available for someone.

Conclusion

The mark of a confident, compassionate, and admired leader is interruptibility. Responding to others' need for your time, energy, and focus is nourishing for relationships.

In fact, relationships are stronger when two people respond to each other's requests for connection. Psychologist John Gottman calls these requests for connection "bids." According to Gottman's research, married couples who regularly turned toward (or engaged) the bid [that is, who responded to this request] versus those who regularly turned away from the bid had much stronger connections.[6] Gottman found specifically that couples who had divorced after a six-year follow-up had "turn-toward bids" 33 percent of the time. Only 3 in 10 of their bids for connection were met with acknowledgment or support. The couples who were still together after six years had "turn-toward bids" 87 percent of the time. Nine in ten of their bids for connection were met with acknowledgment or support.

Interruptibility enriches relationships. Choose people over all the pings, dings, and rings. Trade convenience for connection. Trade your too-important mindset for a relationship.

Move a lonely workforce from isolated to all in by making your attention available to others. And if attention is the planet's most valuable resource, then focus is one of the most valuable skills. In an instantaneous and ever-changing world, the ability to direct and maintain one's attention is a superpower.

Be the hero your team deserves by focusing your attention on them.

Superman

Super Strength, Flight,
X-Ray Vision, etc.

Wonder Woman

Super Strength, Speed,
Healing Factor, etc.

Black Panther

Super Strength, Reflexes,
Hand-to-Hand Combat, etc.

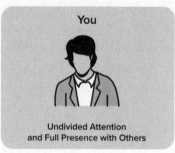

You

Undivided Attention
and Full Presence with Others

Look, up in the sky. It's a bird! It's a plane. It's . . . you!

CONCLUSION

How wonderful it is that nobody
must wait a single moment
before starting to improve the world.
ANNE FRANK

As he gazed out at the quiet and pristine Alaskan landscape, Christopher McCandless couldn't shake the feeling that something was missing. He had accomplished everything he sought to achieve, yet there remained a deep yearning. He took pen to paper to capture his thoughts in that moment. It would be his final words—words we can all live by.

McCandless was an American adventurer and subject of the international bestselling book *Into the Wild*, a nonfiction book by Jon Krakauer that was later made into a full-length feature film. After graduating with honors from Emory University, McCandless gave his life savings of $24,500 to a poverty-fighting charity, abandoned his car, burned any remaining cash in his wallet, and began traveling across North America.[1]

Seeking an increasingly nomadic and isolated lifestyle, McCandless hitchhiked to Alaska in April 1992. He headed down the snow-covered Stampede Trail, hiking for 28 miles into the deep wilderness of central Alaska. The only supplies he had were 10 pounds of rice, a .22 caliber rifle, several boxes of rifle rounds, a camera, and some reading materials—including a field guide to the region's edible plants.

At the beginning of his journey, McCandless wrote, "Society you're a crazy breed, hope you're not lonely without me." He was determined to disconnect from society, living simply off the land by himself. Finally, he found the isolation he had been searching for his entire adult life. On the eastern bank of the Sushana River, he discovered a rusted, abandoned Fairbanks City Transit System bus and decided to make it his new home. This now famous bus was removed on June 18, 2020, because too many tourists were endangering themselves—including deaths—as they trekked into the Alaskan wilderness to find it. Needless to say, McCandless's new home was remote, surrounded by treacherous terrain.

While living out of the bus, McCandless foraged for edible roots and berries, shot an assortment of game—including a moose—and kept a journal of his activities and reflections. Eventually, he got sick after ingesting a poisonous seed. Weak and in need of help, he tried to retreat back into town but found his route blocked by a river raging with snow-melt. Dejected, he retreated to the bus, where he eventually starved to death after approximately 113 days. A few weeks later, a moose hunter found McCandless and notified authorities. They soon recovered his body, his belongings, photos, and a journal.

The final words McCandless penned in his journal read, "Happiness is only real when shared." McCandless achieved everything he *thought* he longed for in life. He thought disconnection from others would quench his yearning spirit, but the thing the soul thirsts most for is connection.

Seeing a sunrise, watching a moose drink from a river, or hearing the rain patter on a metal roof doesn't have the same significance without someone to share it with. Per his unique experience and final words, his happiness was nonexistent because he was alone.

No matter how hard an exterior you have, or how task-focused, introverted, or results-driven you are, at the end of the day, we pine for people. No matter the barriers we intentionally or unintentionally put between ourselves and others, life is better together.

Work Is Better Together

As a leader, you've probably wanted to disconnect from people. At times, the issues of the team seem too complex and daunting, and you'd rather kick them all off the bus and retreat into the wilderness on your own.

That's OK. You're allowed to feel that way. Besides, solitude is healthy. Just don't go too far. Your team needs you. And you need them. Together we heal. Together we perform better. Together we belong.

As Johann Hari writes in his book *Lost Connections: Why You're Depressed and How to Find Hope*, "Loneliness isn't the physical absence of other people, . . . it's the sense that you're not sharing anything that matters with anyone else."[2]

Did a promotion even happen if you didn't share and celebrate it with someone? Eventually, the new office and team will make it real, but the achievement rings hollow without others involved. The highest of highs in life include people. The lowest of lows in life exclude people.

Belonging is the gift your team needs, whether they know it or not. It's also the gift your bottom line deserves.

Loneliness isn't a black eye, it's a birthmark that we all have—one that comes in different shapes and sizes. Since we all have it, there's no sense in hiding it.

So, gather your team close and share in the struggle, vision, and wins together. Share your time, appreciation, and attention. Share to shed loneliness.

Lessen Loneliness in 0.6, 1, and 5

Wolves hunt more successfully in packs, penguins share warmth in huddles, fish swim in schools for protection, and birds migrate in flocks to conserve energy. Together animals accomplish more. The same is true for humans.

Together animals achieve more. We are simply better together.

Our ancient ancestors gathered together to stay safe from predators. Once they felt safe, they could redirect their efforts toward solving the next problem: in their case, being cold. Together they learned
to control fire. Then on to the next problem. And so on.

Together humanity has solved So. Many. Problems. We get to
live in a world that's better than it's ever been, thanks to the problems
solved by previous generations.

Today your team gathers for the same reasons as our ancestors: to
stay safe and solve problems—the problems of customers, clients, and
users. And to stay safe from much different threats. They are no longer as obvious as weather, large animals, or disease, but inconspicuous
threats, like loneliness, depression, and meaninglessness.

You as the leader are at the helm to address these new threats.
Because if the team isn't safe, they can't readily solve the problem at
hand, let alone the inevitable looming problems out in the not-so-
distant future. The yoke of vision-casting, belonging-building, and
action-spurring rests on the shoulders of leaders.

But don't fret. You're now aware and equipped to address one of
the biggest looming threats to your team: loneliness. To improve your
team's situation, you just need you. No sweeping change management
initiative is needed. No management approval. No team buy-in. Just
you making a commitment right here and right now to create more
belonging among your team.

As we covered in this book, your commitment can take as little
as 0.6, 1, and 5.

- ▶ 0.6 minutes (or 40 seconds) is how long it takes for loneliness
  to lessen during a two-person interaction.
- ▶ 1 person is the number of work friends it takes to feel less
  lonely.
- ▶ 5 minutes is the amount of time it takes in a team meeting to
  share something personal.

Moving your team from isolated to all in requires less than you
might expect. What it does fully require is vigilance. A consistent

mentality of zero tolerance for a lonely workforce. Every person on your team is one person away from a stronger sense of belonging. Might you be that person to deliver for them?

The world is growing lonelier. If we fail to fight for more belonging, we will continue to fracture apart. Instead of banding together to solve important problems, we'll retreat into isolation growing ill, bitter, and unfulfilled. Building stronger communities and stronger companies will require action. Action from you. Action from me. Action from all of us. You can only control you, so start there.

Take Connection to the Bank

Imagine you spent a year of your life building a world-shaping new invention. You toiled away for months in your garage, forgoing regular showers, eating more Cheez-Its than anyone ever should, and creating pet names for your tools to cope with your creeping insanity. When you finally emerged from your cave of creation, who would be the first person you'd share your groundbreaking invention with?

To turn your happiness into something real, you'd be eager to share your achievement with a partner, roommate, parent, son, daughter, or spouse.

Our friend from Chapter 1, Don Wetzel, spent months inventing the world's first ATM. Once it was complete, he was ecstatic to share his creation with his wife, Eleanor.

We imagine that conversation in 1969 went something like this:

> **Don:** "The ATM is finally complete! I can't wait to show you! Come try it out."
>
> **Eleanor:** "I'll pass"
>
> **Don:** "Huh!? Why?"
>
> **Eleanor:** "Because it will never smile back at you."
> (Eleanor actually *said that!*)[3]

Despite ignoring her husband's life's work, Don and Eleanor are still happily married and living in Dallas, Texas, as of this writing. And to this day, Eleanor has never used an ATM even though her husband invented it. "I like my little bank on the corner and I like the tellers," she said.[4]

Eleanor has found one way to be more connectable by trading convenience for connection.

You should too.

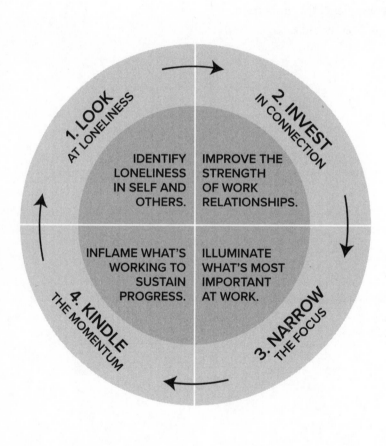

OVERVIEW AND APPLICATIONS

Here is an overview of the four steps of the Less Loneliness Framework™ and the corresponding applications to move your teams from isolated to all in.

1. Look at Loneliness

Identify loneliness in self and others.

Summary: Look at loneliness to gain awareness, look inward to gain perspective, and look outward to gain understanding of where you can lessen loneliness.

Application #1: Look at Loneliness

Reflective Question: *Are You Curious About Loneliness?*

Discuss loneliness as a broad topic with close, nonwork friends or family members. Get their perspective on how they see loneliness showing up at work.

Application #2: Look Inward

Reflective Question: *Do You Have a Healthy Personal Relationship with Loneliness?*

1. **Self-Assess: Look to see what you currently can't see.** Take five minutes to complete the "Loneliness Self-Assessment" highlighted in Chapter 7 or visit LessLonely.com/ SelfAssessment.
2. **Schedule Solitude: Look for opportunities to be still.** Schedule time to isolate your mind from the inputs of other minds in order to freely process, ponder, and/or plan.
3. **Speak Up and Speak Out: Look for the moments to share and be heard.** Share a story with someone at work about a time you experienced loneliness.
4. **Seek Support: Look for people who can help you shoulder the burden.** Identify a trusted advisor (spouse, board member, mentor, or coach), schedule a 30-minute call, and openly share your loneliness journey.

Application #3: Look Outward

Reflective Question: *Are You Aware How Lonely Your Team Is?*

Review the "10 Identifiers of Lonely Workers" in Chapter 7 and write down the names of any team members who meet a few of the qualities. Want more help benchmarking your team and crafting a custom plan to strengthen their connections? Visit LessLonely.com/

Assessment to take The Team Connection Assessment™ and/or share it with your team.

Invest in Connection

Improve the strength of work relationships.

Summary: Invest in connections that are safe, personal, and team-wide so that workers feel connected to their leader and teammates.

Application 1: Invest in Safe Connections

Reflective Question: *Does Psychological Safety Exist on Your Team?*

Start creating more psychological safety among your team members by conducting proportional conversations where every team member has equal opportunity to speak. And in every meeting you attend this week, practice speaking last.

Application 2: Invest in Personal Connections

Reflective Question: *Do You Demonstrate Emotional Intelligence During Conversations with Employees?*

Strive to be relatable to your team by sharing your story and asking to hear a story. Consistently, ask yourself or a trusted advisor, *Am I relatable? What's it like to be on the other side of me?*

Application 3: Invest in Team Connections

Reflective Question: *Are You Actively Facilitating Opportunities for Your Team to Connect with Each Other?*

Create more opportunities for the team to see the human behind the job. Have a "bring your kids or parents to work" day, provide a virtual tour of your home office, or carve out five minutes each meeting to have someone share a personal anecdote.

3. Narrow the Focus

Illuminate what's most important at work.

Summary: Narrow the focus on purpose, clear direction, and growth so that worker engagement overpowers loneliness.

Application 1: Narrow the Team's Focus on Purpose

Reflective Question: *Does Your Team Know the Impact of Their Work?*

Identify the beneficiaries of the labor of each team member. Take an interrogative approach to understand who exactly is benefiting from the team's work by asking "Why?" five times.

Application 2: Narrow the Team's Focus on Clear Direction

Reflective Question: *Does Your Team Have Clarity to Act Swiftly?*

Lead using context, not control. Provide your team with the necessary information so that they can act and decide on their own.

Application 3: Narrow the Focus on Growth

Reflective Question: *Is Your Team Actively Learning and Developing?*

Encourage on-the-job learning by delegating tasks. Have team members run a meeting, lead a presentation, or train a new hire in order to experience new learning and starve loneliness.

4. Kindle the Momentum

Inflame what's working to sustain progress.

Summary: Kindle the momentum by re-Looking, re-Investing, and re-Narrowing so that progress can be maintained toward boosted belonging.

Application 1: Kindle the Momentum by Re-Looking

Reflective Question: *Is There a Structure in Place to Foster Continued Connection?*

Adopt a structure like Citrix's Mental Health First Aiders or the US Army's Comprehensive Fitness Program or purchase the Connect Deck™ for your team at LessLonely.com/Deck.

Application 2: Narrow the Momentum by Re-Investing

Reflective Question: *What Moments Can You Punctuate in Order to Re-Invest in Relationships?*

Search for the "first" milestones of your team and create unique and memorable moments to punctuate them and unify the team.

Application 3: Kindle the Momentum by Re-Narrowing

Reflective Question: *How Can You Captivate and Re-Narrow Your Team's Attention?*

Invite your team into a compelling narrative by answering the following questions: (1) What are we doing? (2) Why are we doing it? (3) How do I fit in? Then acknowledge progress and appreciate their work advancing that story.

MENTAL HEALTH RESOURCES

While the actions discussed in this book will lessen loneliness among a workforce, sometimes professional help is required. If you or others need help from trained mental health specialists, please explore the resources below.

For Individuals

If you or someone you know is dealing with chronic loneliness, depression, or other mental health issues, use the following free 24/7 support resources.

- ▶ **Crisis Text Line: Text "BRAVE" to 741-741.** Text from anywhere, anytime, about any type of crisis. A real-life, trained crisis counselor will receive the text and respond, all from a secure online platform.

▶ **National Suicide Prevention Lifeline: Call 1-800-273-TALK
(8255).** Call from anywhere. You will be routed to the closest
crisis center in your area. Call for yourself or someone you care
about. Your call is free and confidential.

For Organizations

Visit ActiveMinds.org. Active Minds @Work is the nation's premier
nonprofit organization supporting mental health awareness and education at work.

ACKNOWLEDGMENTS

Achievements are never unaccompanied. We are all standing on the shoulders of those who went before us. And if you're lucky, you have someone personally invested in your work. In our case, we have a whole tribe.

Ryan Jenkins

Ashley, thank you for always prioritizing and cultivating our connection. You work tirelessly to create an environment where our family can feel safe, loved, and encouraged. We are healthier and happier because of you. Without you as my dependable anchor, my solitary writing would be unfruitful.

Ella, Landon, and Meyer, the togetherness we experience while singing and dancing to Drew Holcomb and the Neighbors' song "Family" is pure bliss. Belonging with the three of you is one of the greatest joys of my life. I cannot wait to continue to build each of our connections. I love you.

Bauer, your ability to comfort and support without saying a word is appreciated beyond words. Ella wanted to dedicate this book to you, thanks for understanding, buddy.

Mom and Dad, as far back as I can remember you have gone to great lengths to connect me to a loving family, worthwhile values, and my unique strengths. I'm forever grateful. Thank you for setting an example of belonging that can be carried forward for generations.

Thank you, Jonathan Sommers, JT Maradik, and Ahsan Shah, for your insightful and impactful feedback on this book. And more important thank you for your friendship. I treasure it.

Thank you, Adam Langhals and Brian Schumpp, for lending an ear and eye on all my projects. And for always carving out the time to reconnect and create rich memories.

Jennifer Kahnweiler, thank you for being one of the first people to get me connected in the speaker and author community. You were also one of the first established authors that saw me as a writer. Your kind words and belief helped deliver this book. Waldo Waldman, thank you for generously illuminating the path for me, first with speaking and then by sharing your writing journey. Thomas Koulopoulos, thank you for being an early advocate for this book and calling me when my writing column hit a dead end. Your consoling meant the world. Scott Miller, you were the impetus for my writing career after you recommended that I pursue a career in thought leadership at Steinkeller's in Oxford, Ohio. I'll never forget that moment. Thank you.

Steven Van Cohen, my coauthor and business partner, I kept waiting for the day or chapter where we'd butt heads and want to throw in the towel. That day never came. Collaborating with you was effortless, fun, and rewarding. You make me a better writer. Looking forward to the next book, my friend.

Steven Van Cohen

Jen, you make me feel seen. Thank you for loving me the way that you do. Our connection is what allows me to be my very best self. Without your strength, courage, brilliance, and warmth, I could not do what I do. You hold down the fort, provide me the tough feedback, and make me feel like I can do anything. The gratitude I owe to you is never ending. You are my most treasured connection and the person I love with everything I've got.

Claudia and Colette, your endless energy kindles my fire. Be it playing cheetah police, "keepy uppy," copycat, or Disney karaoke, you always know how to include me in your magic. I am so in awe of your beauty, wisdom, curiosity, and kindness. Thank you for allowing me to be your Dad. I love you more than you will ever know.

Mom, you have been my guiding light since the day I was born. Watching you nurture the connections in your life is a master class in how to sustain meaningful relationships. You have been my biggest cheerleader, my most ferocious supporter, and an inexhaustible optimism replenisher. I owe so much of my success to you, thank you for everything.

Dad, Kevin, Laura, and David, you have been the best family anyone could ask for. Thank you for a lifetime of connection, best friendships, and a memory bank that is almost at capacity. I am so proud to call you my people. I love you so much.

Ellis Ritz, my first business partner and dear friend. You have taught me to shoot for the stars. None of this would have been possible without you. Your "gamble" to bet on me 12 years ago has helped shape the man that I am today. I am forever grateful for all that you've done.

Ryan Jenkins, my other "better half." Building with you has been one of the most rewarding adventures in my life. You, my friend, are incredible. I am so proud of what we have done and look forward to what the next chapter will bring. Thank you for all that you do.

Ryan and Steven

Marilyn Allen, our literary agent, thank you for reconsidering working with us even though your workload told you otherwise. Your experience and expertise made all of this possible. Thank you, Kevin Commins, for helping this important work take shape. Thank you, Amy Li, your vision for this book and passion for addressing mental health at work inspired us from the first time we met. Thank you to our editor, Donya Dickerson, for helping us traverse the complex terrain of book publishing and championing this book the whole way. Thank you to the entire McGraw Hill team for betting on a risky project and going to great lengths to normalize the "loneliness" conversation at work.

Erica Keswin, thank you for writing books that pave the way for more humanity at work and graciously sharing your tricks of the trade. Curt Steinhorst, thank you for pushing the envelope on how to engage audiences and unabashedly sharing how others can do the same. And thank you for making crucial introductions when this project was just budding. John Monahon, thank you for your advice on how to make sure the concepts in this book can be widely shared. Christine Seibold, thank you for anchoring the text in research.

Thank you to the following who gave generously of their time and insight: Felicia White, Deep Mahajan, Eric Lane, Emilie Schouten, Dr. Louise Hawkley, Zack Rubinstein, Darren Good, Josh Turner, Shandee Bowman, Nicos Marcou, Donna Kimmel, Pamay Bassey, Lynda Brown-Ganzert, Derek Lundsten, Dr. Steven Cole, Carter Cast, Shari Perez-Conaway, Anthony Silard, Joseph Loch, David Salyers, Dr. Robin Arthur, and Chelsea Cubero.

NOTES

Introduction

1. CBC, "The Grizzlies Lacrosse Team Is Still Going Strong," February 12, 2020, https://www.cbc.ca/television/higharctichaulers/the-grizzlies-lacrosse-team-is-still-going-strong-1.5456255.
2. CBC, "The Grizzlies: 15 Things About the Groundbreaking New Canadian Film," April 18, 2019, https://www.cbc.ca/radio/q/blog/the-grizzlies-15-things-about-the-groundbreaking-new-canadian-film-1.5101737.
3. Julianne Holt-Lunstad, Timothy B. Smith, Mark Baker, Tyler Harris, and David Stephenson, "Loneliness and Social Isolation as Risk Factors for Mortality: A Meta-Analytic Review," *Perspectives on Psychological Science*, March 11, 2015, https://journals.sagepub.com/doi/abs/10.1177/1745691614568352?journalCode=ppsa.

Chapter 1

1. Kim Zetter, "Sept. 2, 1969: First U.S. ATM Starts Doling out Dollars," *Wired*, September 2, 2010, https://www.wired.com/2010/09/0902first-us-atm/.
2. David Byrne, "Eliminating the Human," *MIT Technology Review*, August 15, 2017.
3. L. A. Peplau and D. Perlman, "Perspectives on Loneliness," in *Loneliness: A Sourcebook of Current Theory, Research and Therapy*, ed. L.A. Peplau and D. Perlman (New York: Wiley, 1982), 1–8.
4. Stephanie Cacioppo, et al., "Loneliness: Clinical Import and Interventions," *Perspectives on Psychological Science* 10, no. 2 (2015): 238–49, https://doi.org/10.1177/1745691615570616.
5. Stephanie Cacioppo, et al., "Loneliness: Clinical Import and Interventions."
6. Stephanie Cacioppo, et al, "Loneliness: Clinical Import and Interventions."
7. Stephanie Cacioppo, et al, "Loneliness: Clinical Import and Interventions."
8. Stephanie Cacioppo, et al., "Loneliness: Clinical Import and Interventions."
9. Stephanie Cacioppo, et al., "Loneliness: Clinical Import and Interventions."

10. Julianne Holt-Lunstad, et al., "Loneliness and Social Isolation as Risk Factors for Mortality: A Meta-Analytic Review," *Perspectives on Psychological Science* 10, no. 2 (2015): 227–37, https://doi.org/10.1177/1745691614568352.

11. John T. Cacioppo and William Patrick, *Loneliness: Human Nature and the Need for Social Connection* (Cambridge, MA: W. W. Norton & Company, 2008).

12. Sanjay Gupta, "Just Say Hello: The Powerful New Way to Combat Loneliness," Oprah.com, February 18, 2014, https://www.oprah.com/health/just-say-hello-fight-loneliness/all.

13. Julianne Holt-Lunstad, et al, "Loneliness and Social Isolation as Risk Factors for Mortality."

14. Sanjay Gupta, "Just Say Hello."

15. Cigna, "Cigna Takes Action to Combat the Rise of Loneliness and Improve Mental Wellness in America," January 23, 2020, https://www.cigna.com/about-us/newsroom/news-and-views/press-releases/2020/cigna-takes-action-to-combat-the-rise-of-loneliness-and-improve-mental-wellness-in-america.

16. Ben Cost, "Americans Have Fewer Friends Than Ever Before," *New York Post*, July 27, 2021, https://nypost.com/2021/07/27/americans-have-fewer-friends-than-ever-before-study/.

17. Darrell Bricker, "Majority (54%) of Canadians Say Physical Distancing Has Left Them Feeling Lonely or Isolated," Ipsos, April 10, 2020, https://www.ipsos.com/en-ca/news-and-polls/Majority-Of-Canadians-Say-Physical-Distancing-Has-Left-Them-Feeling-Lonely-Or-Isolated.

18. Australian Psychological Society, "Australian Loneliness Report," *Psychology Week*, 2018, https://psychweek.org.au/2018-archive/loneliness-study/.

19. "The Facts on Loneliness," Campaign to End Loneliness, 2021, https://www.campaigntoendloneliness.org/the-facts-on-loneliness/.

20. "How Lonely Are Europeans?," EU Science Hub, June 12, 2019, https://ec.europa.eu/jrc/en/news/how-lonely-are-europeans.

21. Statista Research Department, "Share of Italians Who Feel They Do Not Have Someone to Talk with or to Ask for Help to in 2015," May 15, 2020, https://www.statista.com/statistics/726762/feeling-of-loneliness-among-italians/.

22. Sydney R. Sauter, Loan P. Kim, and Kathryn H. Jacobsen, "Loneliness and Friendlessness Among Adolescents in 25 Countries in Latin America and the Caribbean," *Child and Adolescent Mental Health* 25, no. 1 (2019): 21–27, https://doi.org/10.1111/camh.12358.

23. Edd Gent, "Social Isolation Is Often Blamed on Technology, But Could It Be Part of the Solution?," BBC, January 29, 2019, https://www.bbc.com/future/article/20190129-the-plight-of-japans-modern-hermits.

24. Bertha Coombs, "Loneliness Is on the Rise and Younger Workers and Social Media Users Feel It Most, Cigna Survey Finds," CNBC, January 23, 2020, https://www.cnbc.com/2020/01/23/loneliness-is-rising-younger-workers-and-social-media-users-feel-it-most.html.

25. Jamie Ducharme, "More Than 90% of Generation Z Is Stressed Out. and Gun Violence Is Partly to Blame," Time, October 30, 2018, https://time.com/5437646/gen-z-stress-report/.

26. Sophie Bethune, "Gen Z More Likely to Report Mental Health Concerns," *American Psychological Association* 50, no. 1 (January 2019): 20, https://www.apa.org/monitor/2019/01/gen-z.

27. MaryKate Wust, "How Gen Z Can Swap Burnout for Breakthroughs," Penn Medicine News, News Blog, March 21, 2019, https://www.pennmedicine.org/news/news-blog/2019/march/how-gen-z-can-swap-burnout-for-breakthroughs.

28. Ryan Jenkins, "Why Most Employees Are Lonely and Underperforming," Entrepreneur.com, June 25, 2020, https://www.entrepreneur.com/article/352081.

29. Anita Lettink, "No, Millennials Will NOT be 75% of the Workforce in 2025 (or Ever)!" LinkedIn.com, September 17, 2019, https://www.linkedin.com/pulse/millennials-75-workforce-2025-ever-anita-lettink/.

30. Liz Richards and Sam Melissa, "The Voice of Generation Z, What Post-Millennials Are Saying About Work," September, 2018, http://rainmakerthinking.com/wp-content/uploads/2018/09/THE-VOICE-OF-GENERATION-Z_Final.pdf.

31. Service Now, "Think You Know What's Important to Your Gen Z Workers? Think Again," November 4, 2019, https://www.servicenow.com/company/media/press-room/what-is-important-to-gen-z-workers.html.

32. Service Now, "Think You Know What's Important to Your Gen Z Workers?"

33. Center for Decision Research, "Nicholas Epley Partners with BBC to Replicate Groundbreaking Study," July 9, 2019, https://research.chicagobooth.edu/cdr/news/2019/nicholas-epley-partners-with-bbc-to-replicate-groundbreaking-study.

34. Adam Grant, "We Don't Have to Fight Loneliness Alone," WorkLife with Adam Grant, April 2020, TED video, 38:36, https://www.ted.com/talks/worklife_with_adam_grant_we_don_t_have_to_fight_loneliness_alone.

Chapter 2

1. Glen Geher, "My Favorite Psychology Study: The Good Samaritan Is in the Situation," *Psychology Today*, March 16, 2017, https://www.psychologytoday.com/us/blog/darwins-subterranean-world/201703/my-favorite-psychology-study.

2. Ryan Smith, "How CEOs Can Support Employee Mental Health in a Crisis," *Harvard Business Review*, May 1, 2020, https://hbr.org/2020/05/how-ceos-can-support-employee-mental-health-in-a-crisis.

3. "Work and the Loneliness Epidemic," *Harvard Business Review*, September 26, 2017, https://hbr.org/2017/09/work-and-the-loneliness-epidemic?ab=seriesnav-bigidea.

4. Miller McPherson, Lynn Smith-Lovin, and Matthew E. Brashears, "Social Isolation in America: Changes in Core Discussion Networks over Two Decades," *American Sociological Review* 71, no. 3 (2006): 353–75, https://doi.org/10.1177/000312240607100301.

5. Markham Heid, "You Asked: How Many Friends Do I Need?," *Time*, March 18, 2015, https://time.com/3748090/friends-social-health/.

6. Jamie Ballard, "Millennials Are the Loneliest Generation," Yougov.com, July 30, 2019, https://today.yougov.com/topics/lifestyle/articles-reports/2019/07/30/loneliness-friendship-new-friends-poll-survey.

7. Scott Berinato, "What Do We Know About Loneliness and Work?," *Harvard Business Review*, September 28, 2017, https://hbr.org/2017/09/what-do-we-know-about-loneliness-and-work?ab=seriesnav-bigidea.

8. Jamil Zaki, "Kindness Contagion," *Scientific American*, July 26, 2016, https://www.scientificamerican.com/article/kindness-contagion/.

9. https://www.youtube.com/watch?v=9XgAyoyMT4Y&t=45s.

10. "Carvana Lazy 60," January 29, 2015, YouTube video, https://youtu.be/Npc2IQiySK4.

11. Cigna, "Cigna Takes Action to Combat the Rise of Loneliness and Improve Mental Wellness in America," January 23, 2020, https://www.cigna.com/about-us/newsroom/news-and-views/press-releases/2020/cigna-takes-action-to-combat-the-rise-of-loneliness-and-improve-mental-wellness-in-america.

12. University of Wollongong—UOW, "Does Social Media Make Us More or Less Lonely? Depends on How You Use It," n.d., https://www.uow.edu.au/media/2020/does-social-media-make-us-more-or-less-lonely-depends-on-how-you-use-it.php#:~:text=Evidence%20from%20past%20literature%20has.

13. Robert Williams, "Mtn Dew, Papa John's Power up Gaming Fans with Controller That Can Order Pizza," Marketing Dive, December 11, 2020, https://www.marketingdive.com/news/mtn-dew-papa-johns-power-up-gaming-fans-with-controller-that-can-order-pi/592008/.

14. Robert Williams, "Pringles Debuts Chip-Dispensing Gaming Headset on Twitch," Marketing Dive, November 27, 2019, https://www.marketingdive.com/news/pringles-debuts-chip-dispensing-gaming-headset-on-twitch/568148/.

15. Aaron Baar, "Bud Light Taps into Gaming Wars with 6-Pack Console," Marketing Dive, November 18, 2020, https://www.marketingdive.com/news/bud-light-taps-into-gaming-wars-with-6-pack-console/589278/.

16. Hannah Ewens, "What Young People Fear the Most," Vice, September 21, 2016, https://www.vice.com/en/article/nnyk37/what-vice-readers-fear-the-most-hannah-ewens-love-loneliness.

17. "Special Report: State of Women's Wellness 2017," Everyday Health, https://images.agoramedia.com/everydayhealth/gcms/Everyday-Health-State-of-Womens-Wellness-Survey-PDF.pdf.

18. Pricewaterhouse Coopers,"US Remote Work Survey," PwC, January 12, 2021, https://www.pwc.com/us/en/library/covid-19/us-remote-work-survey.html.

19. Kate Lister, "News Releases—Global Workplace Analytics," January 12, 2021, https://globalworkplaceanalytics.com/brags/news-releases.

20. Emily Courtney, "Remote Work Statistics Navigating the New Normal," FlexJobs Job Search Tips and Blog, December 21, 2020, https://www.flexjobs.com/blog/post/remote-work-statistics/.

21. Andrea Alexander, Aaron De Smet, Meredith Langstaff, and Dan Ravid, What Employees Are Saying About the Future of Remote Work, April 1, 20221, https://www.mckinsey.com/business-functions/organization/our-insights/what-employees-are-saying-about-the-future-of-remote-work.

22. Emily Courtney, "Remote Work Statistics Navigating the New Normal."

23. https://www.inc.com/magazine/201802/burt-helm/halo-top-healthy-ice-cream.html.

24. Emily Courtney, "Remote Work Statistics Navigating the New Normal."

25. Staffing Industry Analysts, "More Employees Feeling Burnout Due to Working from Home," Staffingindustry.com, July 17, 2020, https://www2.staffingindustry.com/site/Editorial/Daily-News/More-employees-feeling-burnout-due-to-working-from-home-54520.

26. Ace Casimiro, "Employee Engagement: Out of Office, Seldom Away from Work," Randstad, n.d., https://rlc.randstadusa.com/for-business/learning-center/workforce-management/employee-engagement-out-of-office-seldom-away-from-work?.

27. Jason Shen, "Tech Workers Are Showing the Effects of COVID-19-Related Burnout," Fast Company, June 12, 2020, https://www.fastcompany.com/90515519/tech-workers-are-showing-the-effects-of-covid-19-related-burnout.

28. Staffing Industry Analysts, "More Employees Feeling Burnout Due to Working from Home."

29. CBS Philly, "Survey: Millennials Feel Guiltier About Taking Vacation; More Likely to Check in Outside of Work than Older Generations," June 19, 2014, https://philadelphia.cbslocal.com/2014/06/19/survey-millennials-feel-more-guilt-over-using-their-vacation-days-more-likely-to-check-in-outside-of-work-than-older-generations/.

30. Ben Wigart," Employee Burnout: The Biggest Myth," Gallup.com, March 13, 2020, https://www.gallup.com/workplace/288539/employee-burnout-biggest-myth.aspx.

31. Daniel Roth, "Behind the Top Attractors: How We Discovered the World's Best Hirers and Keepers of Talent," LinkedIn, June 20, 2016, https://www.linkedin.com/pulse/behind-top-attractors-how-we-discovered-worlds-best-hirers-roth/.

32. "Annual Gen Z Research Studies—Trends, Stats, Attitudes & More," The Center for Generational Kinetics, July 27, 2020, https://genhq.com/annual-gen-z-research-study/#:~:text=Gen%20Z%20Becomes%20the%20Fastest.

33. Heidi Erdmann-Sullivan, "The Most Compelling Work-Life Stats of 2017 (So Far)," Benefits.care.com, October 6, 2017, https://benefits.care.com/the-most-compelling-work-life-stats-of-2017-so-far.

34. "TED Conferences on LinkedIn: How to Embrace Emotions at Work | 90 Comments," n.d., https://www.linkedin.com/posts/ted-conferences_you-cant-just-flip-a-switch-when-you-step-activity-6620039193605230592-SBAq/.

35. David Koenig, "A $12 Billion Loss for 2020, Delta Is Cautious in Early 2021," AP NEWS, January 14, 2021, https://apnews.com/article/travel-air-travel-coronavirus-pandemic-e6304e8edfcf83a42a29ce9b5faee542.

36. "2019 Global Human Capital Trends," Deloitte Insights, 2019, https://www2.deloitte.com/us/en/insights/focus/human-capital-trends.html.

Chapter 3

1. Scott Berinato, "What Do We Know About Loneliness and Work?," *Harvard Business Review*, September 28, 2017, https://hbr.org/2017/09/what-do-we-know-about-loneliness-and-work?ab=seriesnav-bigidea.

2. Sarah Louise Wright, "Addressing Loneliness at Work," Chap. 8 in *Addressing Loneliness: Coping, Prevention and Clinical Interventions*, ed. Ami Sha'ked and Ami Rokach (Psychology Press, 2014) 123–34.

3. Sarah Wright and Anthony Silard, "Unravelling the Antecedents of Loneliness in the Workplace," *Human Relations*, February 21, 2020, https://doi.org/10.1177/0018726720906013.

4. Alyssa Place and Evelina Nedlund, "WFH Loneliness Is the Latest Virtual Challenge for Employers," Employee Benefit News, December 7, 2020, https://www.benefitnews.com/news/wfh-loneliness-is-the-latest-virtual-challenge-for-employers.

5. Cigna, "Cigna Takes Action to Combat the Rise of Loneliness and Improve Mental Wellness in America," January 23, 2020, https://www.cigna.com/about-us/newsroom/news-and-views/press-releases/2020/cigna-takes-action-to-combat-the-rise-of-loneliness-and-improve-mental-wellness-in-america.

6. Tom Rath and Jim Harter, "Your Friends and Your Social Well-Being," Gallup, August 19, 2010, https://news.gallup.com/businessjournal/127043/friends-social-wellbeing.aspx.

7. Hakan Ozcelik and Sigal G. Barsade, "No Employee an Island: Workplace Loneliness and Job Performance," *Academy of Management Journal* 61, no. 6 (2018): 2343–66, https://doi.org/10.5465/amj.2015.1066.

8. Cigna, "Cigna Takes Action to Combat the Rise of Loneliness."

9. Cory Stieg, "Half of Millennials and 75% of Gen-Zers Have Quit Jobs for Mental Health Reasons," CNBC, October 8, 2019, https://www.cnbc.com/2019/10/08/millennials-gen-z-have-quit-jobs-due-to-mental-health-issues-survey.html.

10. Hakan Ozcelik and Sigal G. Barsade, "No Employee an Island."

11. Vivek H. Murthy, "Whiteboard Session: The Problem of Loneliness at Work," *Harvard Business Review*, April 24, 2018, video, https://hbr.org/video/5775734185001/whiteboard-session-the-problem-of-loneliness-at-work.

12. Vicky McKeever, "Why Loneliness Lowers Your Performance at Work," CNBC, December 3, 2019, https://www.cnbc.com/2019/12/03/why-loneliness-lowers-your-performance-at-work.html.

13. New 13: https://www.webmd.com/sleep-disorders/news/20170601/can-loneliness-rob-you-of-needed-sleep.

14. Sarah Louise Wright, "Addressing Loneliness at Work."

15. Tom Rath and Jim Harter, "Your Friends and Your Social Well-Being."
16. Hakan Ozcelik and Sigal G. Barsade, "No Employee an Island."
17. Hakan Ozcelik and Sigal G. Barsade, "No Employee an Island."
18. Scott Berinato, "What Do We Know About Loneliness and Work?."
19. Hakan Ozcelik and Sigal G. Barsade, "No Employee an Island."
20. Leigh Campbell, "We've Broken Down Your Entire Life into Years Spent Doing Tasks," HuffPost Australia, October 19, 2017, https://www.huffingtonpost.com.au/2017/10/18/weve-broken-down-your-entire-life-into-years-spent-doing-tasks _a_23248153/.
21. Tom Rath and Jim Harter, "Your Friends and Your Social Well-Being."
22. Thomas J. Saporito, "It's Time to Acknowledge CEO Loneliness," *Harvard Business Review*, February 15, 2012, https://hbr.org/2012/02/its-time-to-acknowledge-ceo-lo.

Chapter 4

1. Naomi I. Eisenberger, "The Neural Bases of Social Pain," *Psychosomatic Medicine* 74, no. 2 (2012): 126–35, https://doi.org/10.1097/psy.0b013e3 182464dd1.
2. Veronique de Turenne, "The Pain of Chronic Loneliness Can Be Detrimental to Your Health," UCLA, December 21, 2016, https://newsroom.ucla.edu/stories/stories-20161206.
3. Naomi Eisenberger, "Why Rejection Hurts," Edge.org, May 9, 2021, https://www.edge.org/conversation/naomi_eisenberger-why-rejection-hurts.
4. Eisenberger, "Why Rejection Hurts."
5. Raio TTS, "People Who Quit Their Job Without a Plan Share Their Story—AskReddit," June 15, 2019, https://www.youtube.com/watch?v=zR-1egxpfU0.
6. "John Cacioppo," John Cacioppo.com, 2018, http://www.johncacioppo.com/.
7. Emily Singer, "New Evidence for the Necessity of Loneliness," *Quanta Magazine*, May 10, 2016, https://www.quantamagazine.org/new-evidence-for-the-necessity-of-loneliness-20160510/.
8. Stephanie Cacioppo et al., "Loneliness and Implicit Attention to Social Threat: A High-Performance Electrical Neuroimaging Study," *Taylor and Francis Online Journal* 7, no.1–4 (2015): 138–59, https://doi.org/10.1080/17588928.2015.1070136.
9. Singer, "New Evidence for the Necessity of Loneliness."
10. Adam Piore, "Why Do You Feel Lonely? Neuroscience Is Starting to Find Answers," *MIT Technology Review*, September 4, 2020, https://www.technologyreview.com/2020/09/04/1008008/neuroscience-loneliness-pandemic-covid-neurons -brain/.
11. Piore, "Why Do You Feel Lonely?."
12. Pascalle L. P. Van Loo, et al., "Do Male Mice Prefer or Avoid Each Other's Company? Influence of Hierarchy, Kinship, and Familiarity," *Journal of Applied Animal Welfare Science* 4, no. 2 (2010): 91–103, https://doi.org/10.1207/s15327604jaws0402_1.
13. Raymond J. M. Niesink and Jan M. Van Ree, "Short-Term Isolation Increases Social Interactions of Male Rats: A Parametric Analysis," *Physiology & Behavior* 29, no. 5 (1982): 819–25, https://doi.org/10.1016/0031-9384(82)90331-6.
14. Livia Tomova et al., "Acute Social Isolation Evokes Midbrain Craving Responses Similar to Hunger," *Nature Neuroscience* 23, no. 12 (2020): 1597–1605, https://doi.org/10.1038/s41593-020-00742-z.
15. Piore, "Why Do You Feel Lonely?."
16. Gareth Cook, "Why We Are Wired to Connect," *Scientific American*, October 22, 2013, https://www.scientificamerican.com/article/why-we-are-wired-to-connect/.
17. Cook, "Why We Are Wired to Connect."

18. Nicholas Epley et al., "When We Need a Human: Motivational Determinants of Anthropomorphism," *Social Cognition* 26, no. 2 (2008):143–55, doi:10.1521/soco.2008.26.2.143.

Chapter 5

1. Robert Waldinger, "What Makes a Good Life? Lessons from the Longest Study on Happiness," www.ted.com, n.d., https://www.ted.com/talks/robert_waldinger_what_makes_a_good_life_lessons_from_the_longest_study_on_happiness?rid=aTDYm8mbamME#t-205553.
2. Waldinger, "What Makes a Good Life?."
3. Margaret Heffernan, "The Surprising Element That Will Make Your Company Thrive," Inc.com, May 12, 2015, https://www.inc.com/margaret-heffernan/the-secret-ingredient-that-will-make-your-company-succeed.html.
4. Margaret Heffernan, "The Secret Ingredient That Makes Some Teams Better Than Others," Ideas.ted.com, May 5, 2015, https://ideas.ted.com/the-secret-ingredient-that-makes-some-teams-better-than-others/.
5. Erica Volini et al., "Creating a Culture of Belonging," Deloitte.com, May 15, 2020, https://www2.deloitte.com/us/en/insights/focus/human-capital-trends/2020/creating-a-culture-of-belonging.html.
6. "Beyond Diversity: How Firms Are Cultivating a Sense of Belonging at Work," Knowledge@Wharton, Wharton University of Pennsylvania, March 26, 2019, https://knowledge.wharton.upenn.edu/article/belonging-at-work/.
7. Yanfei Wang, Jieqiong Liu, and Yu Zhu, "Humble Leadership, Psychological Safety, Knowledge Sharing, and Follower Creativity: A Cross-Level Investigation," *Frontiers in Psychology* 9 (2018), 1727, https://doi.org/10.3389/fpsyg.2018.01727.
8. "Guide: Understand Team Effectiveness," Re: Work, Withgoogle.com, 2011, https://rework.withgoogle.com/print/guides/5721312655835136/.
9. Erica Volini et al., "Belonging from Comfort to Connection to Contribution," Deloitte.com, May 15, 2020, https://www2.deloitte.com/us/en/insights/focus/human-capital-trends/2020/creating-a-culture-of-belonging.html.
10. Sarah Louise Wright, "Addressing Loneliness at Work," Chap. 8 in *Addressing Loneliness: Coping, Prevention and Clinical Interventions*, ed. Ami Sha'ked and Ami Rokach (Psychology Press, 2014) 123–34.
11. BetterUp, "The Value of Belonging at Work: New Frontiers for Inclusion," n.d., https://get.betterup.co/rs/600-WTC-654/images/BetterUpBelongingReport_091019.pdf.
12. Volini et al., "Belonging from Comfort to Connection to Contribution."
13. Volini et al., "Belonging from Comfort to Connection to Contribution."
14. Annamarie Mann, "Why We Need Best Friends at Work," Gallup.com, January 15, 2018, https://news.gallup.com/businessjournal/127043/friends-social-wellbeing.aspx.
15. BetterUp, "The Value of Belonging at Work."
16. BetterUp, "The Value of Belonging at Work."
17. Mina Cikara, "Episode 9: The War for Kindness," n.d., in *The Happiness Lab*, podcast, https://www.happinesslab.fm/season-2-episodes/episode-9-the-war-for-kindness.
18. Veronika Tate, "Turn Empathy into Compassion Without the Empathic Distress," *Psychology Today*, December 5, 2019, https://www.psychologytoday.com/us/blog/pulling-through/201912/turn-empathy-compassion-without-the-empathic-distress.
19. Tate, "Turn Empathy into Compassion Without the Empathic Distress."
20. Andrea Asuaje and Yasmin Amer, "We've Become Less Empathetic over Time. Here Are Some Ways to Improve," wbur.org, November 27, 2019, https://www.wbur.org/kindworld/2019/11/27/empathy.

21. Maxwell Huppart, "Employees Share What Gives Them a Sense of Belonging at Work," Linkedin.com, October 25, 2017, https://business.linkedin.com/talent -solutions/blog/company-culture/2017/employees-share-what-gives-them-a-sense -of-belonging-at-work.

22. Laurie Santos, "Episode 10: How to Be a Better Ally," n.d., *The Happiness Lab*, podcast, https://www.happinesslab.fm/season-2-episodes/episode-10-how-to-be-a -better-ally.

Chapter 6

1. Jian Peng et al., "Workplace Loneliness, Leader-Member Exchange and Creativity: The Cross-Level Moderating Role of Leader Compassion," *Personality and Individual Differences* 104 (2017):510–15, doi:10.1016/j.paid.2016.09.020.

2. Joseph Chancellor et al., "Everyday Prosociality in the Workplace: The Reinforcing Benefits of Giving, Getting, and Glimpsing," *Emotion* 18, no. 4 (2018): 507–17, https://doi.org/10.1037/emo0000321.

3. Chancellor et al., "Everyday Prosociality in the Workplace."

4. "A Hairy Tale - The History of Movember's Early Years," Movember, December 30, 2015, https://us.movember.com/story/view/id/11213/.

5. Wikipedia Contributors, "Movember," Wikipedia, October 29, 2019, https:// en.wikipedia.org/wiki/Movember.

6. Ash Jerberg, "How Movember Raised over $1 Billion Thanks to Walking Billboards," Medium, May 15, 2020, https://bettermarketing.pub/how-movember-raised-over -1-billion-thanks-to-walking-billboards-d3d942a2eeb7.

Chapter 7

1. Ceylan Yeginsu, "U.K. Appoints a Minister for Loneliness," *New York Times*, January 17, 2018, https://www.nytimes.com/2018/01/17/world/europe/uk-britain -loneliness.html.

2. Juliet Michaelson, Karen Jeffrey, and Saamah Abdallah, "The Cost of Loneliness to UK Employers," New Economics Foundation, February 20, 2017, https:// neweconomics.org/2017/02/cost-loneliness-uk-employers/.

3. Vivek H. Murthy, "Work and the Loneliness Epidemic," *Harvard Business Review*, September 26, 2017, https://hbr.org/2017/09/work-and-the-loneliness-epidemic.

4. "Person Overview, Alex 'Sandy' Pentland," MIT Media Lab, n.d., https://www.media .mit.edu/people/sandy/overview/.

5. Thomas J. Saporito, "It's Time to Acknowledge CEO Loneliness," *Harvard Business Review*, February 15, 2012, https://hbr.org/2012/02/its-time-to-acknowledge-ceo-lo.

6. Sarah Louise Wright, "Addressing Loneliness at Work," Chap. 8 in *Addressing Loneliness: Coping, Prevention and Clinical Interventions*, ed. Ami Sha'ked and Ami Rokach (Psychology Press, 2014) 123–34.

7. Wikipedia Contributors, "UCLA Loneliness Scale," Wikipedia, August 23, 2018, https://en.wikipedia.org/wiki/UCLA_Loneliness_Scale.

8. Shawn Achor, *The Happiness Advantage: The Seven Principles of Positive Psychology That Fuel Success and Performance at Work* (Crown Business, 2010).

9. Shawn Achor et al., "America's Loneliest Workers, According to Research," *Harvard Business Review*, March 19, 2018, https://hbr.org/2018/03/americas-loneliest -workers-according-to-research.

10. Cigna, "Loneliness Is at Epidemic Levels in America," 2020, https://www.cigna.com/ about-us/newsroom/studies-and-reports/combatting-loneliness/.

11. Jennifer Moss, "Helping Remote Workers Avoid Loneliness and Burnout," *Harvard Business Review*, November 30, 2018, https://hbr.org/2018/11/helping-remote -workers-avoid-loneliness-and-burnout.

12. Sarah Louise Wright, "Loneliness in the Workplace" (PDF), ResearchGate, January 2005, https://www.researchgate.net/publication/29488030_Loneliness_in_the_Workplace.

13. Wright, "Addressing Loneliness at Work."

14. Heather Buschman, "Do These Genes Make Me Lonely? Study Finds Loneliness Is a Heritable Trait," UC Health–UC San Diego, September 20, 2016. https://health.ucsd.edu/news/releases/pages/2016-09-20-loneliness-a-heritable-trait.aspx.

15. Buschman, "Do These Genes Make Me Lonely?."

Chapter 8

1. Hamdi Ulukaya, "The Anti-CEO Playbook," April 2019, TED video, https://www.ted.com/talks/hamdi_ulukaya_the_anti_ceo_playbook?language=en#t-172100.

2. "Hamdi Ulukaya: Creating the Culture of Chobani," Goldman Sachs, November 14, 2018, YouTube video, https://www.youtube.com/watch?v=ccl_juwM8lI.

3. "Tent Foundation," Wikipedia, October 2, 2020, https://en.wikipedia.org/wiki/Tent_Foundation.

4. "AI @Work Study 2020 as Uncertainty Remains, Anxiety and Stress Reach a Tipping Point at Work: Artificial Intelligence Fills the Gaps in Workplace Mental Health Support," Oracle and Workplace Intelligence, 2020, https://www.oracle.com/a/ocom/docs/applications/hcm/2020-hcm-ai-at-work-study.pdf.

5. Kelly Greenwood, Vivek Bapat, and Mike Maughan, "Research: People Want Their Employers to Talk about Mental Health," *Harvard Business Review*, October 7, 2019, https://hbr.org/2019/10/research-people-want-their-employers-to-talk-about-mental-health.

6. Jonathan D. Schaffer et al., "Enduring Mental Health: Prevalence and Prediction," *Journal of Abnormal Psychology* 126, no. 2 (2017): 212–24, https://doi.org/10.1037/abn0000232.

7. Greenwood et al., "Research: People Want Their Employers to Talk About Mental Health."

8. Jake Herway, "How to Create a Culture of Psychological Safety," Gallup.com, December 7, 2017, https://www.gallup.com/workplace/236198/create-culture-psychological-safety.aspx.

9. "Guide: Understand Team Effectiveness," Re: Work, 2011, https://rework.withgoogle.com/print/guides/5721312655835136/.

10. Yanfei Wang, Jieqiong Liu, and Yu Zhu, "Humble Leadership, Psychological Safety, Knowledge Sharing, and Follower Creativity: A Cross-Level Investigation," *Frontiers in Psychology* 9 (September 2018), https://doi.org/10.3389/fpsyg.2018.01727.

11. "Hamdi Ulukaya: Creating the Culture of Chobani."

12. Greenwood et al., "Research: People Want Their Employers to Talk About Mental Health."

13. "Simon Sinek Explains Why You Should Be the Last to Speak in a Meeting," Ladders, January 8, 2018, https://www.theladders.com/career-advice/simon-sinek-explains-why-bosses-need-to-be-the-last-to-speak-in-a-meeting.

14. Rob Cross, Reb Rebele, and Adam Grant, "Collaborative Overload," *Harvard Business Review*, December 20, 2016, https://hbr.org/2016/01/collaborative-overload.

15. Laura Amico, "Loneliness and the Digital Workplace," *Harvard Business Review*, September 29, 2017, https://hbr.org/2017/09/loneliness-and-the-digital-workplace?ab=seriesnav-bigidea.

16. Virgin, "Simon Sinek on Why You Should Put Your Phone Away," YouTube video, April 10, 2018, https://www.youtube.com/watch?v=C75NyXiiJck.

17. KDM Engineering, "Smartphone Etiquette."

18. Matthew Kitchen, "How to Disconnect from 'Always On' Work Culture," *Wall Street Journal*, October 5, 2018, https://www.wsj.com/articles/how-to-disconnect-from -always-on-work-culture-1538740171.
19. KDM Engineering, "Smartphone Etiquette."
20. "WhiteSpace at Work," WhiteSpace at Work, 2017, https://www.whitespaceatwork .com/.
21. Liz Fosslien, "How to Embrace Emotions at Work," 2020, TED Conferences on LinkedIn, https://www.linkedin.com/posts/ted-conferences_you-cant-just-flip-a -switch-when-you-step-activity-6620039193605230592-SBAq/.
22. Shawn Achor, "The Key to Success on a Team Is Connection," SUCCESS, September 13, 2019, https://www.success.com/the-key-to-success-on-a-team-is-connection/.
23. Stanford, Stanford University, and California, 94305 Copyright Complaints Trademark Notice, "Text of the 2014 Commencement Address by Bill and Melinda Gates," Stanford University, June 15, 2014, https://news.stanford.edu/news/2014/ june/gates-commencement-remarks-061514.html.
24. Brené Brown, "On What Vulnerability Isn't," Taken for Granted Podcast, Episode 1, February 23, 2021.
25. Leigh Campbell, "We've Broken Down Your Entire Life into Years Spent Doing Tasks," HuffPost Australia, October 19, 2017, https://www.huffingtonpost.com .au/2017/10/18/weve-broken-down-your-entire-life-into-years-spent-doing-tasks _a_23248153/.
26. "Hilton Introduces Best-in-Industry Adoption Assistance Program," www .businesswire.com, October 5, 2016, https://www.businesswirecom/news/home/ 20161005005791/en/Hilton-Introduces-Best-in-Industry-Adoption-Assistance -Program#:~:text=Under%20the%20new%2program%2C%20Hilton.
27. Stephen Miller, CEBS, "Facebook's Generous Bereavement Leave Sets a High Standard," SHRM, February 9, 2017, https://www.shrm.org/resourcesandtools/ hr-topics/benefits/pages/facebook-bereavement-leave.aspx.
28. Ryan Jenkins, "How to Create Remarkable Culture That Attracts and Retains Gen Z with David Salyers," Ryan Jenkins (blog), November 18, 2019, https://blog.ryan -jenkins.com/how-to-create-remarkable-culture-that-attracts-and-retains-gen-z -with-david-salyers.
29. Ryan Jenkins, "How to Retain Top Talent according to a Company with a 97 Percent Retention Rate," Inc.com, February 27, 2019, https://www.inc.com/ryan-jenkins/3 -things-top-talent-want-in-a-job.html.
30. "Team Common Information Effect: Encourage Critical Thinking" (blog), December 23, 2018, https://www.vvauban.com/blog/team-common-information -effect#:~:text=Common%20information%20effect%20is%20a.
31. Columbia Business School, "What Really Happens at Mixers?" Ideas & Insights, February 27, 2007, https://www8.gsb.columbia.edu/articles/ideas-work/what-really -happens-mixers.
32. David Ludden, "Does Using Social Media Make You Lonely?" *Psychology Today*, January 24, 2018, https://www.psychologytoday.com/us/blog/talking-apes/201801/ does-using-social-media-make-you-lonely.
33. Miller McPherson, Lynn Smith-Lovin, and Matthew E. Brashears, "Social Isolation in America: Changes in Core Discussion Networks over Two Decades," *American Sociological Review* 71, no. 3 (2006): 353–75, https://www.jstor.org/stable/ 30038995?seq=1.
34. Stewart D. Friedman, "How to Get Your Team to Coach Each Other," *Harvard Business Review*, March 13, 2015, https://hbr.org/2015/03/how-to-get-your-team -to-coach-each-other.

35. Shankar Vedantum, "Why Eating the Same Food Increases People's Trust and Cooperation," NPR.org, February 2, 2017, https://www.npr.org/2017/02/02/512998465/why-eating-the-same-food-increases-peoples-trust-and-cooperation.
36. Vivek Murthy, "Work and the Loneliness Epidemic," *Harvard Business Review*, September 26, 2017, https://hbr.org/2017/09/work-and-the-loneliness-epidemic?ab=seriesnav-bigidea.
37. Murthy, "Work and the Loneliness Epidemic."
38. Jennifer Moss, "Helping Remote Workers Avoid Loneliness and Burnout," *Harvard Business Review*, November 30, 2018, https://hbr.org/2018/11/helping-remote-workers-avoid-loneliness-and-burnout.

Chapter 9

1. "Christina Koch," Wikipedia, April 16, 2020, https://en.wikipedia.org/wiki/Christina_Koch.
2. Sarah Lawrence College, "6 of the Loneliest Jobs in the World," Treehugger, May 23, 2020, https://www.treehugger.com/loneliest-jobs-in-the-world-4863839.
3. "Christina Koch," Wikipedia.
4. Tim Herrera, "How to Deal with Life in Long-Term Isolation," *New York Times*, November 25, 2020, https://www.nytimes.com/2020/11/25/style/coronavirus-tips-for-quarantine-isolation.html.
5. "Astronaut Chris Hadfield's Tips for Being in Isolation," ABC7 San Francisco, May 12, 2020, https://abc7news.com/chris-hadfield-astronaut-nasa-iss/6119589/.
6. "Chris Hadfield: An Astronaut's Guide to Self-Isolation," CBC News, YouTube video, March 26, 2020, https://www.youtube.com/watch?v=_dI458GsIpQ.
7. Elizabeth Howell, "What Astronauts Can Teach Us About Mental Health and Isolation," The Walrus, May 19, 2020, https://thewalrus.ca/what-astronauts-can-teach-us-about-mental-health-and-isolation/.
8. Shawn Achor et al., "America's Loneliest Workers, According to Research," *Harvard Business Review*, March 19, 2018, https://hbr.org/2018/03/americas-loneliest-workers-according-to-research.
9. Mary Lyons, Katherine Lavelle, and David Smith, "Gen Z Rising," U.S. Edition, 2017, https://www.accenture.com/t20170901T080938Z__w__/us-en/_acnmedia/PDF-50/Accenture-Strategy-Workforce-Gen-Z-Rising-POV.pdf#zoom=50.
10. Adam M. Grant, "Does Intrinsic Motivation Fuel the Prosocial Fire? Motivational Synergy in Predicting Persistence, Performance, and Productivity," *Journal of Applied Psychology* 93, no. 1 (2008): 48–58, https://doi.org/10.1037/0021-9010.93.1.48.
11. Adam M. Grant, "The Significance of Task Significance: Job Performance Effects, Relational Mechanisms, and Boundary Conditions," *Journal of Applied Psychology* 93, no. 1 (2008): 108–124, https://doi.org/10.1037/0021-9010.93.1.108.
12. HBR Editors, "Cooks Make Tastier Food When They Can See Their Customers," *Harvard Business Review*, November 1, 2014, https://hbr.org/2014/11/cooks-make-tastier-food-when-they-can-see-their-customers.
13. Monster Worldwide, Inc., "Move Over, Millennials: Gen Z Is About to Hit the Workforce," PR Newswire, August 30, 2016, https://www.prnewswire.com/news-releases/move-over-millennials-gen-z-is-about-to-hit-the-workforce-300319567.html.
14. Ryan Jenkins, "This Is How Similar Generation Z Will Be to Millennials," Inc.com, August 21, 2017, https://www.inc.com/ryan-jenkins/this-is-how-similar-generation-z-will-be-to-millen.html.
15. Wikipedia Contributors, "Five Whys," Wikipedia, October 9, 2019, https://en.wikipedia.org/wiki/Five_whys.

16. Mind Tools Content Team, "5 Whys: Getting to the Root of a Problem Quickly," Mindtools.com, 2009, https://www.mindtools.com/pages/article/newTMC_5W.htm.

17. Frank Graff, "An Astronaut's Advice for Coping with Isolation During a Pandemic," PBS North Carolina, January 11, 2021, https://www.pbsnc.org/blogs/science/reframing-isolation/.

18. Graff, "An Astronaut's Advice for Coping with Isolation During a Pandemic."

19. "Perceptual Narrowing," Wikipedia, September 30, 2020, https://en.wikipedia.org/wiki/Perceptual_narrowing.

20. J. Craig Wallace, "Stop Managing for the Weekend," *Psychology Today*, October 10, 2020, https://www.psychologytoday.com/us/blog/higher-level/202010/stop-managing-the-weekend#:~:text=According%20to%20neuroscience%20research%2C%20the.

21. Steve Urban, "Netflix's 'Context, Not Control': How Does It Work?," LinkedIn, August 20, 2015, https://www.linkedin.com/pulse/netflixs-context-control-how-does-work-steve-urban/.

22. Steve Urban, "Netflix's 'Context, Not Control': How Does It Work?."

23. Jim Harter and Amy Adkins, "Employees Want a Lot More from Their Managers," Gallup.com, April 8, 2015, https://www.gallup.com/workplace/236570/employees-lot-managers.aspx.

24. "Chris Hadfield: An Astronaut's Guide to Self-Isolation," CBC News.

25. Randstad, "How Tech Is Impacting the Workforce of Tomorrow," 2019, https://insights.randstadusa.com/how-tech-is-impacting-the-workforce-of-tomorrow?_ga=2.204150489.831362013.1620773174-1922071977.1620581035.

26. Harvard Business Publishing, 2018 State of Leadership Development, May 2018.

27. Kevin Kruse, "How Chick-Fil-A Created a Culture That Lasts," *Forbes*, December 8, 2015, https://www.forbes.com/sites/kevinkruse/2015/12/08/how-chick-fil-a-created-a-culture-that-lasts/?sh=6551fe723602.

28. Harvard Business Publishing, Infographic Millennials, June 2018.

Chapter 10

1. Polly W. Wiessner, "Embers of Society: Firelight Talk Among the Ju/'Hoansi Bushmen," *Proceedings of the National Academy of Sciences* 111, no. 39: 14027–35, https://doi.org/10.1073/pnas.1404212111.

2. "Firekeeper," Wikipedia, April 25, 2019, https://en.wikipedia.org/wiki/Firekeeper.

3. John T. Cacioppo, Harry T. Reis, and Alex J. Zautra, "Social Resilience: The Value of Social Fitness with an Application to the Military," *American Psychologist* 66, no. 1 (2011): 43–51, https://doi.org/10.1037/a0021419.

4. Suicide Awareness Voices of Education, "Suicide Statistics and Facts– SAVE," SAVE, 2016, https://save.org/about-suicide/suicide-facts/.

5. Amy Novotney, "Strong in Mind and Body," *American Psychological Association* 40, no. 11 (December 2009): 40, https://www.apa.org/monitor/2009/12/army-program.

6. John T. Cacioppo and Stephanie Cacioppo, "The Social Muscle," *Harvard Business Review*, October 2, 2017, https://hbr.org/2017/10/the-social-muscle?ab=seriesnav-bigideav.

7. Novotney, "Strong in Mind and Body."

8. Henneke, "How Vivid Words Make Your Message Unforgettable [Case Study]," Enchanting Marketing, November 21, 2017, https://www.enchantingmarketing.com/vivid-language/.

9. Wikipedia Contributors, "Reminiscence Bump," Wikipedia, November 17, 2019, https://en.wikipedia.org/wiki/Reminiscence_bump.

10. Clint Pulver, "Inspirational Video- Be a Mr. Jensen- MUST WATCH!!" May 4, 2017, YouTube video, https://www.youtube.com/watch?v=4p5286T_kn0.
11. Candice Choi, "Gum Sales Have Been Mysteriously Tumbling for Years," *Business Insider*, May 20, 2014, https://www.businessinsider.com/gum-sales-are-tumbling-2014-3.
12. Phil Simon, "Have Smartphones Caused the Death of the In-Store Impulse Buy?," HuffPost, May 13, 2015, https://www.huffpost.com/entry/have-smartphones-caused-t_b_7272788.
13. Daniel J. Kruger et al., "Cell Phone Use Latency in a Midwestern USA University Population," *Journal of Technology in Behavioral Science* 2, no. 1 (2017): 56–59, https://doi.org/10.1007/s41347-017-0012-8.
14. Michelle King, "Struggling to Get Ahead at Work? Your Mental Load Might Be Holding You Back," *Forbes*, April 18, 2018, https://www.forbes.com/sites/michelleking/2018/04/18/struggling-to-get-ahead-at-work-your-mental-load-might-be-holding-you-back/?sh=65dc1df65030.
15. Alison Escalante, "New Science: Why Our Brains Spend 50% of the Time Mind-Wandering," *Forbes*, January 28, 2021. https://www.forbes.com/sites/alisonescalante/2021/01/28/new-science-why-our-brains-spend-50-of-the-time-mind-wandering/?sh=369dc0c04854.
16. J. Clement, "Number of Gamers Worldwide 2023," Statista, January 29, 2021, https://www.statista.com/statistics/748044/number-video-gamers-world/#:~:text=Gamers%20across%20the%20globe&text=According%20to%20estimates%2C%20there%20were.
17. Hilary Russ, "More U.S. Millennials Subscribe to Video Games than Traditional Pay TV: Survey," Reuters, June 10, 2019, https://www.reuters.com/article/us-usa-videogames-television/more-u-s-millennials-subscribe-to-video-games-than-traditional-pay-tv-survey-idUSKCN1TB2CB.
18. "Number of Hours of Video Games Streamed Online 2021," Statista, April 12, 2021, https://www.statista.com/statistics/1125469/video-game-stream-hours-watched/#:~:text=In%20the%20first%20quarter%20of.
19. Carolyn Wiley, "What Motivates Employees According to over 40 Years of Motivation Surveys," *International Journal of Manpower* 18, no. 3 (May 1, 1997): 263–80, https://doi.org/10.1108/01437729710169373.

Chapter 11

1. Sue Shellenbarger, "The Biggest Office Interruptions Are . . . ," *Wall Street Journal*, September 10, 2013, https://www.wsj.com/articles/the-biggest-office-interruptions-are-1378852919.
2. Melissa Dahl, "Work Smarter: Even a 3-Second Distraction Can Screw You Up," The Cut, May 14, 2014, https://www.thecut.com/2014/05/even-a-3-second-distraction-can-screw-you-up.html.
3. Kristin Wong, "How Long It Takes to Get Back on Track After a Distraction," Lifehacker, July 29, 2015, https://lifehacker.com/how-long-it-takes-to-get-back-on-track-after-a-distract-1720708353.
4. "18 Leadership Communication Trends to Look for in 2021," Smarp, January 5, 2021, https://blog.smarp.com/18-leadership-communication-trends-to-look-for-in-2020.
5. Scott D. Anthony, S. Patrick Viguerie, and Andrew Waldeck, "Corporate Longevity: Turbulence Ahead for Large Organizations," Innosight, 2016, https://www.innosight.com/wp-content/uploads/2016/08/Corporate-Longevity-2016-Final.pdf.

6. Emily Esfahani Smith, "Science Says Lasting Relationships Come Down to 2 Basic Traits," *Insider*, November 7, 2015, https://www.businessinsider.com/lasting-relationships-rely-on-traits-2015-11.

Conclusion

1. "Christopher McCandless, Whose Alaskan Odyssey Ended in Death," *New York Times*, 2019, https://www.nytimes.com/interactive/projects/cp/obituaries/archives/christopher-mccandless; Wikipedia Contributors, "Into the Wild (Book)," Wikipedia, October 14, 2019, https://en.wikipedia.org/wiki/Into_the_Wild_(book).
2. Johann Hari, *Lost Connections: Why You're Depressed and How to Find Hope* (Bloomsbury, 2019).
3. Laurie Santos, "Episode 4: Mistakenly Seeking Solitude," The Happiness Lab (podcast), https://www.happinesslab.fm/season-1-episodes/mistakenly-seeking-solitude.
4. Sean Giggy, "ATM Inventor Still Can't Cash in at Home," August 7, 2018, https://www.khou.com/article/news/atm-inventor-still-cant-cash-in-at-home/285-581480864.

INDEX

ABOUT THE AUTHORS

Ryan Jenkins, CSP® (Certified Speaking Professional)™, is an internationally recognized keynote speaker and three-time published author. He speaks all over the world to companies such as State Farm, Wells Fargo, FedEx, Liberty Mutual, and John Deere. For a decade, he has been helping organizations create engaged, inclusive, and high-performing teams by lessening worker loneliness and closing generational gaps. Ryan's top-ranked insights have been featured in *Forbes*, *Fast Company*, and the *Wall Street Journal*. He is also cofounder of LessLonely.com, the world's first resource fully dedicated to reducing worker isolation and strengthening team connections. He holds a BS from Miami University (Ohio). Ryan lives in Atlanta, Georgia, with his wife, three children, and yellow Labrador.

(◎)(▶)(✔)(in) @theRyanJenks

Steven Van Cohen is a global leadership consultant, executive coach, and two-time published author. He has worked with hundreds of leaders from organizations such as Salesforce, The Home Depot, Komatsu, Bank of America, and Bridgestone. He has spent his career helping organizations humanize their businesses by creating workplaces where people come first. Steven has been featured in *Forbes*, Association for Talent Development, and *Training* magazine. He is also cofounder of LessLonely.com, the premier resource dedicated to lessening worker loneliness. Steven holds a BA from the University of Illinois and a MS from Pepperdine University. Steven lives in San Juan Capistrano, California, with his wife and two daughters.

ⓘ ⓨ ⓘⓝ @StevenVanCohen

HOW TO SHARE THIS BOOK

1. Bulk Buy

- ▶ Buy books at LessLonely.com/Bulk.
- ▶ For every bulk buy, we'll donate a percentage of the proceeds in your or your organization's name to ActiveMinds.org, the premier nonprofit organization supporting mental health awareness and education.
  - 5–24 books = 5% donated
  - 25+ books = 15% donated

2. Read and Discuss Together

- ▶ Sharing a book about loneliness can be tricky.
- ▶ Read it along with your team and use the book as the third party that can keep everyone (including the leader) accountable. This offers an external source that can bond a team itself.

3. Share on Social

- ▶ Join the community of other workplace loneliness fighters by following us at @RyanAndSteven.
- ▶ Use the hashtags: #LessLonely
- ▶ Every month we select a team to attend an exclusive virtual teaching by the authors.

4. Share a Review

- ▶ Please leave a helpful and honest review at your book retailer. This helps other people discover the book and experience the benefits of its content.

ADDITIONAL RESOURCES

Visit LessLonely.com to learn how to take this book from informational to transformational for your team or audience. Here's a snapshot of the additional resources to move your team from isolated to all-in.

Keynotes and Workshops

Inspire your team with wow and know-how. Have Ryan and/or Steven speak at your next event or train your team. Join hundreds of the world's leading companies like The Home Depot, Liberty Mutual, and Catalent Pharma Solutions in creating less lonely and more inclusive workspaces.

Digital Course

Ten interactive 10–15 minute micro-learning lessons proven to lessen loneliness and boost belonging. Organizations can insert the courses into any existing learning management system (LMS), or individuals can access directly through our learning portal. Each course is packed with reflective questions, custom videos, and activities.

Assessments

The Team Connection Assessment™ is the first (and only) tool to effectively measure the strength of relationships among a team. The assessment provides research-backed results and a custom report providing evidence-based strategies to improve a team's connection. Assessments are available for individuals, teams, and/or companywide.

Connect Deck™

The Connect Deck is a one-of-a-kind learning experience that uses 30 simple and fun daily activities to reconnect people with their team and humanity. Reenergize and reconnect an isolated, disconnected, and remote team using these custom playing cards.

App

The Connectable App addresses workplace loneliness at scale, combining research and science to give professionals the skills they need to build meaningful social connections at work and beyond.

Podcast

Listen to the authors of *Connectable*, Ryan and Steven, discuss the latest loneliness research, how it applies to them as an introvert and extrovert, and practical strategies to strengthen your connections in life. Listen to "The Case for Connection" wherever you get your podcasts.

Contact Information

Learn more and contact us at **LessLonely.com**.

@RyanAndSteven | #LessLonely